Purposeful Restructuring

To my parents,
Who gave me the joy of learning
To my husband,
Who encouraged and supported my learning
To my children,
Who inspired me to continue learning.

Purposeful Restructuring:
Creating a Culture for Learning and Achievement in Elementary Schools

Janet Hageman Chrispeels

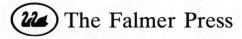 The Falmer Press

(A member of the Taylor & Francis Group)
Washington D.C. • London

| USA | The Falmer Press, Taylor & Francis Inc., 1900 Frost Road, 101, Bristol, PA 19007 |
| UK | The Falmer Press, 4 John St., London, WC1N 2ET |

First published 1992

Library of Congress Cataloging-in-Publication data are available on request

A catalogue record for this book is available from the British Library

ISBN 0 75070 022 x cased
ISBN 0 75070 023 8 paperback

Set in 9.5/11pt Times by
Graphicraft Typesetters Ltd., Hong Kong

Printed in Great Britain by Burgess Science Press, Basingstoke on paper which has a specified pH value on final paper manufacture of not less than 7.5 and is therefore 'acid free'.

Contents

Foreword   ix

Preface   xii

List of Figures and Tables   xiv

Chapter 1   A Context and Framework for Understanding Change   1
            Background of the Study   1
            Theoretical Framework   2
              Strengths of the open-system model   6
              Frames of reference   7
            Recurring Organizational Themes   11
              School organizational structures and procedures   11
              School technology: Curriculum and instructional practices   12
              School climate and culture   12
              Leadership   14
            School Change   15
            Research Design and Procedures   16
              The Sample Schools   16
            Data Sources and Methodologies   17
              Teacher survey data   17
              Teacher interview data   17
              Test data analysis and school effectiveness defined   18
              Archival records   19
              Limits of the study   19
            Chapter Overviews   20

Chapter 2   School Profiles   23
            Context of the Study   23
            Demographic Profiles   25
            Achievement Profiles   29
            Assessing Whitney's effectiveness   31
            Cross Case Comparison of Effective Schools Survey
              Results   40

Contents

Chapter 3 Whitney Elementary: Creating a Culture for Learning and
           Achieving   43
           The Setting: Inputs and Outcomes   43
           School Climate and Culture   45
               Safe and orderly learning environment   45
               Recognition and rewards   47
               High expectations   49
               Home-School Relations   50
               Shared mission   51
               Norms of collegiality   52
           School Technology: Curriculum and Instruction   53
               Use of test scores   53
               Curriculum alignment   54
               Academic focus   54
               Frequent monitoring   55
               Staff development   55
           School Organizational Structures and Procedures   56
           Schoolwide Leadership Team   57
           Summary and Conclusions   58

Chapter 4 Sierra Elementary: the Frustration of Many Efforts and no
           Gains   60
           The Setting: Inputs and Outputs   60
           School Climate and Culture   63
               Safe and orderly learning environment   64
               Recognition and rewards   64
               High expectations   65
               Home-School Relations   66
               Shared mission   67
               Norms of collegiality   68
           School Technology: Curriculum and instruction   68
               Use of test results   68
               Academic focus   70
               Frequent monitoring   70
               Staff development   71
           School Organizational Structures and Procedures   71
               Shared decision-making, collaboration, and teacher
                   empowerment   72
           Instructional Leadership   73
               Shared leadership   74
           Summary and Conclusions   74

Chapter 5 Tahoe Elementary: Healing Divisions, Stabilizing Leadership 77
           The Setting: Inputs and Outputs   77
           School Climate and Culture   79
               Safe and orderly learning environment   80
               Rewards and recognition   80
               High expectations   81
               Home-school relations   82

Shared mission   84
Norms of collegiality   85
School Technology: Curriculum and Instruction   85
Use of test scores   85
Academic focus   87
Frequent monitoring and evaluation of students and
    programs   88
Opportunity to learn and time-on-task   90
Staff development   91
Organizational Structures and Procedures   92
Shared decision-making and collaboration   92
Communication   93
Instructional Leadership   93
Summary and Conclusions   95

Chapter 6   Yosemite Elementary: Coping with the Impact of Tracking 98
The Setting: Inputs and Outputs   98
School Culture and Climate   102
Safe and orderly learning environment   102
Rewards and recognition   103
High expectations   104
Home-School Relations   106
Shared mission   108
Norms of collegiality   109
School Technology: Curriculum and Instruction   109
Use of test results   110
Academic focus   112
Frequent monitoring   113
Opportunity to learn and time-on-task   113
Staff development   114
Organizational Structures and Procedures   116
Shared Decision-Making and Collaboration   116
Problem solving   117
Communication   117
Instructional leadership   118
Summary and Conclusions   120

Chapter 7   Increasing School Effectiveness: Lessons from the Eight
Case Studies   123
School Culture and Climate   123
Safety and order   124
Rewards and recognition   124
Shared mission   125
High expectations   126
Home-school relations   127
School Technology: Curriculum and Instruction   129
Curriculum alignment   129
Use of test results   130
Academic focus   131

Contents

Frequent monitoring   131
Instructional strategies and staff development   133
Organizational Structures and Procedures   135
Committee structures that fostered collaboration   136
Opportunities for shared decision-making   137
Instructional Leadership   138
Shared vision   140
Commitment to change   140
Shared leadership   141
Shared learning   143
Summary and Conclusions   144

Chapter 8 Teacher Views on School Improvement   147
Shared decision-making and collaboration   148
Communication and shared goals   150
Linking school culture and school technology   153
Assessment and monitoring of school and student
    progress   154
The school's culture, home-school relations and student
    achievement   155
Leadership by principal and teachers   156
Summary and Conclusions   157

Chapter 9 Purposeful Restructuring: Lessons from Effective Schools
    Research and Practice   159
Improved Student Outcomes: The Impetus for Change   159
School Organizational Structures and Procedures   163
Curriculum and Instructional Practices   165
Academic focus   165
Instructional practices   167
Time-on-Task   168
Use of test results to assess student progress and
    program effectiveness   169
Staff development   171
School Climate and Culture   172
A safe, orderly, and positive learning environment   173
Home-school relations   173
Stated and shared mission   174
Staff and student rewards and recognition   175
High expectations for students and staff   176
Teacher professionalism and norms of collegiality   176
Summary and Conclusions   180

Appendixes   183
Appendix A   184
Appendix B   195

References   197

Index   214

Foreword

In many countries today, governments are seeking to improve the quality of schooling. The UNESCO World Education Report has revealed that there is an enormous difference in spending levels between the developing countries and industrial nations. Even within the best resourced systems, however, there is a feeling that all is not well. In the United States and the United Kingdom, this feeling has been translated into various programmes of reform and restructuring.

Restructuring of the education systems in many American States and the British reforms following the passing of the 1988 Education Reform Act must be seen — in lots of ways — as very different phenomena, existing in different cultures, prosecuted by different power groups and, sometimes, serving different purposes. But they must also be recognized as stemming from a common dissatisfaction. The reasons for this dissatisfaction are twofold: criticisms of the academic standards reached by school students — especially in the various international comparisons that have been carried out; and the mounting costs of the education service.

For administrators and teachers involved in running schools, all this can seem very unfair. Escalating costs are not restricted to the education service. Furthermore, these people frequently feel they are being blamed and, indeed, scapegoated for the problems of society which — in urban areas — will include crime, vandalism, unemployment and drug abuse. In their eyes, these problems are the manifestation of the societies in which they live and of which they are only one influence. In fact, they may argue, it is just these problems which make their lives in schools so difficult.

The reflexive position of schools within their wider societies, both as products of established traditions working within established cultures, and as agents of socialization and transmitters of values for new generations, can be confusing and stressful. It is especially so at times of change. This is why reforms and restructuring are so difficult to implement. There is, of course, nothing new in this insight for, as the author of this book once pointed out to me, Machiavelli, writing advice to his new prince in 1513, warned that change would be resisted both by those who benefitted from the old order and by those who will not commit themselves until they can be certain that the new order will be more successful than the old.

It is in this context — of change, uncertainty and lack of confidence — that Dr Chrispeels' book has been written. She has set out to do three things:

- identify and synthesize relevant research from a number of related fields;
- clarify the findings from this research in order to create an appropriate conceptual and empirical framework;
- carry out her own study based on eight Californian Elementary schools engaged in school improvement efforts.

The results of these labours are impressive. Over three hundred chapters, papers and books have been studied. This writing has been drawn from studies of change and innovation — from the business as well as the educational world; leadership; management; social science methodology; and parent involvement, as well as — from the rapidly increasing — literature on school effectiveness. Using as her theoretical framework, a view adapted from management theory of 'an open system model' the author establishes four frames of reference which she uses to integrate her literature review:

the climate and culture of the school as perceived by teachers;

the organizational structures and processes which facilitate or inhibited core-group tasks;

the technology of teaching as embodied in the curriculum and instructional practices; and,

the leadership roles within both the school and the district, which direct and orchestrate the transformative process.

Dr Chrispeels' account of her methodology is thorough and includes a description of her sampling process, sources of data, instruments (examples in an appendix) and techniques of analysis. Unusually — and to her credit — she also includes a note of the inevitable limitations imposed by her choice of methodology.

The results of the empirical work are fascinating. The examples of case studies that she provides begin with rich detailed descriptions and are illustrated with data and quotations. They also, however, include the results of Dr Chrispeels' critical analyses which, in turn, enables her to draw tentative conclusions, and to relate these to findings from the more general literature. Amongst the points she highlights, are the importance of common aims, the difficulties for staff in disadvantaged socio-economic areas seeking to maintain high expectations, the need for modest incremental steps forward, the power of school structures to help or hinder progress, and the difficulties endemic to fieldwork in the social sciences of teasing out the influences of confounding variables.

The findings of this careful work deserve to be studied in detail. Certainly this is what is happening in my own research team. We are fascinated by her account of the 'complexity and fragility of the change processes', of the way that teachers reported their views about change, and by the emergence of common perspectives on school improvement.

In her final chapter, Dr Chrispeels provides an interesting discussion of the relationship of the restructuring taking place in many parts of the United States to the findings of school improvement research. Whilst American readers will be more familiar with the history and details of the attempts to restructure, Canadian, Australian, British and other European readers should find the clear and balanced argument helpful in the interpretation of events and changes in their own systems.

At a time when developments in communications make possible almost instant transmission of information across the world, it is right that — despite our cultural and language differences — we take the opportunity to share the fruit of careful scholarship.

Through our common membership of the international Congress of School Effectiveness and Improvement, Dr Crispeels and I have had numerous opportunities to share the findings, hypotheses and — at times — frustrations of working in this complex but highly rewarding field. I am pleased, therefore, to provide a foreword to this impressive study. Whether legislation or restructuring takes place, increasing the quality of learning and teaching in schools must remain our main goal. Dr Chrispeels' scholarship provides further evidence that in the right circumstances, teachers and administrators can succeed in achieving this worthy goal.

Peter Mortimore
Institute of Education
University of London
April 1992

Preface

While the call to restructure schools represents the latest quest for reform and improvement in American public education, efforts to improve have always been ongoing in many schools and districts. The eight elementary schools described in this book have been engaged in the processes of improvement for many years. Most began a systematic effort to improve in the mid-1970s when the California Department of Education initiated the Early Childhood Education program. The improvement process was expanded schoolwide, kindergarten through sixth grade, in 1976, when the Early Childhood Education program became the School Improvement Program. Both programs established decision-making councils in schools long before such councils became a popular cry in the restructuring movement. The stories of the schools in this book begin when the staff turned to the effective schools research as a means of guiding and strengthening their school improvement plans in an effort to achieve both equity and quality of outcomes for students. The goal to increase achievement for all students proved challenging for all, but some schools were more successful than others. The central question is why?

Through the voices of the teachers and principals in the eight schools, the complex and long-term nature of the change process is examined. The framework that is used to guide the analysis is the school as an open-system, buffeted and influenced by the immediate community in which it is located, and by the larger communities of district, state and federal governments. While the inputs (students, staff, and material) into the system are recognized, the focus of the study is on the transformative process of schooling. The heart and soul of school improvement and change occur through the interactions of teachers and students, teachers and administrators, and through the interaction of the school and the larger community. To understand how these interactions brought better student outcomes in some of the schools and not in others, four dimensions of the transformative process — organizational structures and procedures, school technology (curriculum and instruction), school culture, and leadership — were explored. Changes occurred in these dimensions in each of the schools; however, the degree, integration and coordination of the changes proved to be key. In some respects, the changes that occurred in these schools should be regarded as incremental, not radical restructuring. Yet the voices of the teachers revealed that a significant and fundamental restructuring of beliefs was occurring as a result of the changes made in the transformative process. The lessons learned from their efforts are important for all of those now seeking to engage in purposeful restructuring.

Acknowledgment must be made to the district administrators, principals and teachers of the eight schools for the splendid cooperation and support they gave throughout the duration of this study. They opened their doors to me. They endured interviews, completed questionnaires and answered numerous requests for documents with openness, candor and kindness. Without their support and thoughtfulness this study would have been impossible. There is no way to adequately thank them.

My warmest thanks are also due to Sally Pollack, Sammie McCormack, Dave Meaney, Ron Brice, and Dan Watson for being good friends as well as invaluable colleagues, who worked to develop the effective schools program and assisted in the initial effective schools study; to the San Diego County Office of Education for providing the opportunity to not only work with schools, but also to reflect on what was being accomplished; to Peter Mortimore, Charles Teddlie, Sam Stringfield, Joe Murphy, and Phil Hallinger for their encouragement and excellent work, which has been an inspiration and guide for this study; to Desmond Nutall for clarifying my thinking about defining effectiveness; to Larry Lezotte and Barbara Taylor for the many conversations about effective schools that have shaped my thinking; to Peggy Burke, Barbara Taylor and Edie Holcomb for reading Chapter 9 and sharing their thoughts and reactions; to William Foster, Mary Scherr and C. M. 'Mac' Bernd for reading the manuscript in its entirety and offering many helpful suggestions and comments; and to Carol Saumarez, manuscript editor and Malcolm Clarkson, Managing Director at Falmer Press for helping to eliminate as many errors as possible.

Finally, I would like to thank my family. My children, Hanya and Arno, provided the impetus for me to become interested in how schools worked, and why some children were served better by the schools than others. They served as tireless cheerleaders throughout this project. My husband, Maarten Chrispeels, thought what I was doing was important and supported me every step of the way. His insights and suggestions, both of substance and style, are reflected throughout. Even with the wise counsel and significant contributions of all of these people, responsibility for the views expressed remain with me.

List of Figures and Tables

Figures

Figure 1.1   An open-system model of school embedded in larger environments   3

Figure 1.2   Organization of school effectiveness characteristics   7

Figure 1.3   School effectiveness: A model   8

Figure 1.4   A diagram of the transformative process depicting the key components schoolwide effectiveness factors in relationship to student outcomes   9

Figure 1.5   A diagram depicting state and local influences on the school and the school within its social context   10

Figure 2.1   Comparison of student enrollments in relation to overall student achievement   26

Figure 2.2   Comparison of schools in terms of ethnic distribution of students   27

Figure 2.3   Distribution of students by parent occupation and comparison with statewide averages based on third grade CAP data in 1988   28

Figure 2.4   Comparison of per cent of AFDC and limited or non-English speaking (LES/NES) students at each school based on 1987–88 third grade CAP data   28

Figure 2.5   Five-year trend in third grade CAP reading scores   31

Figure 2.6   Five-year trend in third grade CAP mathematics scores   32

Figure 2.7   Five-year trend in sixth grade CAP reading scores   33

Figure 2.8   Five-year trend in sixth grade CAP mathematics scores   34

Figure 2.9   Five-year trend in number of third grade students scoring below Q1 on the CAP reading test   35

Figure 2.10   Five-year trend in number of third grade students scoring below Q1 on the CAP mathematics test — 35

Figure 2.11   Five-year trend in number of sixth grade students scoring below Q1 on the CAP mathematics test — 36

Figure 2.12   Five-year trend in number of sixth grade students scoring below Q1 on the CAP mathematics test — 36

Figure 2.13   Five-year trend in third grade CAP reading scores for lowest SES subgroup and comparison of this group with average statewide score in 1988 — 37

Figure 2.14   Five-year trend in third grade CAP mathematics scores for lowest SES subgroup and comparison of this group with average statewide score in 1988 — 37

Figure 2.15   Five-year trend in sixth grade CAP reading scores for lowest SES subgroup and comparison of this group with average statewide score in 1988 — 38

Figure 2.16   Five-year trend in sixth grade CAP mathematics scores for lowest SES subgroup and comparison of this group with average statewide score in 1988 — 38

Figure 2.17   Comparison of composite mean scores of teacher responses to the effective schools surveys administered in 1989 — 41

Figure 3.1   Comparison of per cent agree scores of teacher responses on Effective Schools Surveys completed in 1986, 1987 and 1989 — 46

Figure 4.1   Comparison of mean scores of teacher responses on the Effective Schools Surveys completed in 1985 and 1989 — 62

Figure 5.1   Comparison of teacher responses on high expectation in 1986 and 1989 bases on the Effective School Survey — 79

Figure 6.1   Comparison of mean scores of teacher responses on the Effective Schools Surveys completed in 1985 and 1989 — 100

Figure 6.2   Five-year trend in Yosemite's third grade CAP score — 100

Figure 6.3   Five-year trend in Yosemite's sixth grade CAP scores — 101

Figure 6.4   Five-year trend in third and sixth grade CAP scores for students from unskilled family backgrounds — 101

Tables

Table 2.1   Comparison of time of entry into the effective schools program and levels of planning and implementation assistance received from the county office of education — 25

Table 2.2   Comparison of school enrollments, grade configuration, SES, and school year schedules — 26

List of Figures and Tables

Table 2.3 Parent occupations and the corresponding SES value 27

Table 2.4 Comparison of each schools' effectiveness score at third and sixth grade 38

Table 2.5 Trend in responses to the Effective Schools Survey based on a composite per cent agree score 41

Table 3.1 Comparison of school and state third grade scaled score results on the 1988 California Assessment Program disaggregated by parent occupation 44

Table 3.2 Comparison of teacher responses regarding school climate based on the Effective Schools Survey given in 1986 and 1989 47

Table 3.3 Comparison of 1986 and 1989 responses to selected items regarding home-school relations 50

Table 3.4 Comparison of teacher responses regarding instructional leadership in 1986 and 1989 57

Table 4.1 Comparison of the ethnic distribution of students in the school, district and state based on the sixth grade CAP data in 1988 61

Table 4.2 Comparison of the school's sixth grade 1988 CAP results disaggregated by family occupation with those students in the state 63

Table 4.3 Comparison of teacher responses on home-school relations in 1985 and 1989 based on the county Effective Schools Survey 66

Table 4.4 Comparison of teacher responses on instructional leadership in 1985 and 1989 based on the county Effective Schools Survey 74

Table 5.1 Three-year comparison of Tahoe's Achievement Scores at third and sixth grade levels with district and state scores on CAP 78

Table 5.2 Comparison of teacher responses on high expectation in 1986 and 1989 based on the Effective Schools Survey 82

Table 5.3 Comparison of teacher responses on home-school relations in 1986 and 1989 based on Effective Schools Survey 83

Table 5.4 Comparison of teacher responses on opportunity to learn based on the 1989 Effective Schools Surveys given at Whitney, Sierra and Tahoe 90

Table 5.5 Comparison of teacher responses on staff development in 1986 and 1989 based on the Effective Schools Survey 91

Table 5.6 Comparison of teacher responses on instructional leadership in 1986 and 1989 based on the county Effective Schools Survey 94

Table 6.1 Comparison of teacher responses on safe and orderly environment in 1985 and 1989 based on the Connecticut and county Effective Schools Surveys 102

Table 6.2   Comparison of teacher responses on high expectations in 1985 and 1989 based on the Connecticut and county Effective Schools Surveys 105

Table 6.3   Comparison of teacher responses on home-school relations in 1985 and 1989 based on the Connecticut and county Effective Schools Surveys 108

Table 6.4   Comparison of teacher responses on items related to use of test results in 1985 and 1989 based on the Connecticut and county Effective Schools Surveys 111

Table 6.5   Comparison of teacher responses from Whitney, Sierra, Tahoe and Yosemite on staff development in 1989 on the county Effective Schools Survey 115

Table 6.6   Comparison of teacher responses on items related to instructional leadership in 1985 and 1989 based on the Connecticut and county Effective Schools Surveys 119

Chapter 1

A Context and Framework for Understanding Change

This book contains a description and analysis of concerted efforts by teachers and principals to make their schools better places for students to learn. As the case studies and cross-case analysis show, not all of the schools succeeded equally well, and that is the reason for telling their stories. The road to school effectiveness and improvement was strewn with organizational barriers that interfered with teacher collaboration. New instructional and curriculum changes mandated by the district or the state frequently required mastery by teachers before mastery could be expected by students. Traditional school structures have created ingrained cultures of isolation and self-reliance by teachers that limit teacher understanding of their school as an organization and make change more difficult. The core purpose of this study is to follow these schools over a four-year period and to gain insights into why some succeeded and others faltered in their work to sustain a course of school improvement. A second purpose is to show that in their efforts to increase school effectiveness, the call of the 1980s, these schools were engaged in a fundamental restructuring of their belief systems and of their workplace, a growing concern in the 1990s.

Background of the Study

Research into school effectiveness has played an important role in bringing about school improvement in the last fifteen years. The early studies documenting characteristics of effective schools serving low-income students, served as the basis for developing school and districtwide improvement programs (Austin, 1978, Brookover and Lezotte, 1979; California State Department of Education, 1980; Edmonds, 1979; Kiltgaard and Hall, 1974; Lezotte, Edmonds, and Ratner, 1974; New York State Department of Education, 1974a, 1974b, 1976; Rutter, Maughan, Mortimore, Ouston, and Smith, 1979; Spartz, Valdes, McCormick, Meyers, and Geppert, 1977; Weber, 1971). Educational agencies at all levels — state departments of education (e.g., Connecticut, South Carolina, New York), intermediate service units (e.g., San Diego, Orange, Los Angeles, Riverside, and Sacramento County Offices of Education in California) and hundreds of local school districts (e.g., Glendale, Arizona; Milwaukee, Wisconsin; Pontiac, Michigan; Seattle, Washington; Montgomery and Prince Georges Counties, Maryland) — launched school effectiveness programs. The staff responsible for implementing these programs developed school effectiveness surveys that were based on the early research findings. They assisted local schools in administering the surveys and collecting disaggregated student test and other outcome data, and helped schools to develop improvement plans. The goal of the plans was to increase overall student achievement and achieve equity for each student subgroup within the school population.

The school effectiveness programs undertaken by state and local educational agencies resulted in a second generation of research studies (McCormack-Larkin, 1985a, 1985b; McCormack-Larkin and Williams, 1982; Pollack, Chrispeels, and Watson, 1987 and 1988; Rossman, Corbett, and Firestone, 1988; Taylor, 1990, Weiss, 1984). These case studies focused, in general, on examining the process of change occurring in the schools engaged in school improvement. Thus, these studies are longitudinal rather than cross-sectional snapshots of effectiveness. The case studies also have addressed organizational variables that document *how* improvement is achieved, trying to move beyond a list of 'effectiveness characteristics'. The goal of the new studies is to understand how the effectiveness characteristics came to be, and how they interact within the dynamic process of school life in ways that lead to greater student learning. Another distinguishing feature of the case studies is that they have typically been conducted by practitioner/researchers who are attempting to reflect on their work and the work of the schools with which they are involved. The study documented in this book falls into this genre of research.

Theoretical Framework

The concept that underlies this study is that schools are complex social organizations with numerous internal and external interactions and processes (Handy and Aitken, 1986; Hanna, 1988; Perrow, 1970, 1979; Rosenholtz, 1989). The way one thinks about an organization is strongly influenced by the metaphors used to describe it (Morgan, 1986). The metaphor used here is that of the school as an 'open-system', as shown in Figure 1.1. In this figure, the school is at the center, embedded within the district, state and federal government systems which shape and influence the daily worklife of teachers, students and administrators. This open-systems model, especially the transformative process, serves as the theoretical framework for this study.

The term open system is drawn from biology and implies that an organization is like a living organism that exists in, influences, and is influenced by its environment (Hanna, 1988, Morgan, 1986). The organization, like an organism, is made up of interrelated parts. To understand the whole, one must have studied both the whole as well as its parts and their relationships. Hanna characterizes an open-system as having seven essential elements which are restated here in a school context (pp. 9–16).

1 *Boundary.* Each system is differentiated from other systems by a boundary. The distinguishing feature of an open-system is that the boundary is permeable, permitting interactions with the environment and

Figure 1.1   An open-system model of school embedded in larger environments.

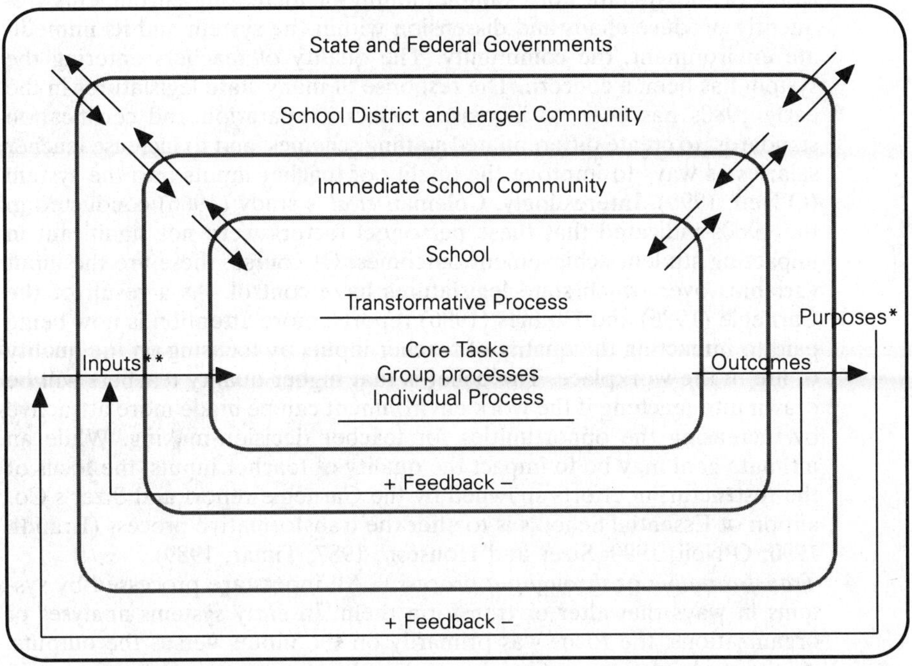

State and Federal Governments

School District and Larger Community

Immediate School Community

School

Transformative Process

Core Tasks
Group processes
Individual Process

Inputs**

Outcomes

Purposes*

+ Feedback –

+ Feedback –

Source: Adapted from Hanna, 1988.

with other systems. Unlike an independent company or organization, an individual school is nested within other systems — the school district, the community, state, and federal governments. This nesting phenomenon is depicted in Figure 1.1. In addition, the physical structures of schools, which establish essentially autonomous classroom units, create significant barriers within a school. These physical barriers frequently lead to psychological boundaries that prevent interaction among teachers.

2 *Purpose and goals.*   Each system has a purpose — a reason for being. The organizational life of schools is made more complex by the multiple purposes of schooling — custodial, certification (or sorting of students), teaching for learning and mastery of subject matter content, and perpetuation of the culture and traditions of society. In addition, multiple players are involved in defining the purpose — federal, state and district, the larger community, and teachers and parents within a given school community. The lack of consensus on the purpose of schooling has profound implications for school improvement and school restructuring. Furthermore, how the purpose is defined dramatically effects the internal workings of the school (the transformative processes, see number 4 below).

3 *Inputs.*   Resources — material, facilities, equipment, people, financial — enable the system to operate. School staff and communities typically complain that financial resources are never adequate; yet it is the human

resources, especially teachers and students, that are the most significant assets of the system. For example, falling or increasing enrollments frequently produce chaos and dissension within the system and its immediate environment, the community. The quality of teachers entering the system has been a concern. The response of many state legislatures in the early 1980s has been to increase teacher preparation and certification standards, to create differentiated staffing schemes, and to increase teacher salaries as ways to improve the quality of teacher inputs into the system (O'Neil, 1990). Interestingly, Coleman *et al.*'s study (1966) conducted in the 1960s indicated that these personnel factors were not significant in impacting student achievement outcomes. Of course, these are the input variables over which state legislatures have control. As a result of the Carnegie (1986) and Holmes (1986) reports, more attention is now being paid to impacting the quality of teacher inputs by focusing on the quality of life in the workplace. The belief is that higher quality teachers will be drawn into teaching if the work environment can be made more attractive by increasing the opportunities for teacher decision-making. While an ultimate goal may be to impact the quality of teacher inputs, the focus of the restructuring efforts spawned by the Carnegie report and Sizer's Coalition of Essential Schools is to alter the transformative process (Brandt, 1990; O'Neil, 1990; Sizer and Houston, 1987; Timar, 1989).

4   *Transformative or throughput process.*   All inputs are processed by systems in ways that alter or transform them. In early systems analyses of organizations, the focus was primarily on the inputs versus the outputs. As the study of organizations has matured, far more attention is now paid to what happens within the system — the transformative process. Both school-effectiveness programs and school restructuring are concerned with the transformative process. According to Hanna (1988), the transformative process consists of three core elements: core tasks, individual processes and group processes. During transformation, core tasks are organized to accomplish the organization's purpose. Individuals within the organization devote energy and talents to accomplish the core tasks, which are usually determined by group processes. Group processes are shaped by the structure, culture, information-processing system, technology, and the rewards of the internal system. The balancing of tasks, individual, and group processes are seen as the role of leadership within the organization.

As was discussed earlier, in most schools there is a lack of consensus about the purpose of schooling, a fact which confounds the establishment of the core tasks for schools. A major thrust of school-effectiveness efforts have centered around defining core tasks. One of the criticisms of school effectiveness is that the core instructional task has been defined too narrowly, as the teaching of basic skills. Those involved with school restructuring also struggle with an effort to define the core tasks of schools. Since there is often disagreement about the definition of a restructured school, defining the core tasks has also proved challenging (Elmore, *et al.*, 1990; Timar, 1989). Both school effectiveness and restructuring involve changes in all aspects of the transformative process in an effort to increase the outcomes or outputs of schooling.

5 *Outputs.* Every system has outputs. How the outputs of schools are viewed and defined by the environment and teachers within the system is closely related to the purpose and is critical in shaping the transformative process. For example, if the purpose of schooling is to sort and certify students, students (inputs) are seen as raw materials. At the output end, students will then more likely be seen as graded products certified to perform differential tasks (Kearns and Doyle, 1988). Under these conditions, during the transformative process, teaching will be viewed as a routine task with a focus on standardized procedures. The primary role of the teacher is that of the worker who delivers the curriculum (Kearns and Doyle, 1988; Seeley, 1981). An alternative view of the purpose of schooling will similarly impact all aspects of the system. For example, if the primary purpose of schooling is the development of learners able to process and evaluate vast amounts of information, students must be seen as 'knowledge workers', who are as actively engaged in the learning process as the teachers (Schlechty, 1990). The system's output will be 'students as thinkers, problem solvers, and creators' (Schlechty, p. 41). With this purpose, the transformative process of schooling must focus on teaching for learning. Many aspects of the process are likely to be non-routine, including the relationship between teachers and students (Rosenholtz, 1989; Schlechty, 1990). School effectiveness research has drawn attention to the fact that the outcomes of schooling, especially for students from low-income or diverse ethnic backgrounds, could be different than they currently are in many schools. Redefining the outcomes of schooling as a way of clarifying the purpose of schooling is the challenge facing those who would restructure schools.

6 *Feedback.* To remain viable, all systems need feedback. Feedback requires information about accomplishments in relation to the purposes, goals and output of the system or organization. The multiple and sometimes conflicting purposes of schools and the imperfect measures of outcomes have often meant that corrective action or feedback does not occur. Data on outcomes are usually available, but the teachers and administration may be unable or unwilling to take steps that will constitute the feedback and result in modifications of the teaching processes. Since the inputs to schools are not easily alterable, feedback about the transformative process is especially important to school improvement and change. For example, if children are not learning to read and the children or their parents (inputs) are seen to be at fault, then possible shortcomings in the teaching process are ignored, and no changes are made in the instructional process regarding the reading program (i.e., the transformative process which teachers can alter).

7 *Environment.* Everything outside the boundary of the system is the environment. As mentioned earlier, schools are nested within a series of systems. The impact and interactions of the environment on an individual school will depend on a large number of factors. For example, a school in a large district may feel the weight of many rules and regulations promulgated in an effort to control and standardize such a large system. However, the same school may have more freedom of action in the

transformative process because it cannot be supervised by district administrative personnel to the same degree that a school in a small district will be supervised.

Schools are also significantly affected by their community environment. In a high socio-economic district, as long as community expectations are met, school staff generally feel secure and comfortable in their environment, because there is considerable congruence in values, norms, and expectations between the teaching staff and the community. However, if a crisis of confidence erupts, the school is quite vulnerable, because of the political clout of the community. In contrast, in low socio-economic communities, school staff typically feel estranged from their communities, yet the community rarely has the political and financial ability to actually effect changes at the school, even if community expectations are not being met.

Strengths of the Open-System Model

While no one theory can capture all aspects of a complex organization, the open-system model seems appropriate for several reasons. First, the model helps to show why different researchers arrived at different conclusions regarding school effects on student outcomes. In their studies, Coleman, *et al.* (1966) and Jencks, *et al.* (1972) focused primarily on the input side of the organizational system. Inputs such as number of books in the library, teachers' years of experience and training, quality of school facilities, teacher salaries, and family background were assessed against outputs in terms of student achievement on standardized tests. Jencks and his colleagues concluded that 'everything else — the school budget, its policies, the characteristics of teachers — is either secondary or completely irrelevant' compared to family background in predicting student achievement or outcomes (p. 256). These data have not been refuted by school effectiveness research. Rather the focus of research has shifted from inputs to the transformative process. The conclusion of the school effectiveness researchers is that the transformative process will make a difference in student outcomes when inputs in terms of student family background are controlled (Armor, *et al.*, 1976; Brookover and Lezotte, 1979; Edmonds, 1979; Levine and Stark, 1981).

A second strength of the model is its broad, inclusive nature. With an open-system perspective, it is easier to capture the complex nature of schooling and the interaction of the school with its environment. Third, the breadth of the model facilitates examining the component parts from a variety of frames of reference (Bolman and Deal, 1986). This is particularly significant in studying each component of the transformative process of the model, which encompasses the structure, technology, culture, leadership and political aspects of all organizations. Fourth, by focusing on the transformative process of the model, it will be possible to examine the relationship between school effectiveness efforts of the 1980s and the current attention to restructuring. Finally, the open-system model reflects the tension in any organisms to grow and develop, and at the same time to remain in a state of homeostasis. The tension is a major factor contributing to the difficulty of organizational change.

Frames of Reference

In this book four major frames of reference are used to examine the transformative process of schools. These are the climate and culture of the school as perceived by teachers; the organizational structures and processes which facilitate or inhibit core-group tasks; the technology of teaching as embodied in the curriculum and instructional practices; and the leadership roles within both the school and the district, which direct and orchestrate the transformative process. Each of these four broad frames encompasses key variables that interact to give shape and definition to each frame.

The contents of each frame has been illuminated over the last fifteen years in a series of school effectiveness studies. The early effective schools research focused on identifying effective schools and enumerating factors that distinguished effective from ineffective schools. Five to seven factors or correlates were typically identified, with the list suggested by Edmonds (1978), being the most widely used. His correlates included: 1) emphasis on student acquisition of basic skills; 2) high expectations for students; 3) strong administrative leadership; 4) frequent monitoring of student progress; and 5) orderly climate conducive to learning. The second phase of school effectiveness research has attempted to cluster the factors or correlates into logical groupings or patterns for program development (Murphy, Hallinger, and Mesa, 1985). In addition, teacher effectiveness findings and organizational-change literature have been integrated with the school effectiveness factors. Purkey and Smith (1983) grouped the characteristics into two major categories: *Structure* and *Process* (Figure 1.2).

Figure 1.2 Organization of school effectiveness characteristics

Structure	Process
school site management and leadership	collaborative planning
staff stability	collegial relationships
curriculum articulation and organization	sense of community
staff development	clear goals
parental involvement and support	order and discipline
schoolwide recognition of students	shared high expectations
maximized learning time	
district support	

Source: Purkey and Smith, 1983.

Murphy, *et al.* (1985) refined this model by organizing the fourteen factors they identified into two major categories; *School technology* and *School environment*. Figure 1.3 presents their organizing model of school effectiveness factors (p. 620). This model helps to more clearly define the transformative process of schooling. School technology consists of two main actions: *Organizing for Curriculum and Instruction* and *Supporting Curriculum and Instruction*. School environment in this model includes *Structures, Norms and Organization Processes*. The model links the transformative process to student outcomes, the goal of school-effectiveness efforts. One of the problems with the model is that instructional leadership is

Figure 1.3   School effectiveness: A model

Organizing for Curriculum and Instruction
   tightly coupled curriculum
   opportunity to learn
   direct instruction
 	
Supporting Curriculum and Instruction
   clear academic mission
   instructional leadership
   frequent monitoring
 	
   structured staff development
	Norms
	   expectations
	
	Organization Processes
	   collaborative processes
	
	Structures
	   opportunity for involvement
	   rewards and recognition
	   safe, orderly environment
	
	   home-school support

School Technology	*School Environment*
student achievement student behavior student outcomes	

Source: Murphy, Hallinger and Mesa, 1985.

mentioned as only one aspect of *Supporting Curriculum and Instruction*. All aspects of school technology and environment are surely affected by leadership. It is through leadership that both technology and environment are shaped.

Based on their study of ten effective, improving, and ineffective schools, Pollack *et al.* (1987) built on Murphy's model by grouping their findings into three major components: School climate and culture, Curriculum and instructional practices, and Organizational structures and processes. This study has attempted to elaborate on the nature and interrelationship of the three components and to explore the role of leadership in relationship to the components and their variables.

Figure 1.4, an interactive model of the school effectiveness transformative process, depicts a hypothetical relationship among the four organizational frames or components schoolwide and in classrooms. The variables that comprise each frame or component are also listed. Scheerens and Creemers (1989) have argued that many of the effective school characteristics are really aspects of leadership. 'We might wonder whether "frequent evaluation" and "orderly climate" could not better be seen as aspects of strong instructional leadership, than as independent causes.' (p. 3) Frequent monitoring is an action that an instructional leader or a group of teachers may take, and an orderly climate may be an outcome of leadership; in this sense they are related to leadership. For purposes of this study, it is argued that the components should be seen not as separate factors, but as interrelated parts of the whole organization. They encompass the actions and outcomes that are shaped and molded by leadership of the principal and school staff, district and state administrators, and the community in ways that enhance or limit student learning and achievement. Through leadership, the schoolwide components are altered in ways that create a context as well as the parameters for learning in the classroom. It is also hypothesized that the relationships among the components are reciprocal rather than causal: change in one component or

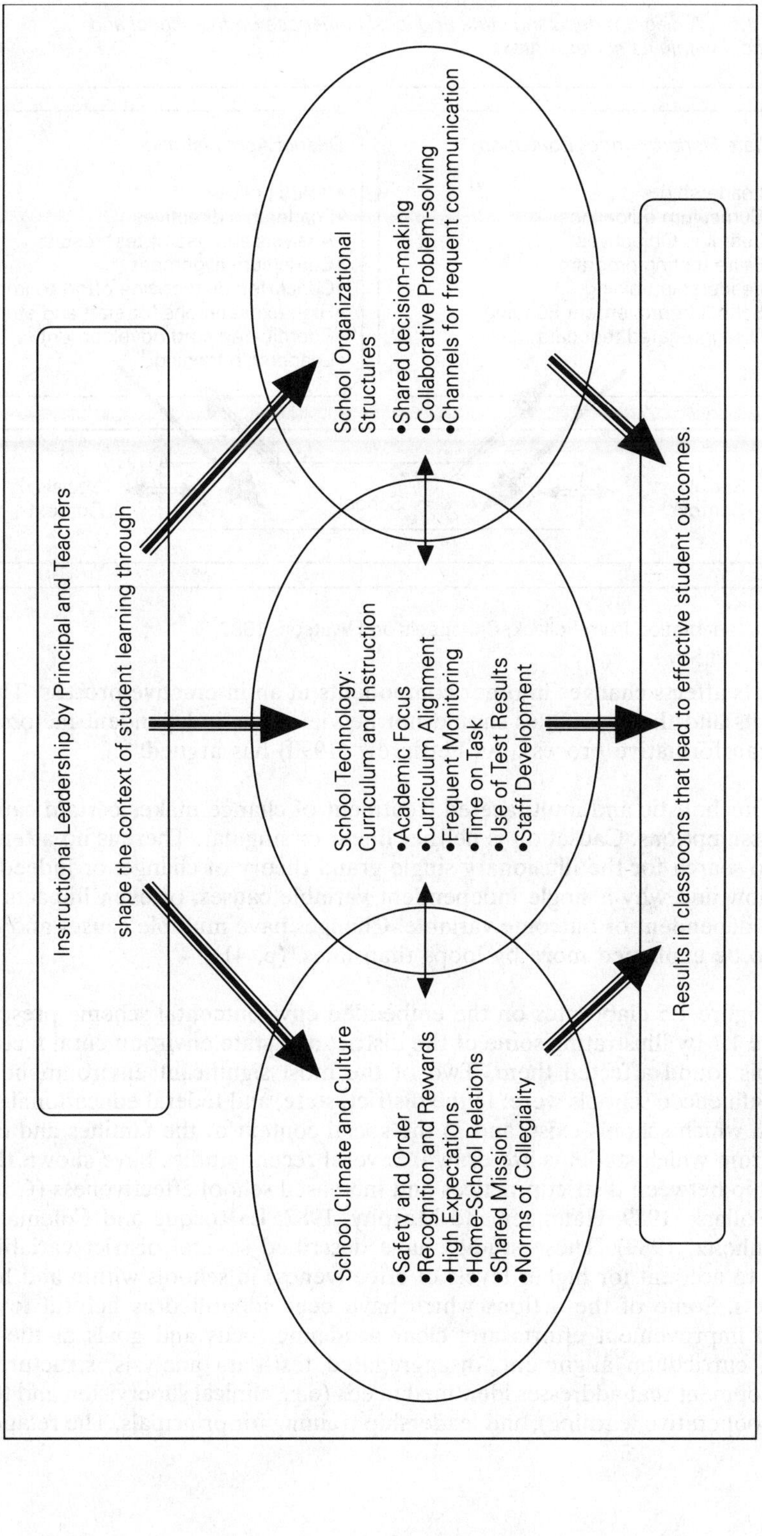

Figure 1.4   A diagram of the transformative process depicting the key components schoolwide effectiveness factors in relationship to student outcomes.

Instructional Leadership by Principal and Teachers

shape the context of student learning through

School Organizational Structures
• Shared decision-making
• Collaborative Problem-solving
• Channels for frequent communication

School Technology: Curriculum and Instruction
• Academic Focus
• Curriculum Alignment
• Frequent Monitoring
• Time on Task
• Use of Test Results
• Staff Development

School Climate and Culture
• Safety and Order
• Recognition and Rewards
• High Expectations
• Home-School Relations
• Shared Mission
• Norms of Collegiality

Results in classrooms that lead to effective student outcomes.

Built on Murphy's model by Pollack, Chrispeels and Watson, 1987.

Figure 1.5   *A diagram depicting state and local influences on the school and the school within its social context.*

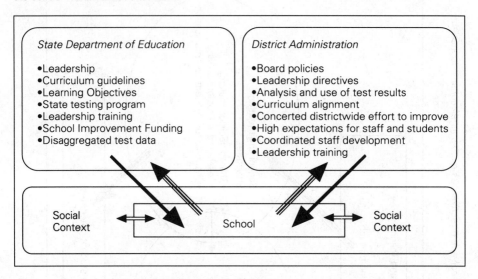

State Department of Education

- •Leadership
- •Curriculum guidelines
- •Learning Objectives
- •State testing program
- •Leadership training
- •School Improvement Funding
- •Disaggregated test data

District Administration

- •Board policies
- •Leadership directives
- •Analysis and use of test results
- •Curriculum alignment
- •Concerted districtwide effort to improve
- •High expectations for staff and students
- •Coordinated staff development
- •Leadership training

Social Context   School   Social Context

Source: Adaptation from Pollack, Chrispeels and Watson, 1987.

its parts affects changes in other components in an interactive process. The components and their variables should not be viewed as independent factors during the transformative process. As Pettigrew (1990) has argued:

> Our holistic and multifaceted treatment of change makes certain causal assumptions. Causation is neither linear or singular. There is no attempt to search for the illusionary single grand theory of change, or indeed of how and why a single independent variable causes, or even impacts on a dependent or outcome variable. Changes have multiple causes and are to be explained more by loops than lines. (p. 41)

Figure 1.5 elaborates on the embedded environmental scheme presented in Figure 1.1 by illustrating some of the district and state environmental factors that schools found affected them. Two of the most significant environment factors that influenced schools were: 1) the district, state, and federal educational systems within which schools exist, and 2) the social context of the families and community from which students are drawn. Several recent studies have shown the relationship between district practices and increased school effectiveness (Chrispeels and Pollack, 1989; Hallinger and Murphy, 1982; LaRocque and Coleman, 1987, Rosenholtz, 1989). These studies have described several district variables that seem to account for higher levels of effectiveness in schools within and between districts. Some of the actions which have been identified as helpful to school-based improvement efforts are: clear academic focus and goals at the district level, curriculum alignment, disaggregated test-data analysis, structured staff development that addresses identified needs (e.g., clinical supervision and teaching and cooperative learning), and leadership training for principals. The relationships between the schools and their districts were explored in this study, especially in the individual case studies.

The second environmental factor is the social context of the school community. While the study of the social context of schooling has existed for some time, only recently has attention been given to the relationship between the social context of the school and school effectiveness (Andrews, Soder, and Jacoby, 1986; Chubb and Moe, 1986; Estler, 1985; Hallinger and Murphy, 1986, 1989; Miller and Sayre, 1986; Rowan and Denk, 1984; Teddlie and Stringfield, 1985).

> The studies suggest that high SES [Socioeconomic status] and low SES effective schools are characterized by different patterns of curricular breadth, allocations of time for learning, school mission, patterns of principal instructional leadership, opportunities for student recognition, expectations for student achievement, and home-school relations. (Hallinger and Murphy, 1989, p. 9)

In their study of high and low SES effective schools, Hallinger and Murphy (1986) found that in a high SES school, the school develops strong links with its environment and the principal's time is often focused on parent/community/school relations; whereas principals in low SES effective schools are highly visible in the classroom and are more task oriented. In essence the school buffers itself from the community environment and works to create a learning climate that is safe and secure and built on high expectations for student achievement within the school walls. The eight schools in this study represented a wide range of socioeconomic levels and provided an opportunity to explore some of the differences in the social context issues raised by the studies cited above.

Recurring Organizational Themes

School Organizational Structures and Procedures

To accomplish their goals, school staff have historically grouped thirty or more students of a similar age together with one teacher. At the elementary level, depending upon the size of the school, there may be several such classes at the same grade level. While at the secondary level, though students rotate throughout the day to different subject specialists, the structure is not markedly different: one teacher with twenty-five to thirty students. The consequences of this structural arrangement on the functioning of the school staff has been profound. Teachers have operated largely in isolation with few opportunities to interact with other teachers. This has two important outcomes: increased teacher uncertainty about their craft and threatened self-esteem (Rosenholtz, 1989). With little time for interaction, teachers do not have the opportunity to develop their teaching skills in ways that enhance their own sense of self-confidence and efficacy. Without a sense of technical certainty, teachers may lack self-confidence and feel their self-esteem threatened when faced with students from diverse backgrounds who do not achieve when taught by the teacher. As will be seen in the case studies, grade level configurations and grouping of students can be altered. Such changes, however, are usually made to accommodate outside environmental pressures, such as increased student enrollments, rather than for pedagogical reasons. In one case-study school, students were organized in lofts (180 students and six teachers in a large open room). This structural decision impacted relations among teachers by increasing interaction at the loft level, but confounded interaction at a schoolwide level. Given the ingrained structures of schools in terms of student groupings, a critical question for this study was: What structural changes have been made that helped to diminish the isolation of teachers? Did any of the schools develop structures that fostered collaboration and increased opportunities for teachers to develop more certainty in curriculum and instructional practices?

School Technology: Curriculum and Instructional Practices

Curriculum and instructional practices represent the technology of schools and the essence of a teacher's craft. Since this study was conducted in California, it is important to understand the state context with regard to curriculum. The trend in recent years has been toward a more standardized curriculum, which is shaped by two forces: the statewide curriculum frameworks in each subject area, and state approved, nationally published textbooks. In the last few years, tensions have emerged between these two determinants of curriculum. During the recent cycle to adopt new mathematics textbooks, the California State Board of Education rejected all that were presented, arguing that they were not in alignment with the new mathematics framework which stressed problem solving. While new textbooks to teach reading have been approved for adoption, there are similar tensions: the state language arts framework urges schools to move away from reliance on basal reading texts and toward the use of trade books. These curricular changes have significant implications for teachers' sense of certainty and efficacy. Mastery of new skills for both teachers and students is being required by the statewide curriculum frameworks.

In addition to changes in curriculum, teachers in each of the sample schools were also under pressure to alter instructional practices. The introduction of cooperative learning strategies, models of effective teaching, and the use of a process model to teach writing were evident in all schools in this study. The ability to handle the technological pressures in ways that enhanced student learning and did not threaten teacher self-esteem appear to be related to three organizational variables: the structures that were established to enhance collaboration, the opportunities for teacher growth through staff development, and increased sense of teacher efficacy that occurred from curriculum alignment and rising test scores. The interrelation of these issues is explored in the case studies and the cross-case analysis.

School Climate and Culture

In recent years, the study of school culture has surfaced as an important dimension of school organizational research (Deal, 1984a and b; Deal, 1985; Deal, 1987; Deal and Peterson, 1990; Joyce, 1990; Morgan, 1986; Rossman, Corbett, and Firestone, 1988; Saphier, and King, 1985; Schein, 1986; and Sergiovanni and Corbally, 1984). The concepts of culture and its use to examine and explain organizational life have been drawn from anthropology. 'In anthropology, culture is the foundation term through which the orderliness and patterning of much of our life experience is explained' (Smircich, 1983, p. 341). This straight forward definition of culture makes sense, but does not adequately capture the multi-dimensional layered aspects of culture. In a similar way, culture is portrayed in Figure 1.4 as one variable of organizational life which intersects with and impacts organizational technology and structures. The aspects of culture delineated in Figure 1.4 (safety and order, rewards, expectations, relations with parents, shared mission and norms of collegiality) can be described in terms of behaviors, shared beliefs, symbols, rituals, and stories of the organization. These aspects are embodied in what Deal and Kennedy (1982) and Smircich (1983) call corporate culture. This view of culture Smircich links to the open-system model of organizations that has been used to frame this study. A corporate culture helps 'to unite individuals into social structures' (Smircich, 1983, p. 342). These social structures in turn adapt and respond to both internal and external environmental pressures in ways that maintain the system. Culture, however, is more than just a variable; it is the organization.

A thesis of this book is that both the structure and technology of schools, which themselves are cultural manifestations, in turn shape the school culture in ways that are often not oriented toward learning and achievement. School structures, including the use of time, and a physical plant that separates teachers into individual classrooms and rarely provides adequate common meeting spaces for teachers, have led to the isolation of teachers and prevented their collaboration and cooperation in ways that foster maximum learning by all students. Technological aspects of schooling, especially a standardized curriculum determined by nationally published textbooks, norm-referenced tests, frontal teaching in teacher-centered classrooms, and the tracking of students, also have had a profound influence on school culture, that is, the daily 'orderliness and patterning' of instruction in the classroom. It is argued that to shift the focus of schools towards beliefs and practices that would maximize learning by both students and teachers will require changes in culture, technology, and organizational structures. It is also argued that changes in structures and technology will eventually lead to changes in teacher beliefs about students and about their own abilities as teachers, which represent fundamental aspects of culture.

The elements of culture outlined in Figure 1.4 (see p. 9) are aspects that in large measure can be shaped by the principal (Deal and Peterson, 1990). An important theme that emerges in the case studies is that staff development is a change strategy that potentially can alter the culture of the school (Joyce, 1990). Staff development impacts organizational cognition and organizational symbolism, two other layers of culture that are not entirely captured in the corporate cultural model, by gradually changing the rules by which the system operates and by creating new shared meanings and understandings (Smircich, 1983). Both effective schools programs and school restructuring are predicated on the belief that schools are purposeful instruments that can be altered often through rational planning and through leadership. Corporate culture, organizational cognition and symbolism are all aspects of culture that are seen to be influenced and shaped through planning. Smircich, however, introduces yet another dimension of culture which she refers to as unconscious processes and organization, 'a projection of mind's universal unconscious infrastructure' (Smircich, 1983, p. 342). This dimension of culture is far more pervasive and because it is unconscious is generally unexamined. The last chapter of this book attempts to examine this more illusive aspect of culture and its influence on schools by presenting a 'root metaphor' of schooling (Smircich, 1983, p. 353). The metaphor that is introduced is schooling as a household and teaching as an extension of women's work. Is the isolation of teachers in the classroom a mirror of the isolation of women in the home? Is the lack of professionalism among teachers a result of the low status of women's work in general but especially in terms of homemaking? It is argued that only by probing and examining the unconscious, unstated cultural determinants that have shaped schools will we begin to understand them as they are and why schools are extremely difficult to alter or restructure in any fundamental way.

Leadership

The schools in this study and in the United States, generally, are managed by principals who oversee the day-to-day operations of the school. The range of management activities is vast, encompassing everything from bus and lunch schedules to supervising teachers and students. The organizational-change literature has recognized that to change an organization require leadership — not management (Bennis and Nanus, 1985; Peters and Waterman, 1982). Strong leadership has been consistently listed as one of the characteristics of an effective school (Armor, 1976; Benjamin, 1980; California State Department of Education, 1980; Edmonds, 1979; Eisner, 1980; Levine and Stark, 1981; Murphy, 1988; Reilly, 1980; Weber, 1971). The principals in these studies were frequently referred to as instructional leaders, indicating that they devoted attention to planning, guiding, monitoring, and evaluating instructional issues and student learning (De Bevoise, 1984). In many of the studies of principals there has not been a clear definition of the terms *leadership* or *instructional leadership* (Murphy, 1988, Rost, 1988; Van de Grift, 1990). Some studies described the principals' styles of leadership that were associated with implementation of innovation, change, and improvement (Hall, Rutherford, Hord and Huling, 1984). Others listed specific behaviors of principals which enabled their school to be effective (Blumberg and Greenfield, 1980; Bossert, Dwyer, Rowan, and Lee, 1982; Greenfield, 1982; Huff, Lake, and Schaalman, 1982; Persell, Cookson and Lyons, 1982). Few of these studies have examined the interactive process of leadership, which is the essence of *transforming* leadership. Burns (1978) has defined transforming leadership as the special process of uniting leaders and followers in pursuit of '*higher* goals, the realization of which is tested by the achievement of significant change' (pp. 425–26). Rost (1988) built on Burn's definition by expanding on the reciprocal nature of leadership needed to bring about real intended change.

In their study of successful implementation of innovations, Hord, Stielgelbauer, and Hall (1984) recognized that principals did not carry out their leadership functions by themselves. They identified the important role of a second change-facilitator who worked closely with the principal and teachers to bring about successful change. However, this study still did not explore the interactive process of leadership. Andrews and Bamburg (1989) have shown that teacher perceptions of principal leadership are related to student outcomes. Their study does not discuss whether the interaction between principal and staff is different or whether only the perceptions are different. Pollack, Chrispeels and Watson (1987) found it their study of four effective schools that, while principals played key roles, leadership in the schools was collective and collegial, and reflective of a reciprocal leader-follower relationship between principal and teachers more typical of transforming leadership. Rosenholtz's (1989) study did not specifically address the topic of principal leadership, yet it is clear from her data that there were considerable differences in the relationships between teachers and their principals in the schools with higher student achievement. The comments of the teachers revealed a relationship built on extensive interaction, positive support from the principal, and mutual respect in regard to technological expertise. In additon, one of the major leadership acts of the principals was to create colaborative structures that facilitated the emergence of teacher leadership. Leadership in the present study is examined from the perspective of transforming leadership and addresses the relationship and interaction between principal and teachers in ways that bring about a fundamental change in the transformative process of schooling and in student outcomes.

School Change

The four frames encompassing the transformative process — organizational structures, curriculum and instructional practices, climate and culture, and school leadership — serve as a way of organizing and thinking about change in schools. Much of the literature on school change has focused on planned educational change, describing implementation of innovations, such as a new reading program, individualized instruction, use of learning centers, or teaching 'discovery' science (Fullan, 1982; Hall and Hord, 1987; Herriott and Gross, 1979). The decades of the 1960s and 1970s were noted for the push to implement new programs, many of which were related to technical innovations. The pressures for many of these changes came from the district or outside agencies and not necessarily from the school.

Implementing these innovations proved to be more difficult than anticipated. The impact of the changes were often disappointing to the originators, because there was frequently little evidence of widespread use in the classroom or the changes were short lived (especially if the initiator left). To understand how innovations can be successfully implemented, research on planned changes has focused on the willingness or resistance of individual teachers to adopt the innovation (Coch and French, 1948; Cruickshank, 1981; Fuller, 1969; Hall and Hord, 1987; Zander, 1962) and on how a change is institutionalized (Fullan, 1982; Huberman and Miles, 1984; Miles, 1983). Little attention has been paid to school culture and organizational structures that may inhibit the implementation of changes.

Undertaking school effectiveness and school restructuring processes requires looking at change from an organizational perspective. Two factors differentiate implementation of innovations from school effectiveness and restructuring efforts. First, the scope of the change will be much broader. Fullan (1990) has argued that there is a need to systematically focus on institutional development, as opposed to staff development, although staff development remains an essential element of institutional development. The model presented in Figure 1.4 (see p. 9) represents an effort to depict the full scope of the interactions that must occur in a school-effectiveness and restructuring program, if it is to positively impact student learning. School change must be occurring at both the school and classroom level with the one reinforcing the other. There is also evidence (Chrispeels, and Pollack, 1989; La Rocque and Coleman, 1987, Murphy, Petersen, and Hallinger, 1986; Rosenholtz, 1989) that district effectiveness enhances school effectiveness, which means that school change needs to be examined within the context of systemwide change. Second, the nature of the change will be both political and cultural. The change will be political, because school effectiveness addresses the fundamental issue of the distribution of educational outcomes. In fact, school effectiveness is often referred to as a movement as much as it is a body of research (Ralph and Fennessey, 1983). Rossman, Corbett, and Firestone (1988) have argued that the change will also be cultural because:

> The definition of effectiveness flows from norms, beliefs, and values concerning the way things ought to be. This connection suggests a different and even more fundamental relationship between culture and effectiveness than previously considered in the literature: culture defines effectiveness. Extreme variation in definitions of effectiveness, then, most likely reflect variation in organizational cultures about what is important and worth striving for, about what is true and good, and about what is sacred. (p. 134)

Since a change in the cultural norms and values, especially in terms of how effectiveness is defined, will be required, 'a political strategy that builds coalitions of support might be indicated' (Pfeffer, 1981, p. 446). Coalition building requires leadership and leadership in school change is an intensely political act (Firestone, 1980) involving teamwork, long-range planning, trust, honesty, and subtlety, all of which are political skills.

Research Design and Procedures

The Sample Schools

Eight elementary schools from five different school districts in southern California were asked to participate in this study. (They are referred to from this point onward by pseudonyms.) These schools were chosen in a nonrandom selection process, as is frequently done in a case-study design (Merriam, 1988, Yin, 1984). The staff in the eight elementary schools had been involved in a school-effectiveness effort for at least four years prior to selection for this study. These schools were first selected for review in 1986–87 from a pool of schools which had participated in a school-effectiveness process led by a southern California county office of education. All schools volunteered to participate in the initial effectiveness assessments between 1983 and 1985, using the county's effective-schools survey (Appendix A), in a review of each school's progress in 1987, and again for participation in this study in 1989. These schools, although volunteers, represent the broad cross-section of schools found within the county in terms of size, geographic distribution, and ethnic composition of the student population. The schools, with regard to both student population and student achievement, can be regarded as typical schools, as opposed to outliers. The selection process of outliers for study has been one of the criticisms of the effective schools research (Purkey and Smith, 1983).

The five districts from which these schools were drawn also represent a broad cross-section; however, no unified district (i.e., a district serving kindergarten through twelfth grade students) is represented in the sample. Two of the districts serve students from kindergarten through eighth grade and three of the districts serve students from kindergarten through sixth grade. The districts represented in the sample range in size from six to thirty elementary schools. The three smallest districts had the most stable and long-tenured superintendents, while the largest district had a turnover in district leadership during the course of the study. Per-pupil expenditures in the districts are comparable as are teachers' salaries. All schools in the sample and their districts receive additional funds from the California School Improvement Program. Two of the districts and the sample schools from those districts also receive considerable funding from state and federal programs for non-English speaking and disadvantaged students. The other schools in the sample receive lesser amounts of such funding, because they serve fewer disadvantaged students and have fewer of those students scoring in the bottom quartile.

Data Sources and Methodologies

Teacher Survey Data

Survey data were collected three times from each site using the Effective Schools Survey, once, in 1987, when the school initiated the school-effectiveness program and again in 1989. In each case, the survey was completed by 85 to 95 per cent of the teaching staff. The survey uses a Likert scale to assess opinions of staff in seven key areas: instructional leadership (IL), home-school relations (HSR), clear school mission (CSM), frequent monitoring (FM), opportunity to learn (OL), safe and orderly environment (SOE), and high expectations (HE). A total mean score and total per cent agreement for each effectiveness factor were computed as well as mean and per cent agreement for each item within the factor cluster.

The overall reliability of the survey is high (Alpha + 0.977) and the factor loading between the subsets is strong, approximately 90 per cent of variance was accounted for through the extraction of a principal component — based on a factor subprogram of SPSSX, Inc., 1986 (Watson, Chrispeels, Pollack, 1987). The validity of the instrument has recently been tested in a study that compared teacher survey results with three year gains in third grade reading scores. Using the survey results, 27 schools were grouped with 93 per cent accuracy according to three year reading achievement gains (Micks, 1989). Thus, the survey instrument seems to be a valid predictor of increases in achievement in third grade reading scores.

Teacher Interview Data

To understand how teachers felt their school had changed as a result of their involvement in the effective schools process, a structured interview protocol was developed (Appendix B). In 1986–87, principals at each school were asked to assist in selecting nine teachers to be interviewed. The principal was asked to select teachers who represented the following categories: 1) two teachers who had been actively involved in the improvement process serving either on the school site council or on a special school effectiveness planning committee; 2) teachers that represented the different grade levels in the school; 3) a teacher who worked with special programs, such as, a reading specialist, bilingual coordinator, or Chapter I resource teacher; 4) a teacher that had been at the school for eight or more years; 5) a teacher who was new to the school. These categories were not mutually exclusive; often one teacher represented two or more categories. In all cases the principal followed these guidelines and a diverse cross-section of the staff was interviewed.

In 1989, five teachers were selected to be interviewed. The teachers were drawn from the pool of teachers previously interviewed with care taken to maintain a representative sample in terms of grade levels. In this way it was possible to explore how these teachers perceived the school had changed or remained the same in the intervening two years. The interviews in 1987 and 1989 lasted approximately one hour. All staff members interviewed freely agreed to be interviewed. The interview data provided a check on survey data and a rich comparative data base to analyze how the eight schools had changed during the last four years. The interview data were analyzed using the four organizational frames presented in Figure 1.4 (see p. 9).

Test Data Analysis and School Effectiveness Defined

Test data from the California Assessment Program (CAP) from 1983–84 to 1987–88 were collected. CAP is a norm-referenced test given to third, sixth, eighth, and twelfth grade students in all California schools. The scaled scores allow cross-school comparisons. In addition, the schools are rated according to a socio-economic index based on parent education levels, Aid to Families with Dependent Children, and language proficiency which allows further comparisons among schools and provides a way to take into account background factors. The California Assessment Program is also unique among state tests in providing disaggregated test data according to family occupation at the elementary level. This subgroup analysis provides an easily accessible and important measure of school effectiveness. Using CAP data, the effectiveness of each school was determined. For purposes of this study the following criteria were used to assess effectiveness and rank the school at both third and sixth grade:

1 A growth of 25 scaled score points in reading and mathematics over four years, or scaled scores that are maintained above comparison bands. (The comparison band represents the range of scores that would be expected in schools serving similar socio-economic status students).

2 A decrease in the number of students scoring in the bottom quartile in reading and mathematics of 10 percentage points over four years, or the number of students scoring below Q1 remains at 15 per cent or less.

3 An increase of 25 scaled score points over four years in the achievement of the lowest SES subgroup in reading and mathematics, or
achievement above the state average in reading and mathematics for
the lowest SES group.

Archival Records

Other archival records and documents were collected to serve as another data
source. School Improvement Plans and Program Quality Review documents were
read and analyzed for each site. The findings of the Program Quality Review
team were compared with the data collected through interviews and surveys. This
provided an independent source of data and description of school program
strengths and weaknesses.

Limits of the Study

There are four major limitations to the methodology used. First, the small sample
size, the geographic confines of the study, the limited number of interviews conducted, the lack of match among schools in terms of size, socio-economic status
and ethnic composition, and the limitation of the study to elementary schools
restricts the ability to generalize the findings of this study, especially to other
parts of the country or to other levels of schooling.

Second, the use of aggregated standardized achievement test results as the
primary measure of effectiveness limits the potential for making inferences about
cause and effect relationships among leadership efforts, programmatic or institutional change, and student outcomes. As Guba and Lincoln (1985) have pointed
out, there is the danger of oversimplifying or exaggerating the situation, 'leading
the reader to erroneous conclusions about the actual state of affairs' (p. 377). To
avoid this danger, the analysis has focused on offering insights into relationships
rather than asserting cause and effect links between variables.

A third limit of the study stemmed from the nature of case-study methodology
which allows the researcher to make only analytical, rather than statistical, gener-
alizations by linking particular events to a broader theory (Yin, 1984). If the case
studies had been drawn from a larger sample size, it would have been possible to
make statistical generalization to corroborate the case study findings as Rosenholtz
(1989) was able to do in her study of schools and teachers in Tennessee.

A fourth limitation arose from the nature of qualitative research which
presents significant problems in maintaining reliability and validity, because it
depends heavily on the interviewing, observational and interpretive skills of the
researcher. Using multiple sources of evidence, establishing a chain of evidence,
and having key informants review the analysis helped to enhance the construct
validity of the study (Yin, 1984). Comparisons of data from this case study with
results from other similar studies (Mortimore, Sammons, Stoll, Lewis and Ecob,
1988; Hallinger and Murphy, 1986, 1989, Rosenholtz, 1989; Teddlie, Kirby, and
Stringfield, 1989; Teddlie, and Stringfield; 1985, Teddlie, Stringfield, and Suarez,
1985) were also used to provide a check on reliability and validity of conclusions.
The opportunity to explore issues in depth and to examine substantive aspects of

organizational change do not overcome the limitations, but they do counterbalance them. The chapters that follow attempt to make sense of the wealth of data that were collected for this study and to present it in a way that will increase understanding of the complex nature of change and organizational development of schools that are working to increase student achievement.

Chapter Overviews

An examination of the schools in this study begins in Chapter 2 with a look at the demographic data, student achievement results, and teacher survey responses in each of the eight elementary schools. This chapter is important in setting the context of the study and bringing to the fore some of the confounding variables. The schools are not all alike. They differ in size, grade configurations, ethnic distribution and number of students who are non-English fluent. They are similar in one important respect: they all had principals who chose to lead the school in a school effectiveness process and to utilize the resources of the county office of education to assist them in that process, at least in the initial stages. In this chapter the criteria for determining a school's effectiveness are applied to the third and six grade California Assessment Program (CAP) scores and a ranking of schools is presented.

Chapter 3 begins the case-studies by describing Whitney Elementary. The primary purpose of this chapter is to show the steps that the principal and staff took to create a culture of learning and achievement. Three important points regarding change emerge in this chapter: 1) the importance of time in the change process; 2) the need for a myriad of little steps to bring about change; and 3) the significance to the change process of enabling teachers to be reflective practitioners by teaching them to analyze and use data. The principal at Whitney served the longest tenure of any principal in the sample schools. The length of his tenure coupled with yearly efforts to improve seemed to have an important impact on the ability to bring about a fundamental shift in teacher beliefs. The multitude of small steps taken at Whitney, including teaching teachers to analyze both test data and survey results, also contributed to a restructured belief system about teachers' ability to teach and students' ability to learn.

Chapter 4 presents the struggles of Sierra, a school which did not experience the achievement gains of Whitney in spite of considerable efforts on the part of the principal and staff. A significant theme addressed in this chapter is the power of structures to foster and limit teacher collaboration. Sierra was unique among the schools in having a loft class structure and combined grade levels (1–2, 3–4, and 5–6). On the one hand, the loft structure provided unique opportunities for the teachers within each loft to cooperate, although not all lofts did. On the other hand, the loft structure interfered with creating schoolwide structures for collaboration and cooperation and diminished the opportunities to establish an academic focus and school mission. Another important theme that emerges in this case-study is the frustration and threat to self-esteem that occurs when teachers feel they are working to improve and do not see the desired results. The social context of the community (which was not the poorest among sample schools) began to be seen by some teachers as an insurmountable barrier to increased student achievement.

Chapter 5 describes Tahoe Elementary, a school serving one of the lowest socio-economic status communities. This school illustrates the problems of initiating and sustaining change when there is administrative turnover at both district and school levels. Important collaborative structures were being established in the final two years encompassed by this study, but part of staff viewed them as creating an *in* and an *out* group. Curriculum and instructional practices also are important themes in this chapter. A lack of curriculum alignment, minimal staff development, frustration over pressures to follow a particular model of instruction, more frequent monitoring of both teaching practices by the principal and increased pressures to raise student test scores were causing considerable concern and uncertainty among teachers, threatening their sense of self-esteem.

Chapter 6 illustrates the power of structures to impact school improvement and effectiveness. Yosemite Elementary between 1983 and 1986 provided a textbook example of bringing about successful change. All four components of the transformative process seemed to be working in coordination to increase student achievement and staff enthusiasm for their work. However, rapidly increasing enrollments, an outside environmental pressure, forced the school to implement a four track year-round school schedule. Challenging though it was, the structural change might have been manageable had the students not been segregated, with all of the gifted students being placed on one track and all limited-English speaking, lower socio-economic students being placed on another. Collaborative and problem-solving structures that had been carefully built in the previous two to three years began to disintegrate. The structural change had a ripple effect on all other components. Teachers in each track felt isolated from their counterparts in other tracks, communication among tracks was difficult, and a gulf emerged between those teachers on the bilingual track and the other three tracks affecting the culture and climate of the school. While many strengths in the curriculum and instructional area remained strong, the academic focus of the school weakened because the principal's time was drawn away from curriculum and instruction and focused primarily on addressing community concerns about the placement of children. In the last year of the study, structural changes were again underway to heal divisions and enhance collaboration among tracks by redistributing students in a more heterogeneous pattern.

The difficulty, complexity, and fragility of the change processes is the major theme of Chapter 7, which summarizes the data from all eight schools using the four frames of reference. While each component is addressed separately, the interrelations among the components are also illustrated. Many active steps were being undertaken to bring about increased effectiveness. These steps were sometimes undermined or failed to reach their full potential if other key aspects of organizational life were not addressed. The data indicate that to have the greatest impact on a school's climate and culture or curriculum and instructional practices, structures that fostered collaboration, cooperation and shared decision-making among teachers need to be in place. A shared mission, an academic focus, and a culture of learning and achievement emerged when teachers had multiple opportunities to interact in grade level teams, on school curriculum or problem-solving committees, and at staff meetings.

A major lesson from this study and other studies (Barth, 1990; Lieberman, 1986, 1988; Rosenholtz, 1989; Schlechty, 1990) is that teachers are critical of the school improvement and restructuring process. Chapter 8 summarizes data from the teacher interviews regarding successful change strategies. Teachers were asked if they were helping other schools to improve, what would they recommend be done? What were the lessons they had learned that they would want to share with others? The themes have been heard before: the need for collaboration and shared decision-making opportunities, the need to have a schoolwide focus, goals and channels of communication, the need to regularly assess school programs and student progress, and the need for parent involvement. What is significant is that teachers in all schools, regardless of their own school's level of success, shared these perspectives.

The relationship between school effectiveness research and restructuring is the theme of Chapter 9. The lessons learned from this study and other school effectiveness studies are applied to current efforts to restructure schools. The impetus for school restructuring is examined in relation to the driving forces behind school effectiveness efforts. Each component of the transformative process is explored for the lessons that may be useful to schools engaged in restructuring. The critical role of school culture is discussed as well as large societal/cultural issues that may impede school restructuring, especially calls for increased collegiality and greater professionalism among teachers.

Chapter 2

School Profiles

This chapter describes the eight elementary schools, the context for their involvement in an effective school process, their demographics, and achievement results
based on the California Assessment Program. The effectiveness formula, presented
in Chapter 1, is applied to the test data to establish an effectiveness scale for each
school at third and sixth grade. The effective schools survey results are assessed
and compared. The data presented are used to answer three questions:

1   Applying the effectiveness formula, did the school effectiveness and
    improvement process have an impact on student achievement during
    the duration of this study?
2   Were there significant differences in attitudes among teachers in the
    more effective schools compared to the less effective schools?
3   Did the opinions of staff members change during the course of the
    study?

In addition, the portraits sketched in this chapter provide the background for the
four more detailed case studies which follow and for the cross-case analysis presented in Chapter 7.

Context of the Study

In 1982–83, several staff members at a southern California county office of education became interested in the research on effective schools. After reviewing the
effective schools surveys developed by several groups, it was decided to base the
county office's Effective Schools Program on the model developed by the Connecticut State Department of Education (Gautier, 1983; Pecheone and Shoemaker,
1984; Villanova, Gauthier, Proctor, and Shoemaker, 1981).

The first schools to participate were volunteers whose principals shared an
early interest in the effective schools reseach. In 1983 and 1984, only a few schools
assessed staff and parent opinions using the Connecticut Questionnaire. By June
1987, over a hundred schools in the county had used either the Connecticut or the
new survey developed by county office (See Appendix A). The new survey was
based on the Connecticut Questionnaire, but added questions to provided data
needed for school improvement reviews. In addition, the new survey had parallel
forms for parents and staff at the elementary level and for parents, students, and
staff at the middle school and high school levels. The surveys enabled the school
to gain insights into staff and parent opinions regarding the presence or absence

of effective schools characteristics. The data was then combined with test data and other documentation about school effects, such as absences or discipline infractions, to help the school develop and an effective schools profile. The profile was used by the staff to develop an improvement plan. Schools were not charged for the service and participation remained voluntary. The amount of follow-up with schools using the surveys varied considerably, depending on the commitment and interest of the principal and the skills and involvement of the county staff member assigned to the school. No new county staff members were hired to specifically direct the effective schools program and many staff members had curriculum specialties that occupied most of their time.

The eight schools involved in this study represent a non-random sample of schools that participated in the effective schools assessment and planning process. The schools entered the program at varying times, with one beginning as early as 1983, and another not administering their first surveys until 1986. All schools, through the actions of their principals or a combination of principal and staff consensus, volunteered to participate in the effective schools process. Between 1983 and 1986, the staff at each school completed the effective schools survey (either the Connecticut or the county version). The survey results were reported to the staff by a staff member from the county office of education; and the data were used by the staff to plan improvement strategies. Not all of the schools received equal assistance and support in the planning and implementing stages. Three of the schools received considerable assistance in terms of interpreting the data, assisting in planning, and organizing follow-up activities, such as staff development. Three schools received moderate amounts, and two schools received little assistance other than the initial assessment and report back to staff. The two schools that received minimal assistance had some extenuating circumstances that help to explain the lack of follow-up. In the case of Lassen, the assistant superintendent for curriculum and instruction of the district had been a member of the county office of education's effective schools team and was well versed in the effective schools process. He provided considerable assistance to all the schools in the district by establishing grade level objectives and expectancies, developing new systems to test and monitor pupil progress, and aligning the district's curriculum. The staff at Tahoe, the second school receiving minimal assistance, did not volunteer to participate and felt pressured into the process by the principal. There was considerable conflict between the staff and principal during his two year tenure and little opportunity for involvement. A new principal was assigned to school in 1986.

All eight schools voluntarily agreed to have a sample of their staff members interviewed (see Appendix 'B') in the late fall early winter of 1986–87, as part of a follow-up study being conducted by the author and two other county office staff members. Six of the eight schools readministered the effective schools surveys. Two schools did not because they had already completed the survey twice prior to 1987. In 1989, again, all eight schools agreed to assist the author in participating in the current study by completing the effective schools surveys and by allowing a sample of staff members to be reinterviewed. Table 2.1 lists the eight schools by the pseudonyms they have been given for purposes of this study, shows the years each school completed the effective schools surveys, and the degree of assistance received in the initial stages of the effective schools process.

Each school has been involved in the California School Improvement Program. This means that the schools received additional state funds, were required

Table 2.1 Comparison of time of entry into the effective schools program and levels of planning and implementation assistance received from the county office of education

School	1st Survey	2nd Survey	3rd Survey	Level of Assistance
Whitney	1/86	3/87	1/89	High
Yosemite	10/83	10/85	5/89	High
Pinyon	2/85	4/87	5/89	Moderate
Lassen	1/85	2/87	4/89	Minimal
Sequoia	3/85	2/87	5/89	Moderate
Shasta	3/85	3/87	6/89	Moderate
Sierra	1/85	2/87	3/89	High
Tahoe	4/85	3/86	5/89	Minimal

to establish a school site council (with equal representation of school staff and parents), and to develop a school improvement plan that was updated each year and rewritten every three years. In most instances, the effective schools survey data were used as documentation to support specific school improvement plan activities. Once specific needs were identified, school improvement funds provided a means for the schools to address identified needs such as training in Teacher Expectations and Student Achievement (TESA), a program designed to raise teacher expectations for students and increase learning.

In all schools, most of school improvement funds were allocated for classroom instructional assistants rather than for staff development or other improvement strategies. As a result of the effective schools surveys, however, one school changed its budget and allocated a significant proportion of their funds to establish reading and math labs that were staffed by teachers, as opposed to noncertificated instructional assistants, as a means of better meeting the needs of the school's low-achieving students.

Demographic Profiles

The schools in this study reflected the diversity in the county in terms of size, grade configuration, and other demographic variables. On the one hand, the diversity of the sample was a confounding factor in the study; on the other hand, the diversity addressed one of the criticisms of the effective schools research that only urban schools with either very high or low achievement have been studied (Purkey and Smith, 1983).

Six of the eight schools served students in kindergarten through sixth grade. During the course of the study (1987–88), two schools transferred sixth grade students to nearby middle schools. All of the schools have had to cope with enrollment growth, and the movement of sixth grade students represented one type of response. Establishing year-round, multiple track schools was another way of handling the surge in student enrollments. During the course of the study, Yosemite, Sequoia, and Pinyon had to implement multiple track year-round programs. In 1986–87 Sequoia returned to a single track, as did Pinyon in 1988–89. Both have retained a single track year-round schedule. In addition to having multiple tracks, Pinyon also had to accommodate a second school on its campus for one year while a new school was being built. Based on interview comments and analysis of test data, all of the shifts in grade configurations impacted the instructional program and the achievement of students. Dips in the California

Table 2.2 Comparison of school enrollments, grade configuration, SES, and school year schedules

Schools	Enrollment	Grade	SES Index	School Schedule 1989
Whitney	522	K-5	2.02	Traditional
Yosemite	755	K-6	3.38	4 Track Year-round
Pinyon	514	K-6	2.07	Modified Year-round
Lassen	792	K-5	1.60	Traditional
Sequoia	762	K-6	1.62	1 Track Year-round
Shasta	655	K-6	1.82	1 Track Year-round
Sierra	642	K-6	1.89	1 Track Year-round
Tahoe	665	K-6	1.46	Traditional

Assessment Program results for Sequoia, Yosemite, and Pinyon can be seen in each school during the year when a four track year-round schedule was implemented. The case study of Yosemite in Chapter 6 explores the issue in more depth. Table 2.2 summarizes the information on size of enrollment, grade configuration, socieconomic index, and school year schedule.

Figure 2.1 graphically presents each school's enrollment for 1988–89. The schools are arranged on the graph in approximate order of their overall level of student achievement as measured at third grade by the California Assessment Program (CAP). The school with the highest third grade achievement (Whitney) is on the left and the school with the lowest achievement (Tahoe) is on the right. (Achievement results are discussed in detail in Achievement Profiles section below). As can be seen from the graph, the two schools with the lowest enrollment (under 525) are at the top end in terms of overall achievement. Three other schools with over 750 students, however, are also at the higher achievement end. Thus, size will not prevent a school from becoming effective. All three schools with enrollments over 750 have an assistant principal. This is not true for the schools with enrollments in the six hundreds. Without further study it is not possible to determine whether the presence of an assistant principal in schools with enrollments over 700 represents a significant difference to improvement efforts compared to the schools with enrollments between 600 and 700 but without an assistant.

Figure 2.1 Comparison of student enrollments in relation to overall student achievement

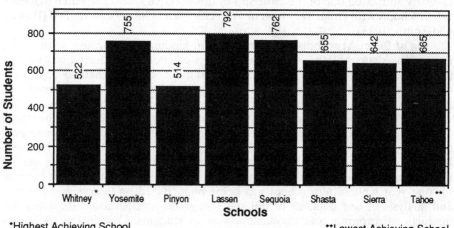

*Highest Achieving School

**Lowest Achieving School

Figure 2.2   Comparison of schools in terms of ethnic distribution of students

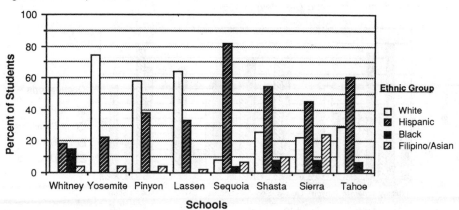

The schools also differed in the ethnic and racial composition of their student bodies. Figure 2.2 shows the ethnic distribution in each school as recorded on reports submitted to the state in the fall of 1988. Again the diversity reflected the diversity in the county. The data in Figure 2.2 show that student achievement is higher at the four schools with the largest White, non-Hispanic populations.

Socioeconomic data.   The index of socioeconomic status (SES) for each school was computed by the state of California based on the occupations of the parents of students in either the third or sixth grade. Teachers, using a list of occupations, categorized parents into one of five groups. On the basis of this classification, an SES value of one, two or three was assigned and an SES index computed. Table 2.3 presents the SES values assigned each occupational group.

Table 2.3   Parent occupations and the corresponding SES value

SES Value	Occupation
1	Unknown
1	Unskilled
2	Skilled and semiskilled employees
3	Semi professional, clerical, sales workers, and technicians
3	Executives, professionals, and managers

The SES index is the average (mean) of the SES (shown in Table 2.3) for all third or sixth grade students in the school. A high SES value indicates the school serves a community with a large percentage of people engaged in professional and semiprofessional occupations.

Figure 2.3 (p. 28) presents the percentage of students in each parent occupational category. (The unknown category is not shown since it was less than 4 per cent in all schools.) The distribution of parent occupations in Figure 2.3, with each school's SES index, supports a general correlation between the index, the per cent of students from each parent occupation category, and overall student achievement (See Figure 2.1). The relationship, however, is not a one to one correspondence. In other words, Whitney, Yosemite, and Pinyon had the highest

Figure 2.3 Distribution of students by parent occupation and comparison with statewide averages based on third grade CAP data in 1988

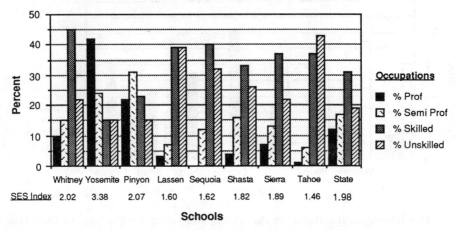

	Whitney	Yosemite	Pinyon	Lassen	Sequoia	Shasta	Sierra	Tahoe	State
SES Index	2.02	3.38	2.07	1.60	1.62	1.82	1.89	1.46	1.98

Schools

Occupations
- % Prof
- % Semi Prof
- % Skilled
- % Unskilled

SES indexes and the highest overall achievement. Lassen and Sequoia, however, had lower SES indexes compared to Shasta and Sierra, and yet out-performed them on the California Assessment Program. As will be shown below, when test scores are disaggregated, the results for the lowest income students in Yosemite and Pinyon were not as strong as for Whitney, Lassen, Sequoia and Shasta which had lower SES indices.

In addition to SES, another economic and demographic variable affecting the schools was the per cent of students receiving Aid to Families with Dependent Children and the per cent who were classified as limited or non-English speaking at third grade. Figure 2.4 presents this data. Again there was variability among the eight schools. Except for Pinyon, the four schools with the highest overall achievement had fewer limited and non-English speaking students. Except for Whitney, three of the four top performing schools had very low percentages of students receiving AFDC.

Figure 2.4 Comparison of per cent of AFDC and limited or non-English speaking (LES/NES) students at each school based on 1987–88 third grade CAP data

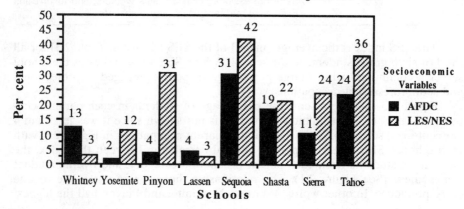

Schools

Socioeconomic Variables
- AFDC
- LES/NES

Each of the graphs presenting the demographic profiles helps to illustrate that family background variables are correlated to a school's overall student achievement. Significantly, the graphs also illustrate that there is not a one to one correspondence between home background or ethnicity and student achievement; therefore, other school factors need to be identified to explain the differences in student achievement. The following points summarize the socioeconomic data for the eight schools and their relationship to student achievement:

- Size of student population did not prevent a school from becoming effect- ive; however, the schools with student populations between 600 and 700 and without an assistant principal had lower levels of achievement. (Figure 2.1)
- Schools serving a higher socioeconomic student population had higher overall achievement, but there was not a one-to-one correlation between SES and achievement, pointing to the significance of other school factors. (Table 2.3 and Figure 2.3)
- Schools with fewer non-English speaking students had higher overall achievement levels, but not necessarily higher achievement for the school's limited and non-English speaking subgroups, as will be shown in the next section. (Figure 2.4)
- Demographic changes, such as rapid growth in student population or shifts in the ethnic composition of student populations required new grade configurations or implementation of multiple track year-round school schedules. The impact of these external environmental factors on teacher attitudes, school programs, and student achievement is explored in depth in the case studies. (Figure 2.2)

The demographic data presented in the graphs raise several critical questions that the case studies and cross-case analysis attempts to answer. Why was Whitney able to achieve both excellence and equity even though it was not serving the most affluent population? Why were Lassen and Sequoia, schools that served large disadvantaged populations, able to achieve good results with their students, while Sierra, Shasta, and Tahoe, with similar populations, have been less successful? In addition to its low-income and largely LES/NES student population, what school factors seemed to contribute to Tahoe's poor achievement profile?

Achievement Profiles

While standardized tests have been criticized as too narrow a measure of student achievement (Rowan *et al.*, 1983), their value is that they allow comparisons among schools. In this study, the California Assessment Program (CAP) was used as the means of comparing and measuring overall student achievement at third and sixth grade. In addition, the results from the CAP test were disaggregated by parent occupation levels providing a means to assess effectiveness and equity issues across all groups of students. A five-year analysis of test scores provided the data needed to answer the first question posed for this study: Applying the effectiveness formula, did the school effectiveness and improvement process have an impact on student achievement throughout the duration of this study? The trend analysis allows both an assessment of the degree of effectiveness at- tained by the schools and a comparison among schools in terms of overall achievement in reading and mathematics at third and sixth grade.

As presented in the definition of an effective school in Chapter 1, three criteria were used for describing each school's degree of effectiveness. The criteria are:

1   A growth of 25 scaled score points in reading and mathematics over four years, or scaled scores that are maintained above the CAP comparison band as indicated on the California Assessment Program (CAP).
2   A decrease in the number of students scoring in the bottom quartile (Q1) in a standard distribution of achievement in reading and mathematics by 10 percentage points over four years, or the number of students scoring below Q1 remains at 15 per cent or less.
3   An increase of 25 scaled score points over four years in the achievement of the lowest SES subgroup in reading and mathematics, or achievement levels of the lowest SES subgroup that are above the statewide average in reading and mathematics.

Each criterion could be met in one of two ways: either by demonstrating change in the desired direction (i.e., higher achievement or fewer students scoring below Q1) or by maintaining a high level of achievement. Allowing schools to meet the criteria of effectiveness in two different ways recognizes that a high growth rate and a high level of performance are often mutually exclusive. Maintaining a high level of performance also requires continuous effort.

For the first criterion of effectiveness, a growth of 25 scaled score points in reading and mathematics over four years was selected, because it represented a realistic growth rate of 10 per cent and indicated a one-half standard deviation gain in achievement. Prior to 1988, the California Assessment Program School Report indicated whether or not the school was scoring above its comparison band (i.e., scoring above what would be expected when the socioeconomic status of the students were taken into account). Scoring above band was the achievement level by which schools could also meet the first criterion.

For the second criterion, a 10 per cent decrease over four years in the percentage of students scoring in the bottom quartile was set as the degree of desired change. Again this number represents a reasonable, yet significant improvement. A school with 15 per cent or fewer students scoring below Q1 was considered to have attained a high level of achievement.

An important dimension of effectiveness is achievement gains of students from the lowest SES group. Therefore, the third criterion of effectiveness focused on this subgroup. A gain of 25 scaled score points over four years in both reading and mathematics was set as the standard. An increase of 25 points would not necessarily bring the lowest SES group to full equity with higher SES groups, but it would show movement in the direction of equity, especially when coupled with the second criterion. To meet the criterion by level of achievement, this subgroup had to be at or above the state average for all students in reading and mathematics.

Using data collected from the California Assessment Program, the eight schools were rated on these criteria and an effectiveness index computed. Figures 2.5 through 2.16 present the data that was used to assess each school's progress toward achieving school effectiveness. The following analysis shows how the criteria were applied to one school to assess its degree of effectiveness.

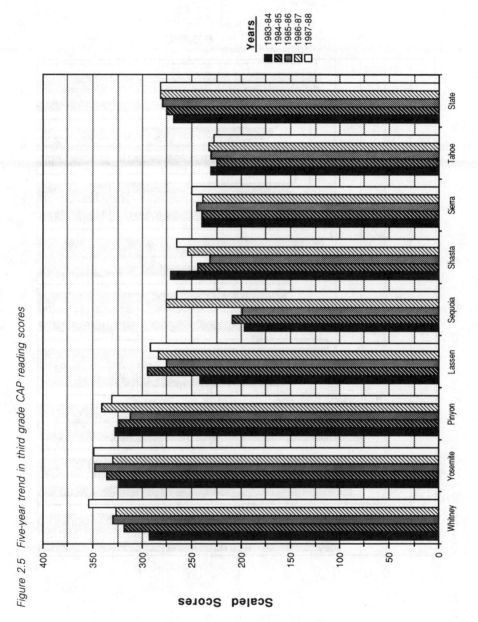

Figure 2.5 Five-year trend in third grade CAP reading scores

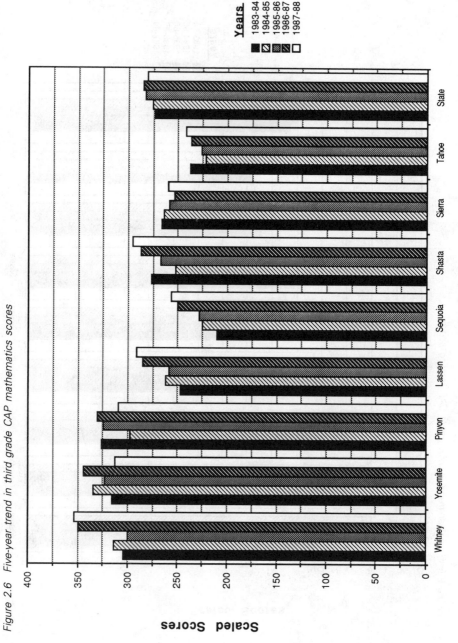

Figure 2.6 Five-year trend in third grade CAP mathematics scores

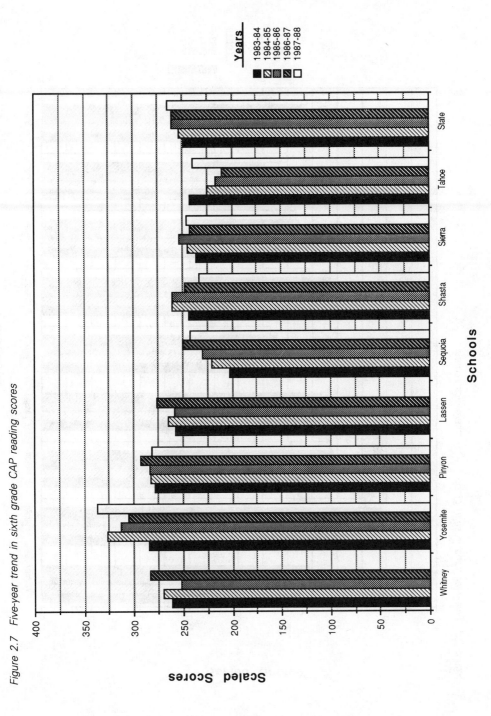

Figure 2.7 Five-year trend in sixth grade CAP reading scores

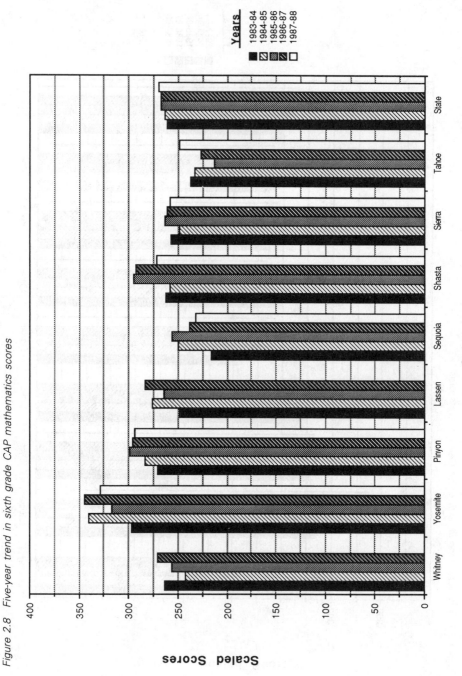

Figure 2.8 Five-year trend in sixth grade CAP mathematics scores

Figure 2.9   Five-year trend in the number of third grade students scoring below Q1 on the CAP reading test

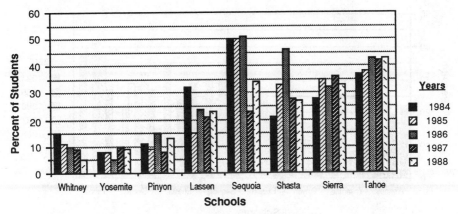

Figure 2.10   Five-year trend in number of third grade students scoring below Q1 on the CAP mathematics test

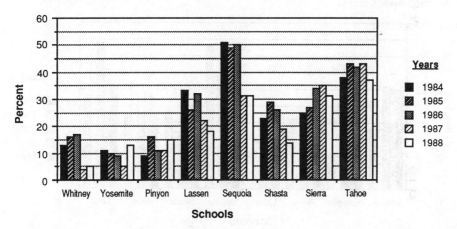

Assessing Whitney's Effectiveness

Based on the data presented in Figures 2.5 and 2.6, Whitney has met the first criterion of effectiveness at third grade. There has been a gain of over 25 points in both reading and mathematics. In addition, the level of scaled scores placed Whitney above the third grade comparison band. At sixth grade, Figures 2.7 and 2.8 show there has been growth in both reading and mathematics, but the gains are below 25 scaled score points. Only in reading did the school meet the alternate criterion of being above the comparison band. In terms of the second criterion of effectiveness — decreases in the number of students scoring below Q1 — Whitney again was highly successful at third grade, but not at sixth. Figures 2.9 and 2.10 show that at third grade there has been a ten point decrease in the percentage of students scoring below Q1 in reading and mathermatics. Also the per cent of students in the bottom quartile was well below 15 per cent in 1986–87 and 1987–88. Figures 2.11 and 2.12 show that there has been over a 10 point

Figure 2.11 Five-year trend in number of sixth grade students scoring below Q1 on the CAP reading test

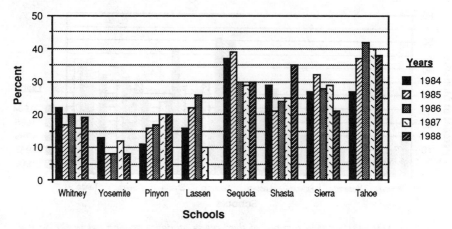

Figure 2.12 Five-year trend in number of sixth grade students scoring below Q1 on the CAP mathematics test

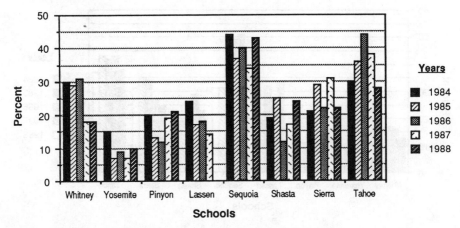

decrease in the percentage of sixth grade students scoring below Q1 in mathematics, but not in reading. In neither reading nor mathematics is the percentage of sixth grade students in the bottom quartile below 15 per cent.

The third criterion of effectiveness is the achievement gains of the lowest SES subgroup. Figures 2.13 and 2.14 show that students whose parent occupation is unskilled or unemployed (Lowest SES Subgroup, see Table 2.3) made an achievement gain of 25 or more scaled score points over the four year period. In addition, the level of achievement for these students was above the statewide average score in third grade reading and mathematics. Figures 2.15 and 2.16 show that as in the other criteria, the sixth grade did not meet either part of this criterion in reading. In mathematics, the lowest SES group gained over 25 points in achievement.

To summarize the data and establish a school effectiveness score, a value of one was assigned to each criterion and its alternate if the criterion was met, and a value of zero when the criteria were not met. For each grade level a maximum

Figure 2.13   Five-year trend in third grade CAP reading scores for lowest SES subgroup and comparison of this group with average statewide score in 1988

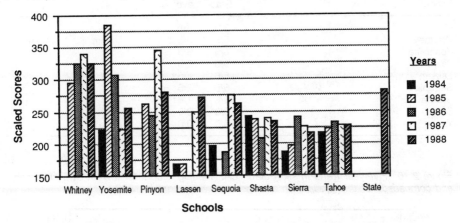

Figure 2.14   Five-year trend in third grade CAP mathematics scores for lowest SES subgroup and comparison of this group with average statewide score in 1988

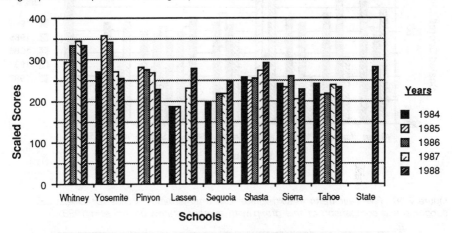

of six points could be achieved. Whitney received a score of six out of six for its third grade performance and three out of six for its sixth grade performance. Based on this scale, Whitney's improvement efforts have resulted in a high level of effectiveness for third grade students and a lesser degree of effectiveness at sixth grade. In a similar manner, the data were analyzed for each school and evaluated against the three criteria. The effectiveness scores derived from this analysis are presented in Table 2.4.

Based on the degree to which the criteria were met, Yosemite and Lassen can be seen to have achieved a relatively high degree of effectiveness for both grade levels. Whitney, on the other hand, has a higher degree of effectiveness at third than at sixth. Like Whitney, Pinyon and Sequoia have met the criteria for effectiveness at third grade, but did not meet all the criteria for sixth grade. Pinyon met the criteria as a result of high levels of achievement, rather than changes or gains in achievement. In fact, the graphs at both third and sixth show

Table 2.4   *Comparison of each schools' effectiveness score at third and sixth grade*

School	Grade Level	
	3rd	6th
Whitney	6/6	3/6
Yosemite	6/6	5/6
Pinyon	5/6	3/6
Lassen	6/6	4/6
Sequoia	6/6	2/6
Shasta	3/6	1/6
Sierra	0/0	0/0
Tahoe	0/0	0/0

Figure 2.15   Five-year trend in sixth grade CAP reading scores for lowest SES subgroup and comparison of this group with average statewide score in 1988

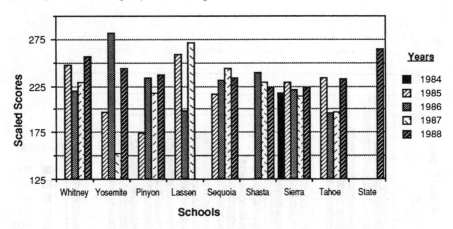

Figure 2.16   Five-year trend in sixth grade CAP mathematics scores for lowest SES subgroup and comparison of this group with average statewide score in 1988

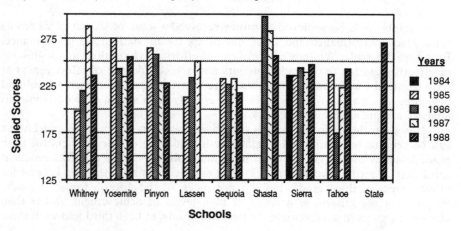

there have been minimal gains except in sixth grade mathematics (Figure 2.8) and third grade reading by the lowest SES subgroup (Figure 2.13). Sequoia, on the other hand, met the criteria more through gains, especially at third grade, as is clearly shown in Figures 2.5 and 2.6. Based on the three criteria, Shasta achieved some degree of effectiveness at third grade, but met only one criterion at sixth grade. Tahoe and Sierra remain ineffective schools in terms of the three criteria.

The five-year trend in CAP data shows that the school improvement process had an impact on student achievement in five of the eight schools and provides a basis for describing some schools as more effective than others. Presenting a five-year trend is also important for three other reasons. First, by examining the data over a five-year period setting criteria by which to evaluate it, a more reliable picture of a school's degree of effectiveness emerges. While the data tend to confirm Rowan, Bossert and Dwyer's (1983) criticism of relying on test scores to determine effectiveness, because they fluctuate from year to year, the data also show that there is a fairly consistent pattern of either improvement or non-improvement in achievement results.

Second, the five-year trend helps to illustrate that school effectiveness cannot be approached as an event, but must be viewed as a long-term process and commitment. None of the schools experienced overnight success, especially at sixth grade, where increased test scores seemed much harder to achieve. Five of the eight schools, however, achieved significant increases in achievement over the five years (i.e., gained a half of a standard deviation or more in reading and mathematics at third or sixth grade). Furthermore, the five schools met the most important criterion of an effective school — significantly raising the achievement of the students from the lowest economic subgroup in one or more subject areas.

Examining the gains and losses within the school context is a third reason for analyzing achievement data over time. When each school's history was explored, possible explanations for the fluctuations or lack of gains began to emerge. Of particular interest were the perturbations in the environment that may be influencing the schools' ability to increase or even sustain achievement gains. For example, Yosemite and Pinyon experienced considerable growth in student population and a shift to a four track year-round school schedule. Both schools remained at a relatively high level of overall performance (see Figures 2.5–2.8). However, at Yosemite, when the scores are disaggregated, the achievement scores in reading and mathematics at both third and sixth grade declined for the lowest socioeconomic subgroup the year that the four track year-round schedule was implemented. This sudden drop in achievement scores for the lowest economic subgroup is explored in depth in Chapter 6 in the Yosemite case-study.

The staff at Sequoia worked for the three years to improve its program for its largely poor and Hispanic population before it began to see real gains. During the first three years, it also coped with shifting to a four track year-round schedule. In 1986–87, the school retained its year-round schedule, but operated with a single track. At this point, reading scores improved dramatically, especially at third grade, while math scores continued their steady, but less dramatic, increase. Shasta's scores showed a more erratic pattern. After several years of significant gains, there was a drop in scores in 1984–85, when a new principal came to the school. Then after a settling-in period, the scores began to improve slightly once again.

Over the last five years, at the third and sixth grade level, the scores at Sierra improved only slightly in reading and sixth grade mathematics and declined slightly in third grade mathematics. During this five year period, the school experienced a shift in population from an English-fluent Filipino population, representing the dominate ethnic group, to limited-English-speaking Hispanics, now representing over a third of the school's students. Unless extra efforts are made, a population shift such as occurred at Sierra can slow improvement efforts. Other reasons for the lack of gains are explored in Chapter 4 in the Sierra case-study.

Except for a slight increase in sixth grade mathematics, Tahoe's third and sixth grade scores remained at fairly constant and low levels over the last five years. The school has also had two changes in principals in this time frame. The impact of the personnel shifts and other school cultural, curriculum and organizational dimensions are discussed in Chapter 5 in the Tahoe case-study.

Cross-Case Comparison of Effective Schools Survey Results

An analysis of the survey results is necessary to answer the second and third research questions: 2) Were there significant differences in attitudes among teachers in the more effective schools compared to the less effective schools? 3) Did the opinions of staff members change during the course of the study? As noted above, the staff at each school completed the effective schools surveys three times over a period of several years (generally from 1984–5 to 1989). The survey results were used to help the staff gain insights into how each staff member perceived the operation of the school, based on seven characteristics of effective schools: instructional leadership (IL), home-school relations (HSR), clear-school mission (CSM), frequent monitoring (FM), opportunity to learn and time-on-task (OLTT), safe and orderly environment (SOE), and high expectations (HE).

The survey data, especially the initial survey results, were used for planning purposes by the school improvement team. The survey was not designed to discriminate among schools based on achievement. Micks (1989), however, found that when the county's effective schools survey was given to staff members in 27 low income schools scattered throughout California, (i.e., 30 per cent or more AFDC students, but less than 30 per cent non-English speaking students), there was a correlation between significant three-year gains in reading achievement at the third grade and a high composite score on the effective schools survey. He did not find that the mean score for any individual correlate could be used to predict achievement gains.

In this study, to see if a similar relationship existed, a cluster analysis was completed on the 1989 effective schools survey results for the eight schools. From the analysis, only Tahoe was identified as being significantly different from the other schools. Figure 2.17 presents the composite scores for each school and shows that the composite mean of Tahoe's effective schools survey results is lower than the other schools, as was shown in the cluster analysis. The graph also shows that Sierra and Shasta, the other two schools that test data analysis showed to be in the less effective category, had higher mean scores than did Lassen, Yosemite, and Pinyon, three schools that had much higher degrees of effectiveness. Thus, based on this small sample size, the survey results do not discriminate between the more effective and less effective schools, except in the case of Tahoe.

The third research question was whether or not the attitudes of the school staff, as assessed by the effective schools surveys, had changed over time. Table 2.5 presents a composite per cent agree score for each school each year the survey was given.

The data show that from the base year there were changes in a positive direction

Figure 2.17   Comparison of composite mean scores of teacher responses to the effective schools surveys administered in 1989

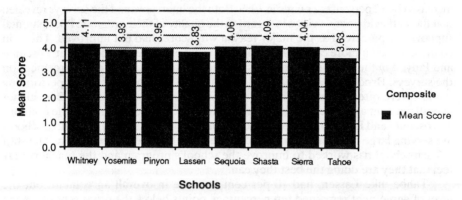

(i.e., more teachers agreed with the survey items). It is interesting to note that Whitney, the school with the greatest achievement gains, especially at third grade, also had the largest gain in agreement among teachers (18 percentage points). Yosemite's agreement increased by 16 percentage points, the second highest change over the five years. Pinyon had the least change in opinions. The one area that dramatically increased in agreement was the area of high expectations moving from 55 per cent to 85 per cent agreement. The interviews revealed that this area had been one of considerable focus by the principal and school staff. The other correlates stayed relatively the same, except for 'frequent monitoring' which decreased from 92 per cent to 69 per cent agreement. In the case of Pinyon, there seems to be a parallel between the moderately high agreement that stayed constant since 1985 and the moderately high, but similarly stable, test scores.

Table 2.5   Trend in responses to the Effective Schools Survey based on a composite per cent agree score

| Schools | Per cent Agree by Years | | |
	1985	1987	1989
Whitney	67 (1986)	80	85
Yosemite	62 (1984)	74 (1985)	78
Pinyon	76	78	80
Lassen	67	75	76
Sequoia	*data lost*	*data lost*	84
Shasta	79	91	85
Sierra	69	69	81
Tahoe	56	54 (1986)	66

Since 1985, there was a ten per cent increase in the overall agreement level among staff members at Lassen. As in the case of its test scores, there have been steady increases in the per cent agreement among staff members, indicating that more aspects of the effective school correlates are in place. Lassen did not attain the high achievement gains of Whitney, a school serving a similar student population, neither has it experienced substantial shifts in opinions regarding the effective schools characteristics assessed by the survey.

Shasta, a school with the most erratic achievement gains, also was the only school in which the per cent agreement increased in 1987 and decreased in 1989. Sierra's per cent agreement stayed the same through two administrations of the survey, but increased by 12 percentage points in 1989. Both the interviews and the surveys revealed that the staff held positive views in regard to the quality of their program. Poor parental support was perceived as the major reason why scores had not improved. This is in contrast to the far more critical and analytical views expressed by the staff at Yosemite and Pinyon in the interviews and substantiated by the lower per cent agreement on the surveys. Brookover and Lezotte (1979) found that teachers in high performing schools were often less satisfied than teachers in less effective schools. The higher overall per cent agreement at Sequoia, Shasta, and Sierra compared to the opinions at Yosemite and Pinyon may be a reflection of this phenomenon. These three schools are serving large numbers of poor and limited-English speaking children. The staff in each school has worked to improve the school's program and the teachers may feel that they are doing the best they can.

Tahoe, like Lassen, had 10 per cent increase in overall agreement, but the level of agreement remained ten percentage points below the other schools. As in the case of Sierra, the staff expressed concern about the low educational levels of parents and lack of family assistance provided to students. The survey results and the interviews, however, revealed that the staff recognized that there were problems with the school as well.

In summary, the views of staff members have changed over time. These changes could be a function of repeated administering of the survey. A detailed review of the survey data, however, showed that views have changed most in those areas where the staff has placed an emphasis, such as high expectations at Pinyon, home-school relations at Sierra, instructional leadership at Whitney. Other areas that were not a focus of the improvement process, tended to remain the same.

The four case studies, Chapters 3–6, discuss in more depth the kinds of changes that have occurred. In addition, the case studies seek to answer a fourth question: What factors best explain the ability of schools to initiate change and to sustain school effectiveness over time? To answer this question, the four frames presented in Figure 1.4 are used to analyze the opinions of teachers and the other documentation collected from each site. Each case study is organized in five sections: 1) The Setting, which describes school inputs in terms of student demographics and school plant as well as the district context in which the school operates; 2) School Climate and Culture, which encompasses school safety and discipline, recognition and rewards for students and staff, teacher expectations for students, home-school mission, shared mission and norms of collegiality; 3) School Technology, which includes academic focus, frequent monitoring of progress, time-on-task, use of test results, curriculum alignment, and staff development; 4) Schoolwide Organizational Structures and Procedures, which addresses structures for shared decision-making, collaborative problem-solving and communication; and 5) School Leadership, which embodies the role of both principal and staff in guiding and shaping the culture, school technology, and organizational structures and procedures to bring about change. Through the individual stories of school change, similarities and differences in school improvement processes will be highlighted. Comparisons will be made between the opinions of teachers when they first began the school effectiveness process, and in 1989, the conclusion of the study. The words of teachers and principals and analysis of survey and interview results will be used to explain how each school has or has not increased its effectiveness.

Chapter 3

Whitney Elementary: Creating a Culture for Learning and Achievement

The Setting: Inputs and Outcomes

Whitney Elementary is located in a small school district consisting of seven elementary schools and two middle schools. The district serves 3,423 students, 54 per cent of whom are White, non-Hispanic, 11 per cent Black, non-Hispanic, 22 per cent Hispanic, 2 per cent Asian, and 2 per cent other. In 1988–89, Whitney Elementary had an enrollment of 525 students and was fairly representative of the district's overall socioeconomic and ethnic makeup. For example, at Whitney, 10 per cent of the students came from professional families. At the district level 7 per cent fell into this category. The parents of most students at both the school and district level fell into the skilled and unskilled categories with Whitney having 45 per cent and 20 per cent respectively, and the district having 39 per cent of its student parents in the skilled category and 25 per cent in the unskilled group. At both the school and district level there are very few non-English speaking students. Sixteen per cent of the students at Whitney were classified as fluent in English plus a second language, and 1.3 per cent were designated as limited or non-English proficient students. Twelve per cent received Aid to Families with Dependent Children, which represented an increase over the previous years and 25 per cent received free or reduced price lunches. The school has a socioeconomic index of 2.02 which made it middle to low-middle class compared to other schools in the state.

The school's physical plant consisted of nineteen classrooms, a media/library center, a room for the resource specialist, an auditorium, a volunteer lounge, a teachers' workroom, and lunch area. There were twenty-one certificated teachers, two of whom worked with special education students. The school had several additional resource personnel including a full-time reading specialist, a full-time library technician, and the part-time assistance of a social worker, a nurse, a psychologist, and a speech therapist. Throughout the year the school was also assisted by several student teachers, and social worker and psychology interns from local colleges and universities. Classified support staff included two full-time special education aides, a school secretary, a health clerk, custodian, two cafeteria personnel, eleven classroom aides, and a volunteer coordinator. In 1987–88, the school received $54,000 in School Improvement funds which were used to fund classroom aides and purchase instructional materials.

In a previous study (Chrispeels and Pollack, 1990), the district was identified as an effective district with achievement for all students being higher than expected based on the SES of the district. More importantly, test data disaggregated at the district level showed that students from all socioeconomic groups were outperforming their counterparts in the state. While the district's leadership team of superintendent and the assistant superintendent of instruction and personnel have guided the district's improvement efforts, not all schools in the district have achieved effectiveness.

The district was one of the first in the county to utilize the county office of education's effective schools program on a systemwide basis. A retreat was held in the fall of 1985 for all principals, district administrators, and the board of education, in order that they might learn about effective schools research and how it might assist the district and its schools in their improvement efforts. The district supported individual school efforts through assistance with test analysis, articulation of the state curriculum frameworks and guidelines, and staff development that addressed district needs and facilitated implementation of the state curriculum frameworks. Schools were required to develop thorough improvement plans. The superintendent was proud of the fact that the district had maintained personnel and programs that other districts had cut, such as social workers, and music and art programs. Districtwide student academic competitions, such as spelling bees, writing and mathematics contests, were used to encourage a focus on achievement. Support from the district facilitated the efforts of Whitney to increase its effectiveness.

The principal at Whitney Elementary led the school from 1979 and throughout the duration of this study. He was the longest serving principal in this study. When he assumed the principalship, Whitney had the worst performance of any school in the district; it had a high rate of vandalism (e.g., there were three incidents of arson in the principal's first year), and the school was not regarded as a desirable place to teach. Under the principal's leadership the school moved from being the lowest to one of the highest achieving schools in the district. In 1989, Whitney was identified as being a Califormia Distinguished School.

Table 3.1   Comparison of school and state third grade scaled score results on the 1988 California Assessment Program disaggregated by parent occupation

Occupation	School					State			
	Students		Scaled Score			Students	Scaled Score		
	No.	%*	Reading	Writing	Math	%	Reading	Writing	Math
• Professional	9	10%	359	438	387	12%	346	341	334
• Semi-professional	14	15%	384	365	368	17%	308	309	301
• Skilled	41	45%	359	313	348	31%	276	279	276
• Unskilled	18	20%	326	356	335	17%	238	243	247

* Per cents for state and school do not add up to 100 per cent because the parent occupation is not identified for all students.

In the beginning, the principal's goal was to restore order and raise student achievement at least to the fiftieth percentile. That goal has been far surpassed, especially at the third grade level. Based on results from the California Assessment Program in 1988, at the third grade level, only five per cent of the students fell into the bottom quartile in reading, writing, or math, a decrease of 15 percentage points from 1983–84. Table 3.1 shows that when student achievement data were disaggregated by family income, all Whitney students did extremely well, with scores well above students in comparable groups in the state.

At the sixth grade, as was shown in Chapter 2, student achievement had not increased as dramatically as third. In 1987 the sixth grade students were transferred to a middle school. Since the sixth grade students from Whitney were mixed with students from other elementary schools, it was not possible to know specifically whether the achievement of Whitney's students had increased or decreased in 1988. The 1988 result for the middle school showed that achievement in reading declined slightly, while achievement in math increased for all middle school students.

The principal and staff at Whitney have been intensely involved in a school effectiveness process since a 1985 orientation. As can be seen from the teacher responses to the effective schools surveys presented in Figure 3.1, not all teachers agreed that the effective schools characteristics were fully in place even though test scores had begun to improve. Of particular concern were the areas of instructional leadership and safe and orderly environment where only slightly more than 50 per cent of the teachers agreed with the components of these characteristics. Figure 3.1 also shows that by 1989 many more teachers agreed that effective schools characteristics were being implemented. From the graph it is easy to see that each year as the principal and staff addressed areas of concern, the staff perceived that changes were taking place. Each year the staff completed the survey, they were extensively involved in analyzing their own responses. From discussions with the principal and the staff, it was clear that they took the survey results seriously and targeted areas in greatest need of improvement.

The remainder of this chapter addresses the transformative process that occurred at Whitney from early 1986 through 1989. Each component of the transformative process is discussed in an effort to understand which changes were undertaken and how they impacted staff working relations and student achievement. While each component is addressed separately, ripple effects, spin-offs, and direct impacts on other components will be noted in an effort to capture the interactive nature of the process of change.

School Climate and Culture

In 1989, if one word was used to describe the culture of Whitney, it would be achievement. This had not always been the case. Ten years ago the staff and community had little to cheer about in terms of school climate or student achievement. By 1989, a number of significant and fundamental changes had occurred that altered both the climate and the culture of Whitney.

Safe and Orderly Learning Environment

While the effective schools research has not established a hierarchy among the correlates that are associated with effectiveness, a safe and orderly learning environment is considered by many to be a prerequisite for improvements to be made in other areas. The principal at Whitney saw the creation of a safe and orderly environment as his first task. While those years of concentration on safety

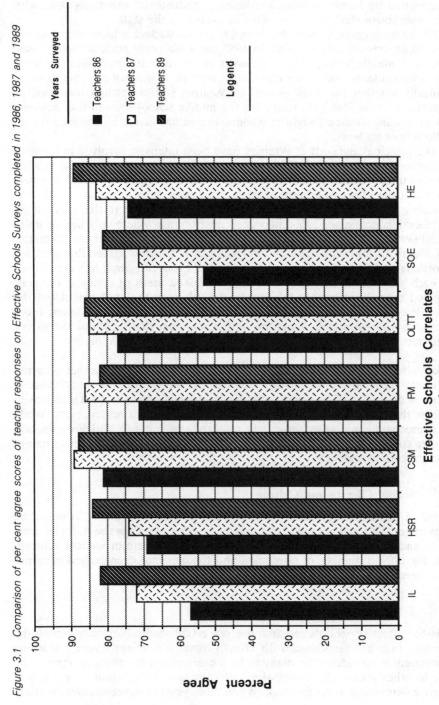

Figure 3.1 Comparison of per cent agree scores of teacher responses on Effective Schools Surveys completed in 1986, 1987 and 1989

Legend: IL = Instructional Leadership, HSR = Home-School Relations, CSM = Clear School Mission, FM = Frequent Monitoring, OL/TT = Opportunity to Learn and Time-on-Task, SOE = Safe Orderly Environment, HE = High Expectations and order lie outside the purview of this study, they laid the foundation for the school to become more effective, because some degree of order was restored to the school, incidents of vandalism declined, and a schoolwide discipline code was initiated. A special celebration for Martin Luther King's birthday, which highlighted the values he stood for, was begun as a way of easing racial tensions in the community and building racial harmony and respect for others among students. Even with this effort, when the first effective schools survey was administered to the staff in 1986, the correlate of safe and orderly environment was ranked lowest, with only 53 per cent of the staff in agreement that the school had a safe and orderly environment. Between 1986 and 1989 the principal and staff continued efforts to improve the school climate and discipline. The overall per cent agreement in the 1989 survey rose to 81 per cent, showing that considerable improvement had been made. Table 3.2 summarizes the results of the surveys given in these two years, and shows how opinions have changed as a result of the efforts of principal, staff, and students. The staff still has concerns about verbal abuse, security of property, and vandalism.

Table 3.2 Comparison of teacher responses regarding school climate based on the Effective Schools Survey given in 1986 and 1989

Survey Item	Per cent Agree 1986	1989
• Students are taught the school rules	89%	100%
• Teachers treat students with respect	95	100
• Few discipline problems are referred to the office	79	65
• This school is a safe and secure place to work	63	90
• Teachers, administration, parents, students share discipline responsibility	32	85
• It is safe to work after students are dismissed	52	80
• There is a positive school spirit	58	90
• Vandalism by students is not a problem	11	50
• The school buildings are kept in good repair	42	85
• Repairs/Alternations responded to in reasonable time	21	70
• Property of students is secure	21	55
• Property of staff is secure	37	60
• Students are respectful and not subject to verbal abuse	11	55
• Staff treated respectfully/not subject to verbal abuse	47	80
• Administration supports teachers in dealing with discipline matters	42	90
• Administration enforces student rules consistently/equitably	42	90
• Student rewarded/praised by staff for following rules	63	90

The principal was pleased that the greatest concern expressed by the staff now was in regard to verbal abuse by students of each other. He could remember the days when breaking up fights occupied much of his time. This view was echoed by one of the teachers when she said, 'Before we were at a primal level. Could we make it through a day with out being called some very gross names, or being hit, or not having to break up a fight? Now we are to the point where we are saying, "Couldn't you find a nicer way to say that to another student?"'

Recognition and Rewards

Obviously there is a critical and cyclical link among student achievement, student recognition and rewards, and sense of self-esteem. All schools in this study recognized and rewarded student achievement. According to the effective schools surveys, the teachers at Whitney felt that they were now recognizing and rewarding students more that they were in 1986. The interviews with the staff and a review of documents indeed showed that Whitney Elementary was unique in the enormous variety of rewards that students could receive. Awards were given for participation in schoolwide extracurricular activities such as Family Literature, Family Math Night, Spring Olympics, Lemon Grove Fun Run, Book Character Parade, St. Jude Math-A-Thon, and so forth. In addition, there were recognition programs for grade specific extracurricular activities such as the cross-age tutor program, Just Say No to Drugs Program, student council, safety patrol, media helpers, cafeteria helpers, winter performances, districtwide competitions, tri-annual homework awards (grades 2–5), rhythm band, American History Week, Presidential Academic and Physical Fitness Awards. Most significant and unique to Whitney, were the tri-annual awards given by the principal, which recognized achievement in each academic area such as math, reading, science, social studies, problem-solving, and writing. Teachers in each class nominated their students who had grown or achieved the most in each academic area. This approach to recognition greatly expanded the number of students who could be recognized. Unlike typical student-of-the-month awards, these academically targeted awards conveyed to students and their parents the range of academics taught in the school, the importance of each area, and the variety of academic skills that needed to be learned and recognized. Thus, the simple act of altering the recognition program had important implications for the areas of academic focus, high expectations, and home-school relations. There were also many classroom recognition activities and awards as well, including the principal's program to call parents at home with positive messages, when classroom teachers alerted him that such a message should be sent. The extensive amount of recognition, especially the focus on achievement in specific academic areas, contributed to creating a climate that stressed learning and achievement at Whitney.

Although most of the teachers interviewed in the eight schools felt that the amount of student recognition was sufficient, many staff members felt that teacher recognition was minimal. Most stated they were recognized for extra efforts, but few felt there was sufficient recognition of their teaching. However, in 1989 at Whitney, four of the five staff members interviewed felt they were recognized for their teaching. A review of the staff bulletins showed that the principal regularly commended the staff for their instructional efforts. For example, in one bulletin the principal commended the following instructional practice.

> First graders in Giza's room were graphing 'apple snacks' at the morning snack break. The activity involved counting, graphing, and predicting. This is a super example of how to take a non-learning activity and get some educational value from it. Could something like this be done with snacks other than green, red, and yellow apples?

One teacher stated that instructional expertise was recognized informally by the teachers' extensive involvement in decision-making and in staff development. Being selected to be a mentor teacher[1] was also seen as a form of recognition. Even though most of the Whitney teachers felt they were recognized for both teaching and extra efforts, one teacher concluded by saying that, 'Given the type of job we have, being asked to give out so much, we can always be recognized more than we are.' Another teacher echoed this view by saying that even if the principal recognized teachers more, for some it would still not be enough.

The interviews revealed some unique ways in which the principal had recognized teacher efforts and linked them to student learning and achievement gains. The first year that the school was above the state comparison band, the principal had a large cake made that said, 'CAP Busters'. Another year, the PTA bought plaques for all teachers to recognize their efforts in increasing student achievement. Last year, when Whitney's CTBS scores were the highest in the district, the Principal asked the Kiwanis Club if they could give some kind of recognition to the staff. The club gave each teacher an attractive paper weight that said, 'BEST in the District CTBS'. These actions to recognize the staff helped to reinforce the ethos and culture of achievement at Whitney. Such extensive recognition of teacher efforts to increase student achievement was not found at any other case-study school.

High Expectations

Establishing a safe and orderly learning environment and recognizing students are necessary, but not sufficient to achieve increased school effectiveness. The schoolwide ethos of safety and discipline and the recognition programs, however, did complement other school efforts to increase expectations for student achievement. In the beginning, the principal set a goal of bringing student achievement to the fiftieth percentile; now according to the principal, the staff is aiming for the ninetieth percentile. In fact, one of the most striking aspects of Whitney Elementary, as revealed through the interviews, was the culture of achievement that permeated the school. A critical shift in opinion has occurred; more teachers now believe that they can successfully teach all students regardless of their home background. When asked if she had changed any of her attitudes as a result of the effective schools process, one teacher at Whitney exclaimed the following:

> Yes, the big difference is now I don't write off any child. I used to very strongly feel that children that didn't have any support, that came from terrible homes, how could I do anything with them when they came poorly clothed, unfed, ill. And over time, with effective schools, I came to realize we can make a difference even in these worst scenarios. That's my biggest change, believing all children can succeed regardless of their home background.

All of the staff members interviewed echoed similar sentiments and stressed the high standards they set for all students. When the survey results from 1986 and 1989 were compared, it showed that more staff members held higher expectations of students in 1989. Since 1986, the overall agreement in this correlate has risen from 74 per cent to 89 per cent.

How did the staff of Whitney Elementary come to develop such high expectations and create a culture more supportive of learning and achievement? The principal clearly had an important role. He said that he typically found teachers to be more concerned with the affective and the affiliation needs of students than with achievement. One strategy he used to help the staff be equally concerned with achievement was to begin recognizing achievements of all types. He was able to do this when several Whitney students won district academic competitions. He linked these student successes back to the efforts of the teachers. He often found areas of strength and pointed these out to the staff. The rewards and recognition programs discussed above were also used to reinforce academic expectations. Once the teachers began to see some gains, achievement became a regular topic at faculty meetings, and views began to shift. At lunch time, on classroom visits and in assemblies, the principal also spent time giving pep talks to students about what they had learned and how they could continue to grow. Through constant reinfocement of teachers and students, an ethic of achievement was created.

Home-School Relations

The interrelationship and interaction between home and school is another key variable that is part of the culture and climate component of school effectiveness. Like many schools, the staff at Whitney traditionally measured parent involvement by the number of parents who volunteered. Whitney experienced the national trend of fewer volunteers, because more and more parents were working full time and fewer were available to volunteer. But, in contrast to teachers at Sierra, Tahoe, and Lassen, the staff who were interviewed did not bemoan the situation; they expressed considerable appreciation for those who did volunteer. In addition, the staff had taken specific steps to make sure that the school was staying in touch with parents who were unable to come to school to volunteer. They initiated regular class newsletters. Telephone calls, notes home, a homework folder, clear policies on homework and discipline that must be signed by parents, invitations to observe the class, back-to-school nights that focused on schools goals, learning objectives and materials, family nights which involved

Table 3.3 Comparison of 1986 and 1989 responses to selected items regarding home-school relations

Survey Item	Per cent Agree 1986	1989
• 90% to 100% of the parents attend parent-teacher conferences	63%	90%
• Most parents are aware of the instructional objectives	26	65
• Most parents have a clear understanding of the school goals	58	70
• Teachers and parents aware of homework policy	89	100
• There is cooperation between parents/teachers re homework	63	80
• Student homework is monitored at home	42	70
• Almost all students complete assigned homework	58	70
• Most parents support school when child disciplined	84	90
• There is an active parent group at this school	84	90
• Parents and community members are frequent volunteers	58	69
• Teachers contact parents on a regular basis	74	80
• 75% plus parents attend open house/back-to-school night	48	69
• Teachers invite parents to observe the instructional program	53	79
• Teachers communicate with parents about good more than the bad	32	75
• Most parents rate this school as superior	63	85

parents and their children in learning activities, giving parents a window on the school curriculum, and parent-teacher conferences were all used to build strong parent involvement and home-school relations. As a result of their concerted efforts, teachers felt that parents were better informed and were more supportive of their children's schoolwork and of the school. The effective schools survey data presented in Table 3.3 show there have been some important shifts in key items regarding parent-teacher contacts.

Work by Johnson, Brookover, and Farrell (1989a) indicated that teacher perceptions of parents' role, interest, and expectations for their children impacted students' sense of futility and student achievement. In other words, if teachers held negative views of parents and believed that they were not concerned about their child's success in school, these negative teacher perceptions were correlated with a greater sense of futility by these students. Epstein and Becker (1982) in their studies found that teacher efforts to communicate with parents and involve them in home learning activities resulted in higher student achievement in reading. Thus, the shifts in opinions about parents and efforts to involve them may be a factor in increasing student efforts and success in the classroom.

The data from Whitney Elementary indicated that three important variables — rewards and recognition, teacher expectations, and parent-teacher relations — were interrelated and helped to lead to a positive achievement spiral. As student achievement increased, especially the achievement of students who frequently had not been successful, teacher expectations for future achievement increased. Rewards and recognition helped to reinforce both teachers and students and to give direction and meaning to the concept of higher expectations. These higher expectations produced higher achievement which demonstrated to the school staff that even students from low-income families could be successful learners. As a result, the school staff moved away, consciously or unconsciously, from blaming the parents for poor student outcomes and was able to focus on positive and substantive parent contacts and communications. In turn, parents felt more involved and knew better how to support their child's learning at home and at school. Thus, a spiral for success more typical of schools serving affluent students was created in a school serving middle and low-income students. This success spiral seemed to have been created at Whitney as reflected in the attitudes of the staff who expressed high expectations for students and for themselves; they viewed themselves as capable of teaching all students and held positive attitudes towards parents as partners.

Shared Mission

When the school initiated the effective schools program, the staff participated in a 'We Agree' process to help develop a mission statement. The following 'We Agree' statements shaped the mission of Whitney and drove their school improvement efforts:

1   We agree there needs to be continuity of curriculum that guarantees each child's involvement in learning the core curriculum.
2   We agree there needs to be an alignment of materials and strategies with the assessment tools.

3 We agree there needs to be a specific set of exit level expectations for each subject at each grade level.
4 We agree there need to be meetings to annually review and discuss expectancies and criteria for indicating that students are 'at or above grade' level.
5 We agree that parents need to be notified of grade level requirements at the beginning of the school year.
6 We agree in helping students develop positive self-esteem.
7 We agree in instilling knowledge, developing skills, and promoting open, inquiring minds, and a desire to learn in students.
8 We agree in helping students become academically sound.
9 We agree to support each other in these endeavors.

From the 'We Agree' statements emerged the following mission statement: 'Our school mission is to help students become responsible citizens in a democratic society.' It is interesting to note that the 'We Agree' statements stress the academic goals of the school more fully than the mission statement.

In the interviews in 1989, a somewhat different mission emerged. Each teacher phrased the mission in his or her own words, however, the mission clearly encompassed a more academic focus compared to the written mission statement developed in 1986. One teacher said the mission was 'To be one of the best schools in the county; to set high goals and standards and communicate them to parents and kids.' Another teacher said 'Provide every child with the opportunity to learn — the low, the high, and the middle.' A third teacher echoed these words by saying: 'Provide all children with a quality education — academically and socially.' The teachers also expressed a firm belief that the parents and students knew and shared the mission. As one teacher said, 'Parents and students share the mission, because all teachers work with parents and send home newsletters, conduct conferences, etc.' This statement shows the close parallel between high expectations and home-school relations. By 1989, many of the teachers at Whitney, not only held high expectations for students, but also were embedding those standards and expectations in the community through regularly communicating the mission and expectations to the parents. At several of the other case schools, especially the least effective schools, more teachers expressed the view that only some of the parents shared the mission — only the higher SES parents. Furthermore, the teachers did not indicate that they or the school was doing anything to help parents develop a shared mission.

Norms of Collegiality

The organizational structures of Whitney — grade level teams, curriculum committees, the School Site Council, *ad hoc* problem-solving committees, and staff meetings — all contributed significantly to the strong norms of collegiality that were evident in the 1987 and 1989 interviews. Teacher-talk centered around schooling, instructional practices, and how to help children be more successful learners. The nature of teacher discussions at Whitney was similar to the findings of Rosenholtz in the more effective schools in her study (1989). The actions of the principal also reinforced these norms, as was evident by the use of staff bulletins to share teaching strategies, the securing of recognition from school and community for teacher efforts, and the extensive involvement of teachers in school decision-making. In other words, all aspects of the transformative process seemed to be working to enhance collegiality and a professional culture in the school.

School Technology: Curriculum and Instruction

While all six variables that encompass the curriculum and instruction component can be shown to have played a role in increasing student achievement at Whitney Elementary, five deserve special attention because of the unique ways they operated at Whitney. These elements are: the use of test results, academic focus, curriculum alignment, frequent monitoring, and staff development.

Use of Test Scores

All schools in the study reviewed and analyzed their test scores. Compared to the other schools, the staff at Whitney seemed to have greater confidence in its ability to analyze and use test results. The staff, with the principal, annually reviewed the results, identified strengths and weaknesses, and then brainstormed ways to address the weaknesses. When the effective schools survey results of 1986 were compared with those of 1989, they showed that the staff was reviewing and using test results more systematically than in 1986. In 1989, a higher per cent agreed with all the items regarding tests results and their use:

- The principal reviews and interprets test results with the faculty.
- Principal emphasizes the meaning and use of standardized test results.
- Principal and staff initiated test results to modify and change instructional programs.
- Test results used for reteaching.
- Test results used to diagnose students strengths and weaknesses.

The interviews confirmed that the test results were carefully reviewed by the staff, and the information used to modify the instructional program. One teacher described the process this way:

A couple of years ago we discovered that test scores in problem-solving were not good. Consequently, we focused on it. We had inservice by the district in problem-solving. We purchased materials, especially Bell Works, and made sure that it was used because it presents a lot of different types of problem-solving strategies. We also found a textbook that was more problem-solving oriented. We supplemented the textbook with manipulatives. So we purchased quite a lot [of] materials and we inserviced our teachers on their use.

In addition to knowing how to analyze and use test data, the staff at Whitney also knew how to analyze and use the effective schools survey data in developing its annual improvement plan. Analysis of the survey data was not done as extensively by teachers in any of the other schools.

Curriculum Alignment

As illustrated by the example given above, the staff at Whitney was sufficiently familiar with what was covered on standardized tests to align the curriculum. The district recently mandated the use of *Explorations*, a new math textbook. Without guidance or direction from the principal, the curriculum alignment committee met to study the new textbook. As one teacher recounted: 'We observed that *Explorations* had a tremendous number of gaps and that if we were going to go strictly with *Explorations*, we were going to have serious pitfalls in test scores.' The teachers then 'red flagged' these weaknesses to the principal who ordered the additional support materials that the teachers requested. This contrasted sharply with the experiences of staff at Tahoe, Sierra and Shasta where the district did not have the new math textbook aligned until very late in the school year. The staff did not know how to align the book, leaving them feeling frustrated and helpless. The principal at Whitney felt that the time and efforts that he and the staff had invested in aligning the curriculum had served as the necessary first steps essential to raising test scores and initiating the success cycle.

Academic Focus

The particular academic focus at Whitney each year was determined by four factors: the textbook adoption cycle; the state curriculum frameworks; the district's academic priority; and the school's identified needs. All schools must address the need to train staff and institute curriculum alignment when a new textbook is adopted. At Whitney the staff was skilled in curriculum alignment and had been able to ensure that new textbooks were integrated into the curriculum and matched with other materials and curriculum areas.

The staff had been given copies of the curriculum frameworks and efforts were underway to modify the curriculum to match the new frameworks. The interviews indicated the staff was well on its way to using a literature-based program to teach reading as has been recommended in the state frameworks. For example, a staff bulletin had the following announcement:

> **Redo the Language Arts Curriculum** We will go over the State Language Arts Model Curriculum at next Tuesdays' meeting. Will the following teachers please be prepared to lead discussion groups at their grade levels:

Each year the district also established an area of academic focus and provided the required staff development to assist each school in implementation. The analysis of test results was the fourth way in which the academic focus for Whitney was determined. For example, when problem solving surfaced as a weakness, it was addressed. The interviews revealed that the staff felt empowered to focus on areas of greatest need as determined by them. They seem comfortable in integrating state, local, and district priorities to create a unified yearly improvement plan.

Frequent Monitoring

Once an area of academic focus has been identified and staff development provided, a critical issue for any school is how to ensure implementation in the classroom and keep the momentum going. The principal at Whitney utilized several unique ways of monitoring implementation that were not found in the other case-study schools. For example, to ensure that writing was a regular part of the instructional program, the principal collected a writing sample from each classroom once a month. On a simple check off-sheet, he asked the teacher to 1) indicate what the goal of the writing activity was, 2) to rate on a scale from one to ten how well the goal was met, 3) to indicate in what phase of the writing process this sample is (e.g., rough draft, rewrite, final), and 4) to inform the principal what should be stressed when the principal discusses the assignment with the students.

Several years ago the school and the district academic focus had been hands-on science. To insure continued implementation, the principal required that each teacher indicate on the trimester lesson planning form which four hands-on science activities they would be doing. Time was given to staff members in grade level teams to discuss and plan these activities together. Similar requirements were made for AIMS — Activities for Integrating Math and Science.

Formal observations represented another monitoring strategy. One-half of the staff was observed formally each year. Previously the principal did one formal observation with a pre-and post-conference and two more informal drop-in observations. The effective schools survey data indicated that the staff felt very few formal observations occurred. He, thus changed his format by conducting three formal observations, one of which focused on the year's academic priorities. He felt this had been very positive in terms of increasing the amount of time spent discussing instruction with teachers and helping them to grow and improve. In addition, teachers used the Stull Bill Objectives (the state required evaluation procedures), which they had written, and their lesson plans were used as vehicles to reinforce the year's academic focus. With a staff that was well-equipped to annually monitor progress and evaluate successes and problems, combined with the principal's monitoring strategies, the staff at Whitney had been able to significantly improve achievement of all students at third grade and to make important, although less dramatic, improvements gains at sixth grade.

Staff Development

Three types of staff development became apparent from the interviews at Whitney. First, the district provided a substantial program of staff development in which teachers were expected to participate. For example, all teachers had been trained in clinical teaching methods and hands-on science strategies. Second, the staff, especially in the last two to three years, had been actively providing its own site-based staff development. As a teacher became trained or skilled in a particular area, she or he in turn would have the responsibility of training other staff members. Third, the principal played an important role in developing staff skills by teaching and empowering the staff to align the curriculum and to analyze test data and survey results. Grade level team meetings and curriculum commit-tees served as important vehicles for the staff to discuss, test out new ideas, and to develop new instructional materials or strategies.

In spite of these important strengths, the school effectiveness surveys in 1986 and again in 1989, identified a number of problems that persisted with the staff-development program. First, 25 per cent of the staff still felt that the staff-development program was not based on school goals. Second, 35 per cent felt that there was not follow-up and assistance by the administration after a staff-development training. Third, 35 per cent felt the principal and staff did not plan staff development together. One of the reasons staff members may have felt they did not have a role is that the district played such a dominant role in organizing formal staff development. Fourth, 60 per cent did not feel that staff development was evaluated on use in the classroom. These issues are significant, because they reflect common problems that have been identified in conducting successful staff development (Hopkins, 1990; Joyce, 1990; Little, 1986).

School Organizational Structures and Procedures

Whitney Elementary has accomplished its goals by putting in place structures and procedures that facilitated growth and change. Every teacher interviewed stressed the importance of the grade-level teams, the cross-grade level committees, and the faculty meetings that focus on instructional issues as important vehicles that have empowered them and enabled the school to improve. As one teacher said: 'These [organizational] changes have had a definite impact on student achieve-ment. We are all sharing, targeting, pulling together, and all working for the same goal.' Another faculty member stressed that the sub-committee structure gave lots of teachers an opportunity for involvement. These committees did the leg work and presented information to the staff in a manageable form. 'That makes us feel not so harried that we have 20,000 decisions to make. Consequently, we are making more effective decisions and I think that is reflected in our test scores and the way children behave in school.' Shared decision making and collabora-tive problem solving was the norm at Whitney.

The extensive committee structure also facilitated constant communication, another key variable of the schoolwide organizational and structural component. All the staff members emphasized that they kept in touch with each other in many ways. As one teacher said, 'It is exciting to go to lunch because it's a time when we can share what's working, compare materials, and offer to assist each other.' This constant communication has resulted in a common goal. The consistency in goals and expectations of the staff has meant that the staff was clearer and more consistent with students about what they must learn and how they must behave. What emerged was a whole school view. The second grade teacher explained how this whole view worked. 'I know exactly what my students need to master so they will be ready for third grade.' She perceived her job not just to teach second grade, but to make sure that her all her students were ready for third.

Schoolwide Leadership Team

The literature on school effectiveness and change indicates that leadership is important if improvement is to occur. All the teachers interviewed agreed that the principal at Whitney played a critical role in the school improvement process. However, the leadership of the principal was not always so clear nor perceived so positively. The principal found that the effective schools process had given him a focus and helped him set priorities. On the first effective schools survey completed by the staff in 1986, the correlate instructional leadership had an overall agreement rate of only 57 per cent; except for safe and orderly environment, it was the lowest ranked correlate. By 1989, the per cent agreement had risen to 82 per cent. Changes had occurred because the principal treated the perceptions and opinions of his staff seriously and took action to change his leadership practices. Table 3.4 summarizes some of the major changes that occurred in teacher opinions regarding instructional leadership.

Table 3.4   Comparison of teacher responses regarding instructional leadership in 1986 and 1989

Survey Item	Per cent Agree 1986	1989
• Principal is highly visible throughout the school	27%	85%
• Principal makes frequent contacts with students and teachers	27	95
• Instructional leadership from the principal is clear, strong, and central	37	80
• Principal seeks ideas and suggestions from staff	64	80
• Principal and faculty can solve most problems	64	95
• Principal is accessible to discuss instructional matters	52	90
• Principal initiates effective coordination of instructional program	37	80
• Administrative leadership effective in resolving education problems	58	75
• Administrative leadership available for disagreements among staff	37	65
• Principal emphasizes the meaning/use of standardized test results	79	95
• Principal initiates test results to modify/change the instructional program	58	90
• Principal active in promoting staff development activities	58	90
• Instructional issues are frequently the focus of staff meetings	47	90
• Principal makes several formal classroom observations each year	47	90
• Before formal observation, principal discusses observation with teacher	79	100
• After formal observation, principal discusses observation with teacher	84	100
• After formal observation, teacher and principal develop improvement plan	79	95

According to the staff, there are still areas for growth, especially in the area of staff development, both in terms of planning and evaluating its impact in the classroom. About a third of the staff declared that the principal did not give sufficient feedback on instructional techniques, and a quarter felt there was a need for more administrative leadership. The survey results indicated that the principal changed considerably during his tenure in ways that contributed to school improvement. In addition, the principal presented an effective model for his staff which encouraged them to grow and develop.

While the leadership of the principal at Whitney has been critical in leading the school's improvement effort, an equally significant element in the school's change process has been the development of a leadership team. The principal not only inspired his staff to do their best, but he also empowered them to do it. One teacher commented, 'It is uncanny how [he] can get you to do what he wants and you think it is your decision.' Another staff member explained the development of the school's leadership team this way.

> [The principal] has really done a tremendous amount of delegating leadership to many other staff members; this was not done ten years ago. These staff members are now taking on major projects and inservicing the staff on such diverse topics as the effective schools process, the Program Quality Review process, cooperative learning, and personality assessments. We've done this for ourselves.

The staff, who were interviewed, respected the role that the principal played in guiding them, and as one commented, 'He is a visionary.' The staff members, however, also knew that they were the shapers of their destiny and that they had the power and capability to take the school to the ninetieth percentile in student achievement if that was their goal.

Summary and Conclusions

The case study of Whitney is significant because it illustrates several key aspects of organizational change. First, applying the open-system model, one can conclude that the inputs into the system remained fairly constant throughout the duration of the study. The socioeconomic status of student's families did not vary substantially, nor did the numbers of students receiving Aid to Families with Dependent Children or entering the school with limited English-speaking skills. There was a growth in the overall number of students, necessitating the transfer of sixth grade students to a middle school. This change did not cause a major disruption in the educational process compared to the movement to a four-track year-round school endured by three of the other case study schools. The experiences of Yosemite in implementing a a four-track year-round school is discussed in Chapter 6. There were some changes in the teaching staff, with a few being initiated or encouraged by the principal. The number of teacher transfers, however, was not greater than would be expected in any other five year period. In terms of inputs, the longevity of the principal's tenure should be seen as an important contributing factor to the school's improvement. The steadiness of the environment as reflected in the consistency in inputs may represent a necessary, but not sufficient condition for changes in both outputs and in the transformative process.

A second conclusion is that the outputs of the system, as measured by the California Assessment Program, showed significant improvements for all students, regardless of family background, especially at third grade. The gains at sixth grade were not as dramatic; however, the last year (1987) that the school had a sixth grade class, it showed gains, especially for its two lowest socioeconomic groups. The 1988 sixth grade class, if it had remained at the school, would have consisted of students who were in third grade in 1984–85, the first year the school showed significant improvement at that grade level.

A third conclusion is that since inputs remained constant, changes in the transformative process need to be studied for possible explanations for improvement in student outcomes. The scope of these changes have been examined in depth in the case study. No one change accounts for the improved outcomes, but changes in each component of the transformative process and the interaction among components as a result of the changes are helpful in illuminating possible explanations for the growth in student achievement. Whitney provides an excellent example of the Peters and Waterman (1982) finding that success results from the accumulated effects of many small actions being done right. Every aspect of the transformative process was altered during the course of the principal's tenure. The leadership role of the principal was documented through the interviews and the changed perceptions about the principal's actions as shown in the effective schools surveys. The role of teachers increased leadership, however, should not be underestimated. The power and authority of teachers to make decisions and affect the life of the school had grown steadily. Without the cultivation of such strong teacher leadership, especially in the areas of curriculum alignment, test and survey data analysis, and staff development, it is unlikely the school would have attained such improved outcomes. This case-study finding suggests tentative insights into the areas where teacher leadership should be encouraged. In addition, it confirms the findings of Rosenholtz (1989) and Bamburg and Andrews (1989) that relationships between principal and staff as manifested in meaningful shared-decision making are critical to the improvement process. Furthermore, the way in which leadership by both principal and teachers were impacting all elements of the transformative process seemed to be approaching Fullan, Bennett and Rolheiser-Bennett's (1990) concept of institutional development.

Note

1   Most school districts in California have a Mentor Teacher Program that is funded through the statewide California Mentor Teacher Program. The mentors are selected by peers and administrators based on criteria established by each district. As will be seen in the case studies, being designated as a Mentor Teacher was considered a significant recognition of curriculum expertise. In addition, these mentors assisted their fellow teachers at their own school site in staff development activities.

Chapter 4

Sierra Elementary: The Frustration of Many Efforts and no Gains

The Setting: Inputs and Outputs

Sierra Elementary is an ethnically diverse, single track year-round school serving 639 students. It is one of thirty schools in a large sized K-6 elementary school district that serves 15,562 students. This attractive, modern looking school was built in 1969 and consists of a main building, a separate kindergarten building and seven portable classrooms. The main building has three large instructional areas called lofts, a well equipped media-library center, a computer lab, and a multi-purpose room. Each loft contains two grades, 1–2, 3–4, and 5–6, 180 students and six teachers. The first and second grade loft has been partitioned into self-contained classrooms, but the other two lofts remain largely open. The seven portable classrooms on the site house two special education classrooms, two self-contained regular classrooms; three portables are used for adult education and parent participation pre-school programs.

The school is ethnically quite diverse with only 13 per cent of the students in the 'White not of Hispanic origin' category (see Table 4.1). As can be seen from Table 4.1, the Filipino population at Sierra is significantly larger than that in both the district and the state. Since 1987 there has been a reversal in the proportion of Hispanic and Filipinos attending Sierra, with the Hispanic student population increasing from 27 to 38 per cent, and the Filipino student population decreasing from 35 to 25 per cent.

These demographic changes have resulted in a large influx of limited-English or non-English speaking students (LES/NES). For example, in 1986–87, 8.2 per cent of the third grade students were classified as LES/NES. In 1987–88, 24 per cent of the students received that classification. In the district as a whole, the percentage of LES/NES students fell from 17 per cent in 1986–87 to 13 per cent in 1987–88. The percentage of students receiving Aid to Families with Dependent Children has remained fairly constant over the last several years at 11–12 per cent. It is equivalent to the district's figures and is comparable to the percentage of AFDC students who attend Whitney Elementary. The percentage of students in each family income category is approximately equivalent to the distribution of students in the district as a whole. The distribution of students at the third grade is as follows: Professional — 7 per cent; Semiprofessional — 13 per cent; Skilled/semiskilled — 47 per cent; Unskilled — 18 per cent, Unknown — 15 per cent.

Table 4.1 *Comparison of the ethnic distribution of students in the school, district and state based on the sixth grade CAP data in 1988*

Ethnic Group	School	District	State
American Indian/Alaskan Native	1%	1%	1%
Asian	8	3	7
Pacific Islander	1	1	1
Filipino	25	8	2
Hispanic	36	40	28
Black, Not of Hispanic Origin	12	4	8
White, Not of Hispanic Origin	13	37	45

Note: per cents in the vertical columns do not equal 100 per cent because not all students are classified.

The faculty at Sierra was similar to the other case-study schools in terms of length of tenure and educational training. Three of the 28 teachers were of Hispanic origin, one was African-American and the remainder were White. The school staff were assisted by a full-time library technician, a part-time nurse, and the occasional services of the district psychologist. Unlike Whitney, the school did not have a social worker. A part-time bilingual community assistant, however, worked with Spanish-speaking parents and organized parent workshops to meet their needs.

In the study of effective districts (Chrispeels and Pollack, 1990), the district in which Sierra is located was identified as a typical district, but did not meet the criteria as a more effective district. The district was trying to improve on many fronts, but the efforts were fragmented. Certain key characteristics that were found in effective districts were less prevalent in this district. For example, in the area of staff development, some excellent opportunities were provided to the staff of each school to attend districtwide staff inservices. The topics, how-ever, were not necessarily ones that were a priority at the school site. Nor was the whole staff of an individual school involved, which would ensure the development of a common understanding and uniformity of implementation. The district ad-ministration did not seem to be extensively involved in aligning the curriculum, as was the case in the more effective districts. In 1987, the district was just begin-ning efforts to enhance the skills of its administrators as instructional leaders. Similarly, training of administrators and key teachers in the clinical teaching model, 'Essential Elements of Instruction' was also just beginning. In contrast, the districts in which Whitney, Pinyon, Yosemite and Sequoia were located had administrators and teachers who had been trained several years before using similar clinical teaching models. Furthermore, such training and other district meetings seemed to frequently occur during the school day, pulling principals away from the school site. Overall in Sierra's district there was less pressure for academic achievement, compared to more effective districts. While this is only a brief summary of some of the findings from the study of effective districts, it helps to set the context in which Sierra launched its effective schools efforts.

The principal was assigned to Sierra in the summer of 1984. The principal whom he replaced had been at the school for seven years and had managed the school with little input from the staff or community. In contrast, the new principal had a reputation for being skilled in working with staff and community and had been the principal at one of the district's few community schools. The new, more open leadership style was readily accepted by the community, but required some adjustment by the staff, who had retreated into their classrooms under the previous administration. Soon after assuming the principalship, the principal contacted the county office of education to utilize its services in conducting an effective schools assessment. The surveys were given to the staff for completion in January of 1985. The data were assembled into a report. The school staff and community members spent a day analyzing the results and using the data to rewrite their school improvement plan.

Over the last five years the staff has continually worked to improve. Figure 4.1 summarizes the effective schools survey data compiled from surveys completed in 1985 and 1989. The graph shows that there have been changes in opinion in a positive direction in all correlated areas. Analysis of items contained in particular correlates, which are presented in subsequent sections in this case study, will show where changes have been made and in which areas changes in perceptions did not occur.

Figure 4.1 *Comparison of mean scores of teacher responses on the Effective Schools Surveys completed in 1985 and 1989*

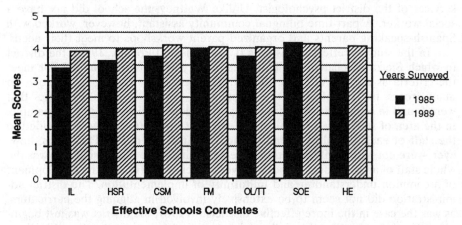

Legend: *IL = Instructional Leadership, HSR = Home-School Relations, CSM = Clear School Mission, FM = Frequent Monitoring, OL/TT = Opportunity to Learn, Time-on-Task, SOE = Safe Orderly Environment, HE = High Expectations.*

In spite of efforts to bring about changes in the school that addressed each of the effective school's characteristics, the results, in terms of standardized achievement, were discouraging, with little or no gains in any subject area. Not only have the test results remained static, but when compared with other schools serving students of similar backgrounds, Sierra consistently scored below these other schools at the third grade and scored within what is called the average expected range of similar schools at sixth grade. If the school had met the definition of effectiveness as presented in Chapter 1, Sierra's sixth grade students would have needed to increase their achievement by half a standard deviation, or its scores would have needed to be above and have remained above the average expected range for similar schools. The number of students scoring in the bottom quartile fluctuated between 42 and 31 per cent in the third grade in reading, written language, and math, and between 31 and 21 per cent in the 6th grade. At the third grade level, average scores in all content areas tested were well below district and state averages. In sixth grade, the achievement levels were also below district and state averages in reading and math, but in 1988, the sixth grade students scored at the state average in written language. The interviews revealed that the failure to make any achievement gains was very discouraging for both principal and staff.

During the interviews, several teachers stated that they were making important gains with their lowest achieving students. This belief was supported at the sixth grade level when scores were disaggregated by family income. Students whose parents fell into the skilled/semiskilled category and comprised 36 per cent of the population were outperforming their district and state counterparts. In the lowest income category, Sierra students outperformed the students in the same category in written language and math and were equal in reading. The 20 per cent of students whose parents were in the professional and semiprofessional subgroups performed poorly in relation to their counterparts in the state. Table 4.2 compares the school's 1988 disaggregated CAP results with those of other sixth grade students in the state.

Table 4.2 Comparison of the school's sixth grade 1988 CAP results disaggregated by family occupation with those of other students in the state

Occupation	School					State			
	Students		Scaled Score			Students	Scaled Score		
	No.	%	Reading	Writing	Math	%	Reading	Writing	Math
• Professional	3	4%	*	*	*	14%	327	327	328
• Semiprofessional	16	16%	233	271	256	17%	292	298	294
• Skilled/Semiskilled	31	36%	283	285	279	35%	257	267	262
• Unskilled	23	27%	223	252	247	21%	224	237	235

*Note: Scores for so few students are typically not reported by the state because the CAP test uses matrix sampling in test administration and the results may not be valid.

Based on an analysis of the data collected from Sierra, it was not entirely clear why the students in the semiprofessional group were doing so poorly. One explanation, however, might be that many of the students who fell into the semiprofessional category were Filipino. While these students were classified   fluent in English, no special effort was made to assess their language proficiency or to develop programs for them, if their language skills were lacking. In contrast, there were Hispanic bilingual resources available and extra programs for these limited and non-English speaking students.

Based on an analysis of achievement data presented in Chapter 2, Sierra remained a less effective school. The interviews conducted in 1987 and 1989 revealed that the school had undertaken a number of improvement initiatives. Teachers felt that changes had been made that were impacting their teaching practices. An analysis of the effective schools survey and interview data provided insights into how the school functioned and some aspects of the school's climate and culture, school technology, and organizational structures and practices that may help to explain why student achievement, as measured by standardized test, had not increased.

School Climate and Culture

The climate at Sierra could be summarized as warm, friendly, and positive. The cultural norms of the school stressed the affective. Many of the teachers at Sierra had been at the school for ten or more years. The school is one of the few remaining open-plan schools with three large lofts (first-second grade, third-fourth grade, and fifth-sixth grade). Initially many of the teachers had chosen to teach at Sierra because it required teachers willing to team-teach and work together. In the early years of the school's existence, teachers had also been actively involved in the selection of their colleagues, but this was no longer the practice. Furthermore, teachers were now assigned to the school based on the agreement negotiated by the teachers' association with the district. This meant that for some teachers the assignment may not necessarily be their first choice. In general, the teachers were satisfied with their work situation. Within two of the lofts there was also a good team spirit among teachers. The first and second grade loft had been divided into self-contained teaching units using portable walls. There did not seem to be much coherence or cooperation among these six teachers. In addition, the teachers in the self-contained classrooms seemed to operate in isolation from the peers in the lofts, further fragmenting staff relations and interactions.

Safe and Orderly Learning Environment

Unlike the staff at Whitney, Sierra's staff felt that discipline, safety, and order were not major issues. In 1985, when the first effective schools survey was administered, the overall rate of agreement with the safe and orderly survey items was a high 90 per cent. In 1989, when the survey was readministered, the rate of agreement was 89 per cent. The only items that had changed negatively were concerns for the safety of student and staff members' property. All felt that a positive spirit permeated the school.

Between 1984 and 1988, the staff, principal, and parents worked hard to maintain a positive school climate as an area of strength. The principal recruited outstanding motivational speakers who addressed the topic of discipline and self-esteem. After one inservice on assertive discipline, a schoolwide committee was formed to develop an assertive discipline plan for the school. In 1987–88, the staff received training in classroom management techniques. All of these activities help to explain why a safe and orderly learning environment was not an issue at Sierra.

Recognition and Rewards

Student recognition was primarily determined in each loft. Students earned recognition for improvements and growth in academic areas as well as behavior. Each loft had its own system of recognizing and rewarding students. At a schoolwide level, behavior and attendance were emphasized more than academic gains. For example, quarterly schoolwide assemblies with movies and popcorn were held to reward students who had had no discipline referrals. There was an end-of-the-year schoolwide awards assembly where students were recognized for outstanding achievement, service on the school safety patrol, or perfect attendance. Other achievements were also acknowledged, such as spelling bee winners.

A collection of student writings was published twice a year and the booklets sent home to parents. Sierra's approach stood in sharp contrast to Whitney's, where students in every classroom received schoolwide recognition for improvement in each academic area as well as other extracurricular activities at both monthly and special tri-annual assemblies. One teacher at Sierra commented on this lack of schoolwide recognition, saying that she thought it was a mistake not to have schoolwide awards assemblies on a regular basis that recognized academic progress and improvement as well as behavior. 'It is not the same when it comes from a teacher they see everyday. It is more meaningful when the principal gives the award.' Whitney had certainly found this to be true.

The fifth and sixth grade loft used a weekly contract system consisting of three categories: independent worker, directed worker, and dependent worker. The number of each type of contract fluctuated from week to week depending on each student's performance. Those on an independent contract earned extra privileges for that week. According to the teachers interviewed, team members urge their fellow classmates to strive to maintain an independent contract. The fifth-sixth grade contract system seemed to serve multiple functions in addition to rewarding students. The system helped the teachers keep in touch with parents. These teachers did not express the same level of frustration in dealing with parents that surfaced in the interviews with teachers from the other lofts. The teachers also felt the contracts helped to train the students to be responsible, independent learners, which linked to their stated mission.

The teachers interviewed at Sierra did not see teacher recognition as a strength. The principal agreed with this perception saying he did not think teachers were recognized as much as he would like. According to one teacher, the principal pointed out honors teachers had received and the district committees on which teachers were serving. The entire staff met only four times a year, primarily for staff development and review of the School Improvement Plan. These infrequent meetings did not provide many opportunities for the principal to recognize teachers and the instructional strategies they were using in their rooms. One teacher expressed the view of several when she said, 'There is a need for more teacher-to-teacher and principal-to-teacher recognition. The principal needs to take the initiative in recognizing teachers and patting them on the back.' Unlike the staff at Whitney, Sierra's staff felt that they have had little to celebrate in terms of student achievement. The principal at Whitney, when he was in a similar situation, however, had used teacher recognition for small student gains and accomplishments as a way to focus on achievement, to impact teacher self-esteem and sense of efficacy, and to motivate teachers to work harder.

High Expectations

On the 1985 effective schools survey, high expectation was the second lowest area of agreement — only 52 per cent agreed. According to the survey, most of the teachers felt that they held consistently high expectations for students, and that they were responsible for students learning the basics. However, 46 per cent did not expect that 95 per cent of the students would graduate from high school. Thirty-four per cent believed that family background determined achievement.

By 1989, the overall per cent agreement with the items encompassing high expectation on the survey rose to 79 per cent. During the intervening years, about

12 staff members had received training in TESA, Teacher Expectations and Student Achievement. This training, designed to help teachers become more aware of how they treated students in the classroom and how their attitudes and practices could be lowering expectations, seemed to have paid off in terms of changes in teacher practices. In 1989, 93 per cent of the teachers agreed that they made sure low-achieving students had equal opportunity to respond. In 1985, only 58 per cent agreed that they did.

Because the staff had not yet experienced success as reflected in standardized test scores, the interviews did not reveal the same upbeat attitude and high expectations found at Whitney Elementary. One faculty member said in regard to test scores. 'We [the faculty] have done all we can to raise scores.' She contradicted this statement, however, later in the interview when she described how she, a twenty-year veteran teacher, had recently changed some of her teaching practices considerably, as a result of the staff development program. She felt that the changes were improving the effectiveness of her teaching.

Home-School Relations

Much energy on the part of the principal was devoted on a schoolwide basis to improving home-school relations. The school received several grants to support its program as well as countywide recognition for its effort. The school held several well-attended parent workshops each year. A monthly newsletter was distributed in English and Spanish. English as a second language classes were held at the school. Systematic Training in Effective Parenting (STEP) classes were conducted for parents in English and in Spanish. A unique cooperative parent involvement program was initiated with the neighboring junior high that resulted in co-sponsoring parent education programs as well as joint staff inservices. These cooperative efforts made transition to the junior high much smoother for Sierra's students and parents. An active core of approximately twenty to thirty parents assisted in the school as classroom and school volunteers. Classroom teachers also instituted a number of ways of staying in touch with parents. As mentioned above, the fifth and sixth grade loft used a weekly contract with students.

There were changes in teacher opinions regarding home-school relations as reflected on the effective schools survey. The overall agreement has risen from 69 per cent in 1985 to 79 per cent in 1989. Table 4.3 show which items changed.

Table 4.3   Comparison of teacher responses on home-school relations in 1985 and 1989 based on the county Effective Schools Survey

Survey Item	Per cent Agree	
	1984	1989
• Parent and teachers cooperate in monitoring homework	85%	92%
• Parents and teacher are aware of the homework policy	81	100
• Multiple methods are used to communicate with parents	89	97
• 90–100% parents attend parent-teacher conferences	69	89
• Almost all students complete assigned homework	78	81
• Parents frequently initiate contacts with classroom teachers	30	63
• Teachers invite parents to observe the instructional program	15	74
• There is an active parent group	52	76
• Most parents would rate this school as superior	85	52

Except for the last item the trend was upward in terms of positive feelings about this correlate. Some additional questions, however, were added to the effective schools surveys in 1986 when the surveys were revised. The questions which were asked on the 1989 survey are significant in giving insights into the issue of home-school relations because of the low per cent agreement on them. They are:

- Teachers communicate with parents about the good more than bad — 41 per cent agree
- Most parents are aware of the instructional objectives — 26 per cent agree
- 75 per cent plus parents attend open house/back to school night — 26 per cent agree

These figures stand in sharp contrast to the much higher per cent agreement among Whitney's staff on these same items (75, 65, 69 per cent agreement respectively). In spite of the schoolwide initiatives and gains in per cent agreement, the interviews revealed that classroom teachers still seemed frustrated by what they perceived as a lack of parent support for children and the educational program. One teacher expressed her frustration this way:

The children have a hard time focusing. There are more at-risk kids. The population has changed considerably. Home life for many of these children is difficult, less structured. They are spending much more time watching TV and playing video games like Nintendo. We need to be working much more with parents to help them see how important education is and what they can do to help. The Filipino parents value education much more than the Anglo and Hispanic parents at the school. They put education first. Hispanic parents don't follow through.

In the winter of 1989, the principal had a portable telephone installed and urged teachers to use it to call parents with positive messages. Several of the teachers interviewed said they were making more positive contacts and sending more positive notes home now. They felt their efforts were having a positive impact on parents. One teacher had even received two positive notes in return. If the teachers continue to use the telephone, to send positive written communications, and to inform parents about specific learning objectives and how they can help their children, there is evidence to suggest that parents, perceived as less supportive, will become more supportive (Epstein, 1987; Henderson, 1987).

As the principal at Whitney said, 'It is critical to get those first gains in student achievement.' Sierra's staff had not been able to achieve a breakthrough in test scores. Consequently the staff was having difficulty developing a psychology of success. It had not developed the positive attitudes towards parents that were found at Whitney which may have been undermining their perceived high expectations of students. The affective culture was strong at Sierra, but there was not yet a culture of achievement that permeated the school.

Shared Mission

When asked about the mission of the school, three significant points emerged. First, the teachers stated that they knew what their loft mission was, but they were not sure that staff members in the other lofts shared the mission. Second, the mission focused more on affective issues — building self-esteem, helping students become independent learners, and learning to accept students from diverse backgrounds — and less on academic achievement. The fifth-sixth grade loft said that their mission was to prepare the students adequately for junior high school socially, emotionally, and academically. Third, most of the teachers interviewed felt that only 30 to 40 per cent of the parents shared the mission. The loft with the weekly contracts felt that they were communicating the mission to parents and students, and they felt most supported the mission; however, the teacher interviewed from this loft felt that this was not happening in the other lofts. Teachers from the other lofts confirmed her view. The fragmentation among the teachers in the first and second grade loft and the two single classrooms meant that these teachers did not even share a mission among themselves. The fractured loft structure seemed to have made it difficult to develop a schoolwide mission.

Norms of Collegiality

Sierra was unique among the eight schools in that there were some very strong norms of collegiality among the teachers who teamed in the third-fourth and fifth-sixth grade lofts. These teachers spent considerable time together (e.g., during most of their lunch hours and frequently before or after school), discussing teaching strategies, planning lessons, discussing children's progress. These regular team meetings created a very strong culture within each loft. This pattern of collegiality represented both strengths and liabilities for the total school.

Prior to the principal coming to the school in 1984, the teachers worked almost exclusively in their lofts with very little total staff interaction. The previous school improvement plan had been put together by a small select committee with little total staff involvement. When the principal assumed his post in 1984, he wanted to change the norm of isolation between lofts. The undertaking of the school effectiveness process was one of his first steps. With the data collected from the surveys and CAP reports, he involved the whole staff and community members in developing a new school improvement plan. The extensive staff development program (see page 71) helped to bring the total staff together. The interviews revealed, however, that there were still factions among the staff. There was very little cross-loft collaboration, except on the four days a year that the principal set aside for reviewing the school improvement plan. Without regular staff meetings or ongoing curriculum committees to bring the staff together, staff cohesiveness did not develop. The result was norms of collegiality among two of the lofts, but absence of sharing, collaboration and collegiality among all the staff members. This weakness seemed to contribute to the failure to develop a shared mission and a coordinated curriculum.

School Technology: Curriculum and Instruction

Like the other schools in the study, the curriculum at Sierra was largely determined by the state curriculum frameworks, textbooks, and the district's curriculum guides. Analysis of several of the key correlates that encompass the school tech-nology component may help to explain why achievement gains had not yet occurred at Sierra.

Use of Test Results

All of the teachers interviewed said they were aware of the test results, and they knew that they were going to have to treat test scores much more seriously because of the new superintendent's views. The district's test evaluator annually reviewed the results with the staff and helped to identify strengths and weaknesses. On the effective schools survey, only 63 per cent of the staff, however, indicated that test results were used to modify the instructional program. The teachers did not appear to be able to analyze and use test results as effectively as the staff at Whitney. The principal said that he had recently learned a great deal about analyzing test scores from the California School Leadership Academy program, and that he felt there was a need to better train the teaching staff in their use.

The principal stated that the staff had a tendency to dismiss the results. This view was also expressed by several of the teachers who were interviewed. A first grade teacher said, 'They don't play a big role for me.' Another teacher said that tools like standardized tests to assess students are needed, but expressed frustration that they measured so little. She went on to say, 'The [state curriculum] frameworks have laid out many good educational concepts and are making good things happen in education. The frameworks are built on the basis of teaching the whole child, whereas the CAP testing covers such a minor part.' The principal at Whitney recognized this teacher's point; however, he had helped his staff to see that CAP covered an essential 30 per cent of the curriculum that students must learn. Once the students have mastered that, the staff would still have ample time to address other educational aspects that they thought were critical to teaching the whole child. In contrast, the staff at Sierra had not yet fully come to terms with the CAP test. One teacher summarized the problem this way:

> This test business needs to be sorted out. CAP is not just a third and sixth grade problem. We say we don't believe test scores are that significant a measure. If that's the case, we won't and don't bother. Unfortunately, the district, state, and superintendent care. We need to, too. We need to see who is embarrassed by this state of affairs and who is going to join together to address the issue. We can bring up the test scores by better teaching to the test. There needs to be an articulated curriculum.

This ambivalence about test scores prevented the school from using the results extensively and vigorously to plan instructional improvements and, more significantly, to engage in curriculum alignment. In 1988–89 the district issued a pacing guide for the new math series, but it arrived too late in the school year to be of much assistance to the teachers. In fact, it seemed to have increased anxiety and tension. Unlike the teachers at Whitney, the teachers at Sierra did not have a committee in place to immediately review the new textbook themselves and align it with the standardized tests.

In addition to not aligning the curriculum, the staff had also done little in the way of test preparation. They had used materials such as 'Scoring High' with the Chapter I[1] students with good results. They had not used these materials with others students, and, in fact, had been discouraged from doing so by the district administrative staff. The principal realized now that the decision not to use the materials was a mistake. He said that if he was staying at the school, he would definitely use these materials with all students in the future.

Academic Focus

When asked why she thought achievement had not improved, one teacher replied: 'The main reason is the lack of unity and focus. We have no common goal or understanding. Everyone needs to be responsible and part of the effort to improve test scores.' Only the principal talked about mastery of essential skills as a part of the mission. Without a clear sense of the academic goals and without systematic use of test scores, there seemed to be less of an academic focus at Sierra than at Whitney. The one area where the staff had come together had been in the area of writing. The whole staff received extensive training in the writing process in 1986–87 and made concerted efforts in their classrooms to increase the amount of writing assignments given to students. However, no other curriculum area had received such concerted attention over the last five years. Each loft and the other self-contained classrooms all seemed to operate independently of each other. There was curriculum planning within two of the lofts by the teachers, but that did not seem to be the case in the other loft or the two single classrooms which operated on their own. This is in sharp contrast to Whitney that had focused on science, on use of math manipulatives and problem solving, and on literature and the whole language approach to reading.

Frequent Monitoring

The teachers in the two most cohesive lofts felt that they monitored the implementation of changes fairly well. As one teacher said, 'In a loft situation one can't hide. Once a decision is made, all of us have to follow through because we observe each other and we talk about it.' However, the first and second grade loft did not appear to be working together as a team, and it was unclear how the two self-contained classrooms were monitored and linked to the other classrooms.

The principal and staff monitored the implementation of their improvement plan four times a year as part of their four staff development days. This served as a significant process to bring the whole staff together and to break down loft barriers. The total staff involvement and the periodic reviews of the plan were a strength and helped to train and empower the staff to examine the instructional program. Unfortunately, this strength was not maximized through ongoing curriculum committees.

The principal played a role in monitoring school programs through formal and informal observations. In the interviews, the staff expressed appreciation for the principal's knowledge of the Essential Elements of Instruction and the feedback he gave them individually after an observation. The 1989 effective school survey results indicated that the staff was in near unanimous agreement that before a formal observation the principal and teacher met to discuss what would be observed and after the observation they met again to review what was observed. Only 75 per cent of the teachers, however, stated that after an observation they developed a plan to improve instruction. While the teachers recognized that the principal was monitoring the program through observation, they did not see it as an active process in terms of the entire instructional program. The lack of regular staff meetings limited the time to discuss instructional issues across lofts and limited the principal's ability to share his observations about the instructional program in the various lofts. In addition, the principal did not use the staff bulletin in the same way as the principal at Whitney to monitor the instructional program by sharing what he observed in various classrooms. The lack of regular discussions and sharing of instructional issues may help to explain the staff's feeling that there was insufficient monitoring.

Staff Development

This aspect of the school improvement effort deserves special mention at Sierra because in the past three years it had served to bring the staff together, to increase collegiality across lofts, and to improve instructional skills. The first schoolwide staff development was a series of workshops on the writing process.

All of the teachers interviewed mentioned the important role the principal played in organizing high quality staff development programs. The staff identified the topics, but the principal recruited the presenters. In addition to training in the writing process, workshops were held on TESA, cooperative learning, the Essential Elements of Instruction, classroom management techniques, and homework strategies. As a result of these presentations, several teachers commented that a common language was developing among them. All of the teachers interviewed were excited and enthusiastic about the acquisition of new skills and the impact these were having on students in their classrooms. This enthusiasm about the teaching and learning process was not found two years earlier when the initial interviews were conducted. The only concern expressed by the staff was that they needed some brief refresher courses and more reinforcement by sharing across lofts to discuss what was working and what refinements teachers were making in the skills they had learned and were now trying to implement. The lack of reinforcement and follow through in implementation are common problems faced by most schools (Little, 1986; Hopkins, 1990). Staff members shared with each other in the lofts, especially if one of them had attended a workshop and learned new information or skills. However, the interviews did not indicate that staff members were extensively involved in conducting schoolwide staff development themselves, as seemed to be occurring at several of the more effective schools.

Nor was the principal as active in monitoring the use of new instructional practices as was the principal of Whitney. Little (1986) found that the active participation of the principal in the implementation phase was key to successful staff development that led to changed teaching practices.

School Organizational Structures and Procedures

The physical structure of Sierra shaped facets of its culture and climate and impacted the school's technology. The loft system resulted in more team-teaching and cooperative planning than was found in most schools and produced teachers who were able to teach in a fish bowl. As one teacher commented, 'The loft system forces us constantly to be looking at the program and how to improve.' Because of the planning time required to work as a team at the loft level, the structure also resulted in teachers who were wrapped up in their own loft's work, and who were less willing to take a whole school view. The loft structure created three schools within one with two isolated classrooms as appendages. As one teacher commented: 'There is no articulation to speak of. The interactions between the lofts seems to be accusatory rather than problem-solving discussion.' The teacher went on to acknowledge, however, that the situation was much better than its used to be.

During his tenure, the principal also had seen changes in the patterns of interaction, with more teachers now associating with each other across lofts during staff inservices and at other meetings. When asked what the staff would recommend to others on how to improve, all of the teachers stressed the need to continue the schoolwide staff-development program. In addition, they recommended the creation of curriculum committees that would cut across grade levels and focus on key academic areas. They also felt the need to more frequently hold all-school staff meetings. Two years ago when the interviews were conducted for the 1987 study, the staff members did not appear willing to give up their loft autonomy. This shift in views represents an important change, and illustrates how long it takes to change the culture of a school.

Shared Decision-Making, Collaboration, and Teacher Empowerment

As mentioned above, teachers collaborated in the lofts. There was a great deal of shared decision-making about the curriculum and instructional strategies to be used within the loft. Teachers felt they had a significant role in shaping the School Improvement Plan, but they were more divided about their role in budgetary matters. One felt that the School Improvement Budget was predetermined, and they had little say about that aspect of school improvement. In the beginning, over half of the School Improvement Budget was allocated for classroom aides. As personnel costs had increased, ever larger proportions were used for personnel, often without a thorough reexamination of the cost effectiveness of these expenditures. Consequently, the staff felt they had little say about the budget. Another teacher, however, mentioned that each loft had received an allocation of lottery funds and it was up to them to decide how to use these funds. She said she did not think teachers in other schools had so much say about use of lottery funds.

Other than the four school-improvement planning days, the school did not have schoolwide committees that brought the staff together to work on curriculum issues. In 1987, a schoolwide discipline committee was established to develop a discipline plan for the school. As one teacher said, 'The discipline plan was one issue we all worked on. We need to do more activities like that.' During the interviews, two teachers expressed a concern that there was a need to update the discipline plan, but the committee no longer existed and there was no vehicle to address the issue. At other points in the interviews, several teachers mentioned the need to develop a schoolwide oral language program, but again they seemed stymied, because structures were not in place for tackling the issue. To address schoolwide issues, the principal met once a month with a representative from each loft and the kindergarten team; however, most of the teachers did not feel this was an adequate system or process for resolving instructional issues. All of those interviewed indicated that there was a need for more ways that would bring them together as a whole staff.

During the past five years, the staff felt empowered to act in their lofts. They learned to play an active role in writing the School Improvement Plan. They learned the value of working together in the staff-development inservices, and they had come to recognize the need to establish some schoolwide curriculum committees.

Instructional Leadership

In 1985 when the first effective schools survey was administered and the principal was new, the results from the instructional leadership correlate showed that the staff was uncertain about the principal's role and leadership. In 1989, when the survey was administered again, the staff opinions regarding the principal's leadership had shifted with far greater agreement about individual items. The overall agreement in 1985 was 49 per cent. By 1989, the agreement rate had risen to 76 per cent. Even with these shifts, it remained the lowest area of agreement among all the correlates assessed by the survey. The area with the most positive shifts centered on the principal's observation of the classroom. In the past two years, the principal has been trained in the Essential Elements of Instruction (EEI), a clinical teaching model. The staff recognized the principal's expertise in this methodology and its use in his classroom observations. In other areas, opinions remained less positive.

On the one hand, the principal modeled the importance of growth and development by his own participation in the California School Leadership Academy, in becoming a trainer in EEI, participating in the Assessment Center run by the county office of education, and in assisting in countywide efforts to increase parent involvement by conducting workshops and organizing conferences. In other words, the principal had continued to update his own skills. The staff appreciated the fact that he was current with educational research and developments and through staff inservices had brought this information to the staff. On the other hand, all of this participation had taken the principal away from the school site. This lack of availability was reflected in the survey results in 1989. Table 4.4 (see p. 74) compares the results of the staff's opinions of the principal's instructional leadership as reflected in the survey items in 1985 and in 1989. It reveals the areas of growth and the areas of slippage.

Table 4.4 *Comparison of teacher responses on instructional leadership in 1985 and 1989 based on the county Effective Schools Survey*

Survey Item	Per cent Agree	
	1985	1989
• Principal is active in promoting staff development	75%	96%
• Before formal observation principal and teacher discuss what to observe	22	93
• Following formal observation principal discusses observation with teacher	33	96
• Classroom observations by principal focused on improving instruction	19	85
• Principal makes frequent classroom observations	26	63
• After formal observations, teacher and principal develop instructional improvement plan	19	74
• Principal emphasizes meaning/use of standard test results with faculty	44	78
• Principal reviews and interprets test results with faculty	63	82
• Principal uses test results to modify and change the instructional program	41	46
• Instructional leadership from the principal is clear, strong, and central	37	58
• Instructional issues are frequently the focus of staff meetings	56	48
• Principal makes frequent contacts with students and teachers	97	89
• Principal is highly visible throughout school	85	65

These survey results show the multiplicity of tasks that are subsumed under the heading of instructional leadership. Balancing all the tasks that must be done is a challenge, especially when asked by the district to assume a number of additional responsibilities, as happened in the case of the principal of Sierra. Furthermore, the size of the school was over 600 but under the number needed to qualify for an assistant principal. During the principal's five year tenure much had been accomplished. If his tenureship had continued the same length of time as Whitney's principal, perhaps increased achievement for students would have followed. This assumption is based on the fact that by the time the interviews were conducted in 1989, both the principal and the staff seemed to have a number of insights about problems facing the school. That recognition by the staff had not been shown in the interviews conducted in 1987.

Shared Leadership

There was good participation at Sierra by teachers, support staff, and parents in the development of the school improvement plan. Teachers in the third-fourth and fifth-sixth grade lofts jointly made decisions for their lofts. Yet, there was not the same sense of shared leadership that led to total school responsibility, as when compared to Whitney. The length of time that the principal at Whitney had had to develop the data analysis and problem-solving skills of his teachers had contributed to their ability to share in leadership. The training of Sierra's staff members and the principal in the Essential Elements of Instruction process offered the potential of developing a leadership team in this area. The development of shared leadership, which would lead to institutional development, however, appeared to be blocked, until organizational and structural barriers created by the combination of lofts and self-contained classrooms was resolved.

Summary and Conclusions

This chapter has presented the story of Sierra Elementary, a school that has worked hard to improve, but has not yet seen the benefits of its labors, especially in terms of standardized test score increases. For the duration of this study, Sierra experienced a small, but perhaps significant change in its student inputs. The overall enrollment has remained fairly stable, but there was a 10 per cent shift in the ethnic background of students, with Hispanic and Latino students now out-numbering Filipinos. Perhaps because of their lack of experience in teaching limited-English speaking students, teachers viewed this population shift some-what negatively. On a schoolwide basis, the principal had responded to these changes in student inputs by developing a bilingual program, hiring Spanish-speaking assistants to work with students and parents, and working tirelessly to break down racial barriers among parents — Filipino, White, Hispanic-Latino and African-American. These responses were not always appreciated by the staff.

Student outcomes at both third and sixth grade did not improve significantly over the course of the study. Sierra remained a less effective school based on the criteria presented in Chapter 1. In an effort to improve the outcomes, the school undertook a number of changes in the transformative process. One of the most significant changes at Sierra was in the area of staff development. Interview data suggested that the staff development program was contributing to the overall institutional development of the school. Through the frequently ongoing staff development activities, such as the training in teaching writing as a process, the staff had become far more reflective about their own teaching practices and had begun to recognize some of the developmental problems besetting the school. A concomitant development had not occurred in the organizational component, which would have enabled the staff to translate its insights and concerns into action. The entrenchment of the loft structure and staff interaction patterns that it had created proved a major barrier to developing a *schoolwide* mission, aca-demic focus, coordinate curriculum, norms of collegiality, and shared decision-making. Glimpses of these existed in the two strongest lofts, but were absent among the other eight teachers, and thus resulted in a fragmented school. While the lofts could solve problems in their own area, they could not solve schoolwide problems, and in fact, tended to be counterproductive in addressing school-wide issues. By 1989, the teachers had begun to recognize the problem, but no solution seemed in sight.

The critical role of leadership and its interface with organizational structures is well illustrated in the case of Sierra. The principal masterfully brought parents and staff together to develop a schoolwide improvement plan; however, he did not or could not maintain that schoolwide momentum in the face of the long tradition of the autonomous lofts. The initiation of the staff development program represented an end run around the loft structure, but it needed to be supported by the creation of schoolwide structures, such as ongoing curriculum committees and regular staff meetings that cut across loft structures and led to the development of a schoolwide leadership team. It is also important to note that in a school of over 600 students, it is clear that the principal's time needs to be totally devoted to the school. Yet, the principal at Sierra found his time frequently occupied in district and countywide programs and issues. These external time demands left little time for classroom observations and curriculum monitoring, areas in which the principal had useful skills. These are important observations, because time is probably one of the scarcest resources of schools. In the push for more site-based management and self-governing restructured schools, the issue of time and how it is used needs to be carefully considered, especially given the generally large size of California schools.

Finally, this case study helps to demonstrate the close interrelationship between the components of the transformative process. Many pieces needed for school improvement and increased effectiveness were put in place at Sierra. Yet key cultural, organizational, and technology elements were not quite right. The incongruities, especially the lack of a whole school view and strong norms of total school collegiality, seemed to prevent bringing all the pieces together in ways that led to improved student outcomes.

Note

1   Chapter 1 is a federally funded program designed to provide supplementary support to local school districts to meet the needs of educational disadvantaged students who are scoring in the bottom quartile as shown on standardized achievement tests. The formula for disbursement of funds to states and localities is based on the number of low-income students living in a school district and the average cost of education per pupil within the state (Doyle and Cooper, 1988, pp. 52–5). Each school community has some flexibility in deciding how Chapter 1 funds are allocated to individual school sites.

Chapter 5

Tahoe Elementary: Healing Divisions, Stabilizing Leadership

The Setting: Inputs and Outputs

Tahoe Elementary is located in a mixed area of small single and multiple family residences adjacent to an industrial and commercial area. The school was built in 1953 in the finger plan common to schools built in that era. The physical plant consisted of a large cafetorium, a kindergarten complex of two classrooms, and five wings containing twenty-two self-contained classrooms and a library. In 1988–89 the school served 651 lower-middle and low income students, many from single parent families. When both parents were present in the home, both of them usually worked outside the home. The ethnic distribution of the schools was approximately 23 per cent White, not of Hispanic origin, 71 per cent Hispanic, 4 per cent Black, not of Hispanic origin, and 0.5 per cent Asian. Forty-seven per cent of the students were limited or non-English speaking (LEP/NEP), and were receiving English as a second language instruction. The low income status of the school was reflected in the socio-economic index of 1.33, which was the lowest of all the schools in the study. The state average was 2.03. Twenty-three per cent of the students received Aid to Families with Dependent Children, which was twice the rate of Sierra and Whitney and of the district as a whole. The school population also had a high turnover in student enrollments partly because many were recent immigrants; the neighborhood was a temporary stopping point. In the 1987–88 sixth grade class, only 29 per cent of the students had been at the school since kindergarten, 31 per cent of the students had entered in the sixth grade. It is important to note, however, that the achievement results of the students who entered in sixth grade were similar to those who had been in the school since kindergarten. Mobility, thus, cannot directly be considered a factor in explaining the overall achievement results.

To meet the needs of this low-income population, the school received Chapter I, Chapter VII[1], State Compensatory Education funds and California School Improvement monies. Most of these resources were used to support extra personnel. In addition to the twenty-two regular classroom teachers, students received the full time services of a resource specialist, two Miller-Unruh Reading Specialists, and a bilingual resource teacher. The students had the part-time services of a nurse, a librarian, a speech therapist, a psychologist, and twenty-nine instructional aides.

Tahoe, located in the same district as Sierra, operated with the same support and constraints. The school had a change of principals in 1984, and again in 1986, when the principal who joined the staff in 1984 was promoted to a district office position. This rapid change in personnel did not make it easy to formulate and implement a school improvement plan. The current principal hoped he would stay long enough to see substantial growth and gains in student achievement.

Tahoe's student achievement levels in all content areas assessed by the California Assessment Program (CAP) remained low in both the third and sixth grade and were well below district and state averages. At the third grade there had been an increase in overall math scores, but not in reading or language arts. At the sixth grade, there were some modest gains in all areas. Table 5.1 compares the school's CAP scaled scores in reading, written language, and mathematics for third and sixth grade for the last three years with the district and the state scores. This table helps to put the school's scores in perspective and to show how the district scored in comparison to the state. As can be seen from the Table 5.1, the district consistently scored below the state at the third grade in reading and language arts, but above the state in mathematics. At the sixth grade level, the district's students scored at or slightly above the state average in reading and language arts, and consistently above in mathematics.

Table 5.1   Three-year comparison of Tahoe's Achievement Scores at third and sixth grade levels with district and state scores on CAP

| Content Areas | Years | Scaled Scores | | | | | |
| | | School | | District | | State | |
		3rd	6th	3rd	6th	3rd	6th
Reading	85–86	231	216	279	262	280	260
	86–87	233	210	276	262	282	260
	87–88	228	239	272	267	282	265
Written Language	85–86	228	228	282	275	285	271
	86–87	229	227	276	270	287	271
	87–88	224	239	274	274	284	273
Mathematics	85–86	226	213	296	280	283	268
	86–87	237	227	297	281	285	268
	87–88	242	249	298	278	281	270

Unlike Sierra, when scores were disaggregated by family occupation, all third grade students at each income level scored well below their counterparts at the district and state levels. At the sixth grade level the results were more mixed. When scores were disaggregated by family occupation, sixth grade scores were below the district levels for comparable groups, except for the students with semi-skilled parents, who were above in written language. The students with unskilled parents, who comprise 69 per cent of the student population, scored slightly above the same group at the state level in reading and mathematics, but below the district in all content areas. At both the third and sixth grade level a large percentage of students were scoring in the bottom quartile. On all three of the criteria Tahoe remained a less effective school.

The school effectiveness program was initiated in 1984, when a new principal was assigned to the school, and the staff and school site council somewhat reluctantly decided to participate in the program. The school had the reputation of being the worst in the district. The principal saw the effective schools assessment as a way of identifying needs and focusing efforts. While the record indicated that the staff voted to participate, the interviews that were conducted in 1987 revealed that several of the staff members felt they were coerced to participate by the principal. The staff seemed to have been particularly threatened by the classroom time-on-task observations which were a part of the assessment process. The time-on-task observations were conducted by teachers from another school with whom the school had been paired. Some of the teachers from Tahoe, in turn, were trained and conducted the time-on-task audits at their paired school.

Figure 5.1 compares the teachers' opinions for the three years that the effective schools surveys were given: 1984, 1986, and 1989. As can be seen from the graph, opinions in the latest survey shifted to a higher per cent agreement, as shown by the higher mean scores. As was learned from the case study of Sierra, however, more positive views regarding the effective schools correlates, did not mean an automatic increase in achievement scores. The very low per cent agreement in 1984 and 1986, however, matched the very low achievement results in those years and did not bode well for accomplishing any gains in achievement. The results in 1989 suggested the beginnings of a more positive view within the school. At the same time, the test scores at the sixth grade level also showed an upward trend.

Figure 5.1   Comparison of Mean Scores of teacher responses on the Effective Schools Surveys completed in 1984, 1987, and 1989

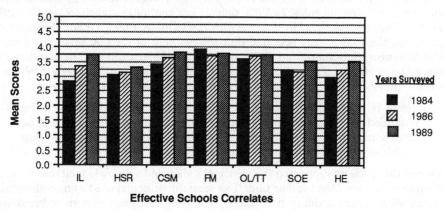

Legend: IL = Instructional Leadership, HSR = Home-School Relations, CSM = Clear School Mission, FM = Frequent Monitoring, OL/TT = Opportunity to Learn, Time-on-Task, SOE = Safe Orderly Environment, HE = High Expectations.

By examining in detail aspects of the school climate and culture, school technology, and organizational structures and procedures, it was possible to identify areas that may be impeding increased student achievement.

School Climate and Culture

Tahoe was serving one of the largest concentrations of low income students of the eight schools in the study. Shasta, located in close proximity and in the same district as Tahoe, and Sequoia, located in a nearby district, were the other two schools serving similar populations. The challenges of creating a culture of achievement and success were considerable for all three. Both Shasta and Sequoia, however, by 1987–88, were able to attain achievement levels that averaged 20 to 40 points above those of Tahoe in reading, written language and mathematics. Several aspects of the school culture point to some of the problems that Tahoe had in increasing student achievement.

Safe and Orderly Learning Environment

Improvement of the physical plant was one of the important changes that occurred at Tahoe during the duration of this study. This change was initiated by the principal in 1985 and continued under the current administration. While only 48 per cent agreed that the school buildings were neat, clean, and kept in good repair in 1985, 100 per cent felt that they were in 1989. There were, however, still other significant issues in terms of school safety. Over 80 per cent of the staff did not believe their property was secure, and 57 per cent felt vandalism was a problem. While most of the staff members felt the school was a safe and secure place to work, 32 per cent did not feel it was safe after students were dismissed.

The school had a schoolwide discipline plan. Teachers reported that students were taught schools rules, they believed that students felt the rules were reasonable and appropriate. Teachers also generally agreed that students were held accountable for following school rules, and that teachers rewarded and praised students for following rules. In 1986, only 42 per cent of the teachers felt that the principal supported them in dealing with discipline matters. Under the current principal, the 1989 survey revealed that 100 per cent of the teachers agreed that the administration supported them in dealing with discipline. The number of discipline problems referred to the principal's office was still seen as a problem. In the interviews, the principal confirmed the problem when he said:

> There is a schoolwide discipline plan, however, I feel it needs to be redefined. A number of teachers deal with discipline problems in the classroom, others are sending them to me. I am the disciplinarian. I am spending a signficant amount of my time on discipline.

Two of the teachers supported the principal's view and acknowledged that he was playing a big role. One teacher said, 'I've seen the principal used as disciplinarian rather than teachers doing it at their level. The discipline system is breaking down, teachers are using him as a leaning post.'

Each year the effective schools surveys were given, there were more teachers who agreed that a positive school spirit permeated the school. In 1985, only 15 per cent of the teachers agreed, in 1986, 31 per cent agreed, and in 1989, 57 per cent agreed that the school had a positive spirit. While the climate was improving, some important safety and discipline issues remained to be resolved before all teachers would fully agree that Tahoe had a safe and orderly learning environment.

Rewards and Recognition

In the last two years the current principal expanded the amount of schoolwide recognition for students. Each month a Good Person Assembly was held. Teachers nominated students from their classes to receive recognition for both academic success and good behavior. Last year, the sixth grade teacher in charge of the student council was instrumental in implementing the Honor Student Award Program which was designed to recognize student efforts, growth, and improvement. In this regard, the program was distinct from more typical honor roll programs which only acknowledge outstanding scholarship. Traditional spelling bees, writing contests and other academic competitions represented other ways the school recognized student achievement. Establishing a good recognition program for students was one important dimension of the school climate that Tahoe had improved.

Recognition of teacher efforts and instructional practices was not seen as a strong part of the culture. Teachers who were interviewed felt they were recognized for extra efforts such as serving on a committee, putting on a play, or organizing the school talent show. Most teachers felt they were not recognized for instructional expertise. One teacher commented that if a teacher was 'selected to be trained to get ahead in the district administratively, they were given a lot of opportunity to do extra jobs and get recognized.' Two other teachers expressed the view that quieter, but competent teachers who were everyday doing a good job in their classroom received little recognition. 'It seems the louder you are the more recognition you get. It's unfortunate.' These concerns about the the lack of teacher recognition and who gets recognized were symptomatic of the divisions that existed among the staff. Several of the interviews revealed feelings that the staff was divided into an *in group* and an *out group*. These divisions will be discussed more fully under the section on organizational structures and procedures.

High Expectations

The effective schools surveys showed that high expectations for student achievement were not a prevalent part of the culture at Tahoe. In 1985, the overall agreement with the High Expectations correlate was 47 per cent; in 1986 it was 48 per cent and in 1989, 61 per cent. According to the survey in 1989, 80 per cent of the teachers said they consistently held high academic expectations for students and that they expected students to be successful in school work. In 1986, 69 per cent of the teachers said they were responsible for helping students achieve identified standards. By 1989, 95 per cent of the staff felt they were responsible. This shift most likely was a reflection of the new emphasis of the district and site administration to hold teachers more accountable for student achievement.

Although teachers said they held high expectations, as in the case of Sierra, other survey items cast doubts about how high their expectations really were. Table 5.2 compares the responses to the surveys in 1986 and 1989, and shows that many teachers still held relatively low expectations both for themselves and for the ultimate success of their students.

The principal felt that expectations had improved. The data in Table 5.2 confirmed his view that expectations had increased in a number of areas. By 1989, a higher percentage of teachers believed that all students could achieve basic skills in reading, writing, and mathematics. Teachers' low expectations for student performance on standardized tests and their feelings of inadequacy in helping

Table 5.2   Comparison of teacher responses on high expectation in 1986 and 1989 based on the Effective Schools Survey

Survey Item	Per cent Agree 1986	1989
• Teachers can successfully teach 90–95% in spite of home background	38%	75%
• Teachers expect most to do well on teacher prepared tests	50	65
• Teachers grade on achievement of subject, not behavior	77	67
• Teachers believe all students can achieve basic math	62	71
• Students can achieve identified standards regardless of home	39	58
• Teachers believe all students can achieve basic writing	46	62
• Teachers believe all students can achieve basic reading	50	72
• Students are given additional help until standards are achieved	56	57
• Low income/high income students retained proportionally	23	27
• Teachers feel capable of helping all achieve identified standards	39	45
• Most teachers believe all students can achieve subject standards	50	45
• Over 90% expected to achieve identified standards	23	25
• Teachers expect students to do well on standardized tests	23	29
• Teachers expect over 95% will graduate from high school	8	15

all students achieve the identified standards, however, remained to be addressed. Research on teacher expectations and student achievement has indicated that considerably less was often expected of students in low tracks (Evertson, 1980). Once patterns of expectations get set they seemed to be difficult to alter. Brophy (1982) states, 'Low expectations are likely to become entrenched norms that channel teacher and student behavior without ever being seriously questioned.' (p. 64)

In many respects, the staff perceived Tahoe as a 'low track' school. The principal highlighted this problem by explaining that a number of teachers, especially a core that has recently left the school, had the attitude of 'Look how great we are, working with these poor kids.' The principal went on the say, 'Yet they held very low expectations for them, especially in the academic area and were actually pulling them [the students] down.' Even though most of the teachers that held this view have left, the school still suffers an inferiority complex. During the interviews, several teachers described the school as being rock bottom in the district. One teacher stated that he believed parents held higher expectations than the teachers. Another teacher who had been trained in TESA and other programs about expectations, commented that she needed constant reminders to keep her expectations high. 'I love them dearly, I see them coming in the way they do, and I know I have been guilty of not expecting them to do their best. Teachers have been lowering expectations because of children's home background. I'd like to change that mentality.' This quote helps to show the close link between teacher expectations for student achievement and home-school relations. The next section addresses home-school relations and demonstrates just how closely these two correlates are intertwined at Tahoe.

Home-School Relations

This is clearly an area of frustration for the school staff. During the interview, the principal lamented that if Tahoe 'was a magnet school, it could be labeled the

Table 5.3   Comparison of teacher responses on home-school relations in 1986 and 1989 based on the Effective Schools Survey

Survey Item	Per cent Agree	
	1986	1989
• Teachers use many ways to communicate with parents	100	100%
• Parent-teacher conferences relate to student achievement	80	90
• Parents are invited and attend school activities	73	95
• Teachers contact parents on a regular basis	61	80
• Parent-teacher conferences result in specific plans for cooperation	69	75
• Parent organization is considered important by administration	65	75
• Parents are aware of the discipline policy	61	65
• Most parents support school when child is disciplined for misbehavior	56	80
• Teachers and parents are aware of the homework policy	48	72
• There is cooperation between parents/teachers re homework monitoring	31	55
• There is an active parent group	35	60
• Teachers invite parents to observe the instructional program	43	43
• Teachers communicate with parents about the good more than bad	12	33
• 90% to 100% parents attend scheduled parent-teacher conferences	27	48
• Student homework is monitored at home	16	35
• Almost all students complete assigned homework	16	34
• Most parents have a clear understanding of school goals	31	25
• Most parents would rate this school as superior	8	20
• Parents frequently initiate contact with classroom teachers	19	29
• 75% plus parents attend open house/back to school night	8	20
• Most parents are aware of the instructional objectives	10	12
• Parents and or community members are frequent volunteers	12	15

School for Dysfunctional Families. There is a heartbreak a minute at this school.' He said that he felt many parents could not support the school's mission or their children because they were so needy themselves. Prevalent in both interviews and surveys was the notion that Tahoe was a low track, low performing school because its children were from low-income income families. The schools low expectations for students were matched by their low expectations for parents.

Similar to the high expectations correlate, home-school relations was consistently an area of low agreement. Since the first survey in 1985, staff views changed very little. The total agreement with the home-school realtions correlate was 45 per cent in 1985, 41 per cent in 1986, and 53 per cent in 1989. Table 5.3 compares staff responses in 1986 with the responses on the 1989 survey. The comparisons show the areas of greatest change, the areas of highest agreement that an action was taking place, and the areas that teachers felt were problems. Teachers were very positive about their own behavior and efforts in reaching out to parents. From their perspective, the problem resided with the parents.

While there was a shift to the positive on almost all items, the percentage agreement remained low in many critical areas. The staff believed that parents were not well informed about school goals and instructional objectives. They felt that most parents were not participating in significant events like back-to-school night and parent-teacher conferences. The staff stated that they were communicating in many different ways with parents, but they also acknowledged that they communicated more about the bad than the good. They believed that parents did not hold the school in high regard.

Even though the communication and involvement problems were identified in the survey in 1985, and again in 1986, the 1989 survey and interviews indicated that little had been done to address these issues. Based on the interviews, most teachers indicated that they had not altered the ways they were working with parents or that they were now making more contacts with them. In discussing homework, one of the teachers recognized that other schools were doing more to link home and school. She said:

> Homework is sent by the teachers. I know that parents help, but I can't honestly tell you how much they help. It is not uniform throughout the school. I know at other schools it is more systematic, such as having a yellow folder on Monday with four pages of homework due on Friday. We don't do that.

The principal and bilingual coordinator mentioned that they were conducting more home visits; however, the primary focus of the visits was to discuss problems such as excessive absences. The principal indicated that home-school relations was going to be one of his priority areas for the 1989–90 school year. He stated that the core leadership team was looking at ways resources might be allocated to work more effectively with families. Tahoe's staff viewed its families as problems rather than resources. As long as families were seen as the problem, expectations for their support and their actual support remained low. The principal expressed a desire for parents to be actively involved on the School Site Council and PTA. He felt, however, that such involvement was unlikely. Lessons from Whitney and Sierra demonstrated that the focus needed to be on improving communications, especially positive ones with parents, if parental support was to be increased. In addition, until teachers' sense of self-esteem and efficacy in working with a large low-income Spanish speaking population was enhanced by seeing achievement gains (as had occurred at Whitney), it was unlikely that the staff would be able to develop more positive views toward parents.

Shared Mission

On the 1986 and 1989 surveys, the staff agreed that the school had a written statement of purpose and that it focused on learning and achievement. In the interviews, however, most teachers said they could not remember what the mission was. One teacher commented, 'The mission has been written up so many times, but I don't really remember it.' When asked to state the mission in their own words, articulation of the mission varied from 'Expect the Best' to have an orderly environment that is safe where children can do optimum learning. One teacher said that the mission of the district was to raise test scores, but that he did not agree with this mission. He thought the primary goal of the school should be to help children get along well together. The very diverse articulations of the mission showed that the staff did not have a shared mission. The long history of cliques in this school no doubt contributed to the lack of a shared mission. Unlike the staff at Whitney and Yosemite, the staff had not participated in a 'We Agree' process or any other team building activity that would have helped it to develop a mission. Also the change in leadership at both the district and school had no doubt contributed to the lack of a coherent mission.

Norms of Collegiality

Tahoe had a long history of being a school plagued with cliques and sub-groups. There were examples of team teaching, but a consistent norm of collegiality did not exist. By 1989, the principal thought he was making progress in bringing the school together by creating a core leadership team, which will be discussed in detail below. After his first year, he had had the opportunity to bring in six new faculty members whom he felt were bringing a fresh perspective to the school and many of whom were now serving on the leadership team. However, the interviews revealed that there were still divisions within the school. A number of the teachers interviewed, who had been at the school for some time, saw themselves in the 'out' group, isolated from the decision-making process. Without a shared sense of mission and with few opportunities to work together in grade level teams and on curriculum committees, the staff did not possess the means to develop norms of collegiality.

School Techology: Curriculum and Instruction

Since Sierra and Whitney were in the same district, the curriculum strengths and problems were similar. For example, both schools shared the experience in 1988–89 of implementing a new math textbook and receiving the pacing and curriculum alignment materials too late in the school year to be helpful. Both had the same kind of district help in analyzing test scores with the same consequences of not developing staff expertise in test data analysis. There were also some critical differences between the two schools, especially in the area of staff development and academic focus.

Use of Test Scores

The interviews at Tahoe revealed a great deal of disagreement about test scores, their importance, and their use. Like the staff at Sierra, Tahoe's staff felt there was increasing pressure to improve test results. The new district superintendent was unwilling to accept the *status quo*, just because Tahoe was serving a very low-income student population. When asked what role test scores play, one teacher replied: 'They are used to hold over our heads.' Another said, 'They are used to harangue us.' The principal said, 'They are the bottom line. Our esteem as a school is perceived on the basis, unfortunately, of student performance as measured by test scores.' Like the staff at most schools in the study, over half of the staff at Tahoe consistently stated that the California Assessment Program was not a valid measure. Only at Whitney was there a significant positive shift in staff opinions regarding this question.

The three effective schools surveys showed that, in general, the two principals had consistently reviewed and interpreted test results with the faculty. In 1985, 66 per cent said the principal reviewed them, in 1986, 92 per cent agree, and in 1989, 86 per cent. There was slightly less agreement that the two principals emphasized the meaning and use of test results. In 1986, 69 per cent of the staff agreed that this was done; in 1989, 90 per cent said the current principal was emphasizing their use. In 1986, 58 per cent and in 1989, 63 per cent of the staff said the principal was using the test results to modify the instructional program. Of those interviewed, 60 per cent of the staff and the principal said that teachers were not using them to modify the instructional program. Those who indicated they were being used cited the staff's involvement in the Writing Project as a example of their use.

Like Sierra, the staff had not used test results to align its curriculum. The staff also had not made much use of testwiseness materials. This year before the test, orange juice was served to the students. However, consistent use of such materials as *Scoring High*, *Bell Works*, *Excel Math*, or *Short Shots* to prepare students for the tests were not evident. The previous principal had purchased *Scoring High*, but it was never implemented before he left. The current principal did not discover existence of the materials until late in the school year. One staff member commented: 'This year it was pulled off the shelf, dusted off, and distributed a month before the test which wasn't long enough to change anything.'

Whitney, Sierra, and Tahoe this year engaged in a systematic process of analyzing individual pupil results for diagnostic purposes. The activity, however, produced quite different results in the three schools, analysis of which reflects important differences in culture and expectations. At Whitney, the principal asked the first and second grade teachers to identify the fifteen lowest achieving students in their grades, to decide what skills these students needed to master, and to identify possible strategies for helping them master them. He felt that just as a result of the discussion itself, these students probably had a more positive experience in the classroom, because the teachers would be more sensitive to their needs. He said that part of his role was to focus constantly on the bottom group and ask teachers how they were meeting its needs. This approach seemed to work for three reasons. First, the principal and staff chose a reasonable number of students to assist. Second, the assistance was provided against a backdrop of teacher attitudes that accepted responsibility for educating all children. Third, the staff looked at what needed to be changed in the curriculum, not what was wrong or needed to be changed in the children by outside resource personnel. One staff member at Whitney summarized the issue this way:

> Achievement of minorities, single families — we have not isolated them *per se* and targeted them as high risk students. We have looked at the concept of high risk students and we have grouped all children together as being entitled to a fair and equal education. All children can be educated regardless of their home environment — that's the premise of effective schools. We've looked at weak areas within the curriculum and said *how can we improve* (emphasis added).

At Sierra and Tahoe this year the principal and each teacher went through a similar process, but they examined the cumulative folders of all their students. Deficiencies were identified. 'We said what is it that we are really lacking, is it this or that — oral language, help in testwiseness, monitoring more closely the child's progress, children-at-risk. We looked at everything and followed up with the Learning Screening Team.' From the perspective of several other teachers at both schools, several problems surfaced with this approach. First, the staff was trying to address the needs of too many students. The task seemed more than the teachers could handle. Second, they felt that they did not have sufficient resource personnel to follow through. At Tahoe, in particular, many students were referred to the psychologist for testing or to Learning Screening Team for review, which produced an overload and backlog of cases.[2] Third, there was little indication that the teachers focused on what needed to be changed in the curriculum at the classroom level to better meet student needs. One teacher at Sierra also expressed frustration at the lack of follow-up by resource personnel. However, at Sierra, students with the greatest needs were referred to the intersession program during the year-round school breaks where they received intensive small group help. This program had two benefits. First, the staff felt that the program addressed the skills that these students were missing, thus helping them to catch up. Second, several of the teachers who worked in the program had the opportunity to get to know these students much better, to appreciate their strengths, and to develop more positive attitudes about their ability to learn, which they carried back to the regular classroom setting. No such opportunities were available for the students or teachers at Tahoe. This comparison helps to illustrate that what appears to be a similar act, using test scores to diagnose students' learning needs, can have different conseqences depending on the school's culture, school technology and organizational structures. The merit or appropriateness of a solution to a problem needs to be evaluated within the context of the school's environment.

Academic Focus

The staff at Tahoe stated that they wanted students to learn, but a consistent sense of what and how much students were to learn did not emerge from the interviews. The survey responses in 1986 and 1989 indicated that there were written standards in all major curricular areas, however, standards of mastery were not specified. Only 31 per cent of the staff agreed that students must achieve identified standards. A comparison of the survey responses on the clear school mission correlate in 1986 and 1989 revealed that problems identified in 1986 still persisted in 1989. Over 50 per cent of the staff identified the following as problems:

- Instructional decisions were not based on the statement of purpose.
- Students were not estimating answers, using mental arithmetic, or doing sufficient problem solving.
- Textbooks and materials did not support learning objectives.
- Teachers were not accountable for skills/concepts in course outline.
- Students were not accountable for clear/accurate writing in all subjects.
- Social studies materials were not matched to reading abilities.

The most recent Program Quality Review, conducted in March 1988, supported the need to address these issues. For example, the report suggested the need to emphasize problem-solving and the use of manipulatives in the math curriculum, provide more direct instruction in the writing process, purchase more Spanish language books, explore resources available through the district and county that would enhance the existing history-social science programs, and strengthen the articulation between grade levels in all areas.

To meet the requirements of the School Improvement Program, the school developed a three year plan for each major curriuclum area. In general, the plan was to implement the district's curriculum. Based on comments from the interviews, there currently seemed to be two areas of academic focus: writing and English Language for Limited English Proficient Student. (ELEPS). The total staff had participated in the Writing Project as a result of the recommendations for improvement in the Program Quality Review. Several of the staff members who were interviewed seemed quite enthusiastic about this staff development program. One teacher, in particular, commented on the fact that the training had been done by district presenters, 'but it was on our campus and with our kids. It was more meaningful and more likely to have an impact.' The ELEPS program had also been initiated at the school, but not all teachers were trained, nor were all using the program to address the needs of limited English proficient students. One teacher expressed the concern that although we know we should be using ELEPS, there does not seem to be a way for the whole staff to come together and say, 'We will do this'. The efforts in both writing and ELEPS represented important first steps in bringing more focus to the academic program. The interviews and open-ended responses to the survey questions indicated the staff would like to see such a focus continue, but the mechanisms to sustain development did not seem to be in place.

Frequent Monitoring and Evaluation of Students and Programs

A review of the items that encompass the frequent monitoring correlate revealed that monitoring of pupil progress was in place. All agreed that multiple methods were used to assess student progress, and that test results were used to diagnose student strengths and weaknesses. Most teachers (80 per cent) agreed that re-teaching and remediation were important parts of the instructional process, and 70 per cent of the staff say they use test results to plan reteaching. Most teachers also gave students specific feedback on assignments and tests.

Parents were not asked to complete a survey; therefore, it is not known if they felt they were kept adequately informed on how their children were doing. The teacher frustrations that were revealed in responses to the home-school relations correlate indicated that there was not sufficient reporting of pupil progress, particularly in regard to what students were to learn and how well they were learning.

Teachers felt there was monitoring of them through classroom observations and through the annual review of their Stull Bill Objectives, but this was a relatively new phenomenon. The new superintendent had recently implemented a system-wide requirement for principals to do more formal classroom observation, which was considerably increasing individual teacher monitoring and teacher anxiety. One teacher commented that the superintendent himself was getting involved. 'The superintendent came dashing in to make his evaluation of two teachers. It had nothing to do with curriculum or teaching, but with behavior and classroom order and discipline.'

The surveys and interviews indicated that close monitoring of the instructional program did not occur. One teacher felt that it was difficult to monitor the program if one was not a curriculum expert (which she felt the principal was not).

The principal acknowledged that monitoring the program was one of the weak areas of his management, and that he was working to improve. Next year he planned more frequent reviews of certain practices, such as grouping practices or teaming efforts. He also saw the core leadership team that he had created as playing a more active role in the monitoring process.

The lack of monitoring resulted in programs that were undertaken, with much enthusiasm and effort, only to be dropped after a year or two. One teacher described how many staff members had participated in a district-initiated drug training program, 'got it going with great fire, and then it just died. No one tells any one they need to teach it.' Another teacher described a similar incident in regard to science:

> About two years ago we got a new science program. I happen to be on the science selection team. I went to all the meetings, piloted a program and learned all about it. But after the program was chosen, it wasn't the one I wanted and piloted. Then everyone had to use the one selected. I think a lot of people weren't happy with it and thought the other one was better. It is the same thing with the math program. We have inservices on the new program, but no one is looking to see if the program is being implemented or is effective. Once materials are purchased, that's it for the next seven years. No one really wants to know if they are any good.

Monitoring of the instructional program at Tahoe was hindered by the lack of curriculum committees that were assigned the responsibility to monitor, check implementation problems, and evaluate new curriculum efforts. The School Site Council at Tahoe was also a very weak group that did not play an active role in monitoring and evaluating the school site plan. Some monitoring and evaluation took place on staff development days (pupil-free days allowed under state legislation, Assembly Bill 777), but the process did not seem to be as systematic and thorough as that of Sierra and Whitney.

Evidence from Whitney, Sierra, and other schools in the study indicated that to successfully bring about curriculum changes required ongoing monitoring of school programs, review and modification at regular intervals, organization of additional staff development, if necessary, and showing a willingness to stick with a new program long enough to have an impact on student achievement. The changes of leadership at Tahoe in 1984 and again in 1986 made it more difficult to develop a consistent academic focus and stay with it long enough to see a payoff in terms of student achievement.

While the loft system at Sierra created some barriers and problems, at least two of the lofts were monitoring and evaluating their own instructional programs to some degree. One strength of the lofts was the speed with which curriculum and instructional strategies learned at staff development inservices were implemented; the lofts provided a natural coaching and support system for teachers trying to learn new skills, such as the writing process or cooperative learning. Whitney, with self-contained classrooms, had developed its monitoring system through curriculum committees, active and cohesive grade level teams, and more consistent involvement of the principal in implementation follow-through activities. Tahoe currently lacked these or other mechanisms to monitor and evaluate the instructional changes it was trying to implement.

Table 5.4   Comparison of teacher responses on opportunity to learn based on the 1989
Effective Schools Surveys given at Whitney, Sierra, and Tahoe

Survey Item	Per cent Agree		
	Whitney	Sierra	Tahoe
• Special instructional programs coordinated with curriculum and instruction	90%	83%	62%
• Class begins promptly	85	96	85
• Students learning until the end of the instructional period	90	96	76
• This school has a written homework policy	95	74	65
• Homework is regularly assigned	100	100	90
• Students receive immediate feedback/suggestions on homework	95	77	70
• Fifty minutes or more for math each day	100	74	50
• Two hours or more for reading/language arts each day	95	81	75
• Essential skills are mastered before proceeding to the next learning task	75	55	39
• Classroom instruction is free from outside maintenance interruptions	85	59	30
• Basic skill time consistently followed in each classroom	95	81	52
• Basic skill instruction is free from interruptions	60	48	33
• Class is rarely interrupted to discipline students	50	71	45
• Pull-out programs don't disrupt basic skill instruction	35	7	20

Opportunity to Learn and Time-on-Task

All schools seemed to struggle with the issue of optimizing the learning time and keeping the classroom free from interruptions. The survey results, however, showed that there was a continuum. Whitney, the school with the best third grade academic results as measured by CAP, also had the least disagreement on several key items dealing with opportunity to learn and use of learning time. Table 5.4 presents the results of the 1989 surveys from Whitney, Sierra, and Tahoe and compares staff responses on a number of items.

As can be seen from Table 5.4, in almost all areas, Whitney had the highest per cent agreement on the items in this correlate, but the staff still felt there were too many times when the instructional program was interrupted for student discipline, and that pull-out programs disrupted basic skills instruction. At both Whitney and Sierra, however, the staff generally felt that the special programs were coordinated with the regular instructional program. Only 62 per cent of the teachers at Tahoe felt the coordination existed. Homework is another way that learning time is extended. All three schools reported that homework was assigned regularly; however, only Whitney reported that the teachers essentially agreed that they had a homework policy and that regular feedback was given to students. Work by Walberg (1984) has shown that feedback on homework is essential to achieve its maximum benefit. Similarly, the existence of a schoolwide homework policy helps to reinforce classroom expectations and provides parents with needed information. Both survey data and the interviews at Sierra and Tahoe revealed that return of homework by students and monitoring of homework by parents were seen to be problems. The absence of a schoolwide policy (or lack of knowledge on the part of teachers that such a policy exists) may be a contributing factor to frustrations with parents and their students about homework. Lack of

Table 5.5   Comparison of teacher responses on staff development in 1986 and 1989 based on the Effective Schools Survey

Survey Item	Per cent Agree	
	1986	1989
• Principal emphasizes participation in staff development activities	80%	90%
• Principal active in promoting staff development	66	85
• There is a staff development program based on school goals	53	90
• Principal and staff plan the staff development program	39	55
• Primary focus of staff development — increase knowledge of topic	39	95
• Primary focus of staff development — acquisition of new skills	27	75
• There is follow-up assistance by administration to support staff development skills	27	53
• Staff development evaluated on evidence of use in classroom	23	40

assignment or completion of homework also gave Tahoe one less tool to use in enhancing student achievement.

Another important difference revealed through comparing the survey results was that basic-skills instructional time was most consistently followed at Whitney. Since mastery of skills is closely associated with the time available to achieve mastery, this is an important difference. In addition, a much higher per cent of the staff at Whitney reported that mastery was achieved before moving on to new skills, which has been documented as a variable in increased student achievement (Block, Efthim, and Burns, 1989).

Staff Development

A comparison of the 1986 and 1989 survey results indicated that the staff held more positive opinions about staff development in 1989. Table 5.5 compares the 1986 responses regarding staff development with those given in 1989 and shows the items where most changes had occurred.

In spite of more positive opinions found on the 1989 survey, Tahoe did not have the same level of staff development that was found at Sierra. As noted previously, staff members at Sierra were physically separated by the loft system. In the last three years, the staff-development program served as a uniting and directing force in the school. Even without the physical separation, the staff at Tahoe seemed to be fragmented. They were divided into cliques by attitude, length of tenure at the school, relations with the principal, involvement with the bilingual program, and whether or not they saw themselves in the *in* or the *out* group. Unlike Sierra, Tahoe had not had an extensive staff-development program at the school site that could bring the staff together. Teachers received staff development, mostly at workshops at the district office or the county office of education. At both Sierra and Whitney comments were made about the school staff members' who were now providing staff development for their colleagues. In contrast, the staff at Tahoe was not involved in facilitating the school's staff development.

A good precedent for schoolwide, school-based staff development was set at Tahoe with training in the writing process. Based on the interviews, though, there was no indication that the school had plans for more whole school staff-development efforts targeted to identified needs. One staff member explained why this was the approach the school needed to take, when she said, 'You can go to wonderful conferences in the district or miles away, but it is very difficult to come back and get that assimilated into the regular program.' Based on the interview and survey data, the Tahoe staff viewed staff development more positively in 1989 than in 1986, but staff development was still not a strong component compared to the programs at Sierra and Whitney.

Organizational Structures and Procedures

The current principal at Tahoe acknowledged that his approach was to come in and take charge, to make the decisions that he felt were needed to get the school moving forward. He solicited imput from teachers, but he selected those teachers. He felt that this more autocratic approach was necessary because of the divisiveness and cliques among the staff. During his first year, he eliminated the Quality Circle Group because it was 'just a bitch session, and very negative'. He announced that he was in control of the school. He eliminated split contracts (i.e., teachers sharing a position), revamped the retention procedures and the referral process to the Learning Screening Team. He set up criteria for team-teaching allowing only two teachers to team. He found that with multiple teaming, students were being sent in many directions with little consistency and follow through. Approximately five or six teachers left at the end of the principal's first year. This gave him the opportunity to bring in some new staff members.

Shared Decision-Making and Collaboration

In 1988–89, the principal began experimenting with ways to involve the staff in the decision-making process. To give the staff more say, he established a core leadership team composed of a representative from each grade level who was selected by the grade level teachers. This group was conducting a thorough review of the school and was given the opportunity to visit exemplary programs in other schools. This group was to develop an improvement plan and bring it to the entire staff for consideration. According to the principal, the teachers who were serving on the committee felt this was the most power they had ever been given. From informal discussions with two of the teachers who were serving on the committee, it was clear they felt quite excited about the process. No one who was formally interviewed for this study was serving on the committee. By design those who were selected for interview were teachers who had been at the school through the past three administrations. The new core leadership committee seemed to be comprised of teachers who were new to the school.

Several problems surfaced during the interviews in regard to this core leadership committee. First, the staff members who were not on the committee had little information about what the committee was considering in terms of changes for the school. This produced some concern and mistrust of their work. Second, there was no formal process for receiving input from the rest of the staff either prior to or during the process. The teachers interviewed, who were not on the committee, felt left out of the process. They knew they would have the final vote on the plan, but there was a sense that this would be a pro forma vote. Third, the core committee of grade level representatives was not supported by regular grade level teams or curriculum committees to whom they reported and who reviewed the plans. Thus, there was no parallel or pyramid structure that extended the involvement to the entire staff. The responses to the open-ended questions on the survey about the school's strengths and weaknesses further confirmed that the process created an *in* group and an *out* group. Some teachers saw the committee as a strength and as helping to evaluate programs and set priorities. Other teachers saw the committee as divisive and stated that the school needed more staff input, unity, team spirit, and they wanted 'changes to be discussed with the total staff instead of a select few'.

The principal created an emerging process for shared decision-making and collaboration. His intentions for the fall of 1989 were to implement more consistent grade level meetings and to change the format of the staff meetings 'from me just spilling out information items to seeking input and leading discussions in a more consensus achieving format'. If these changes were made they could help build the unity and involvement that staff members who were feeling left out would like to see.

An issue that appeared to be unresolved was: If the core team is now developing an improvement plan, what role does the school site council play? It was not clear how the new plan would be merged with the current school improvement plan on which all staff members had worked in 1986. These were not insurmountable problems, but little thought seemed to have been given to how to prevent the establishment of new cliques in the school. The principal and staff had not thought through the relationships and working structures that were now in place and what was needed in the future to enable the school to accomplish its goals.

Communication

The principal disbanded the Quality Circle Group because he felt it created more negative than positive communications. That decision represented an important insight into the critical role that structures and procedures play in promoting or inhibiting communications. The principal most likely was correct in his assessment of the situation; however, alternative systems needed to be installed. New communication structures seemed to have been slow to emerge or to be created at Tahoe. The lack of communication channels such as grade level teams, or curricular committees, made it difficult for Tahoe's staff to develop consensus on goals and objectives.

Instructional Leadership

Over the period in which the effective schools surveys were completed by the staff, instructional leadership was one of the lowest areas of agreement. When the staff completed the survey in 1985, the principal was new. On many items the faculty marked the column 'don't know'. However, even on the first survey, there were many who indicated disagreements with statements such as, 'the principal is highly visible', 'the principal is available to discuss instructional matters', 'the

Table 5.6   *Comparison of teacher responses on instructional leadership in 1986 and 1989 based on the county Effective Schools Survey*

Survey Item	Per cent Agree	
	1986	1989
• Principal reviews and interprets test results with faculty	92%	86%
• Principal emphasizes meaning/use of standard test results	69	90
• Principal encourages teachers to accept student achievement responsibility	77	95
• Principal and faculty can solve most problems	69	75
• Before formal observation principal and teacher discuss observation	35	70
• Following formal observation principal discusses observation with teacher	58	79
• Classroom observations by principal focused on improving instruction	38	75
• Principal makes several classroom observations each year	50	60
• After formal observation teacher and principal develop instructional improvement plan	31	55
• Principal is highly visible throughout school	62	83
• Principal makes frequent contacts with students and teachers	46	100
• Principal is accessible to discuss instructional matters	62	85
• Principal initiates test results to modify/change the instruct program	58	63
• Instructional leadership from the principal is clear, strong, and central	27	50
• Instructional issues frequently the focus of staff meetings	31	57
• Administrative leadership available for disagreements among staff	38	67
• Principal seeks ideas and suggestions from staff	46	70
• Administrative leadership effective in resolving education problems	43	55
• Principal initiates effective coordination of instructional program	39	45

principal provides strong, clear instructional leadership', and 'instructional issues are the focus of faculty meetings'. The overall agreement was 37 per cent, disagreement was 42 per cent.

Approximately a year later the staff completed the survey again. Opinions shifted slightly to the positive with 48 per cent in agreement and 25 per cent in disagreement. In the fall of 1986, the new principal assumed the leadership role at Tahoe. Although interviews were conducted with the staff in 1987 as part of the previous effective schools study, the principal did not feel it was appropriate to readminister the survey. The survey was completed by the staff in late spring of 1989. The results showed that the current principal was beginning to solidify a working relationship with the staff. The total per cent agreement rose to 71 per cent and total disagreement fell to 20 per cent with 9 per cent remaining undecided. These figures indicated that the principal was building a good working relationship with most of the staff. Table 5.6 compares the results for the 1986 survey with those in 1989. It shows the areas where the current principal had introduced some changes, and indicates that the staff was more certain about the leadership of the school. The survey results also highlight some areas of disagreement that remained.

There is no doubt that the two changes of principals in 1984 and 1986 slowed the potential for school improvement. Conditions at the school were not good, in terms of the outcome for students or the teaching and learning environment for staff and students in 1984. Since 1984, growth has occurred in all areas, but not sufficiently to impact student achievement. The current principal expanded the number of staff members who would be involved in problem analysis and decision-making at the school. On the whole, the responses in the interviews and on the open-ended responses in 1989 indicated that staff members saw the expansion of the leadership team as a positive step. Some teachers, however, felt excluded from the process and were not sure about the types of changes that the new leadership team would recommend. The principal was aware of the lack of trust of some of the faculty members and that some were very suspicious of the process. He felt that trust would grow with time, as these teachers saw progress being made.

The principal had a vision of where he wanted the school to be. He knew the vision had not been realized but felt he and the staff were moving in the right direction. He seemed to have been effective in communicating his vision to some of the teachers and in selecting other teachers who shared it. Learning how to build a communications network and to enhance faculty support through greater involvement remained future agenda items. During the interview, the principal commented that he had learned some important lessons about involvement and his own leadership approach.

I shared the real fear that many administrators have in letting go, because you know you are held responsible. I don't want to go to the superintendent and say the teachers voted and well. . . . That won't make it. But I also know I want their involvement in rational, reasonable decision-making. If they are involved, they are likely to show me rational and reasonable things that I hadn't thought of before. Part of the effective schools research has shown me that I need to be a risk-taker and let go of a bit of the autocratic control. The interesting thing is that I am finding as I let go I am actually feeling more in control, and I am gaining support. I flubbed up on the expenditures on the lottery money. I should have put it in writing. I thought I had put it in writing, but I didn't. Someone started complaining about it in the lounge. Another teacher came to my defense and said that 'he said that in staff meeting'. Several others spoke up in support. Six months ago I wouldn't have had anyone come to my defense. They are also realizing, as they get involved, that this is a difficult job.

Summary and Conclusions

During the course of this study, Tahoe's student inputs remained fairly stable in terms of the number of limited-English speaking students and socioeconomic status of the school community. Tahoe remained among the three lowest SES schools in the study. There were new staff inputs. Similar to Shasta and Sequoia, (See Chapter 2), Tahoe experienced a change in leadership in mid-course. At Sequoia, a school located in a neighboring district, the transition was well-planned and did not seem to disturb the improvement process. There were some tensions at Shasta during the changeover, with some faculty choosing to leave the school with the previous principal. The change of leadership at Tahoe resulted in continued turmoil that lasted until 1988–89. Another significant input was an infusion of teachers new to the school. These teachers replaced six teachers who chose to leave after the second principal's first year. The principal looked upon the infusion of new blood as a benefit. He felt the new staff members more closely reflected his thinking about school improvement. Amongst some continuing staff members, however, there persisted a feeling of an 'in' and an 'out' group. Although there were also new staff members at Shasta when the principal changed, the new staff members arrived with the principal. In addition, the interviews indicated that at Shasta there was not a split between the new and remaining staff, as was the case at Tahoe. Norms of collegiality built by Shasta's previous principal remained high.

As with Sierra, overall student outcomes did not change, except in the last year. Sixth grade achievements showed increases in CAP reading and mathematics scores. The changes in principals cannot be overlooked as an important explanation of why outcomes did not improve. Without consistency in leadership, at least in style if not in person, it is difficult to manage the transformative process in ways that lead to enhanced student outcomes.

The transformative process at Tahoe was characterized by both change and stagnation, providing possible explanations for why student outcomes did not improve. One major change in the culture and climate dimension was in the improvement of the physical plant. As in the case of Whitney, this was an important first and necessary step, before other changes could be considered. While changes were made in the student recognition program, other areas remained static — no sense of shared mission had developed, there were weak norms of collegiality, negative perceptions of home support continued, and mixed expectations about students' potential for success and teachers' efficacy in teaching these students persisted. Tahoe's staff seemed a long way from creating the culture of learning and achievement that permeated Whitney.

The school's technology had also undergone only slight modifications. Teachers understood the district's focus on increasing students test scores, but did not have in place curricular and instructional practices that would enable them to meet district expectations. Like Sierra, test preparation materials existed at the site, but were not used. The curriculum was not fully aligned, and teachers had not been trained to engage in their own alignment process. Program monitoring seemed particularly weak and standards of student mastery had not been set. Comparisons of Tahoe survey results with those of Sierra and Whitney revealed considerable deficiencies in the use of time, including homework as a possible extension of student learning time. During the course of the study, the school experienced its first extended school-based staff-development programs when it participated in training to implement the Writing Project. This seems to have been positively received. However, plans for future staff development of this nature did not seem to exist, unlike the continuing staff-development process at both Whitney and Sierra. At Tahoe, the principal did not seem to play an active role in providing assistance and follow-through with implementation of staff development programs.

Organizational structures and systems to ensure active communication and participation among all staff members remained undeveloped. The establishment of a new core leadership team represented a potentially significant change, but there was a need to address staff members' concerns about its operation and role in relation to the school improvement process. As with the principals of Whitney and Sierra, the principal at Tahoe showed a willingness to grow and change. He consciously made an effort to become less autocratic and more participatory in his leadership style. His comments indicated that he was pleased with the change and felt that it bode well for the school and staff.

At the conclusion of the study, too many key elements of the transformative process seemed to be malfunctioning, especially when compared with Whitney. The outcome was a failure to increase student achievement. The interviews conducted in 1989, however, indicated that the school was in ferment. If the principal and staff can capitalize on the ferment and on the winds of change stirred by the core leadership team, there is the potential for growth and development at Tahoe.

Notes

1   Chapter VII is a federally funded program designed to meet the needs of students who enter school with no or limited-English proficiency. Funding is based on the number of limited- or non-English proficient students, but local districts have some flexibility in how the funds are allocated.

2   It is interesting to note, that this problem of sending many students to the Learning Screening Team also existed at Whitney. The principal said that teachers would get angry if students they referred were not given a special educational placement. Now it is no longer a problem. Teachers first exhaust all means in their classroom, then come to the team to find out what additional strategies they might need to try in the classroom, and, finally, in very rare cases ask for additional assistance or an alternate placement.

Chapter 6

Yosemite Elementary:
Coping with the Impact of Tracking

The Setting: Inputs and Outputs

Yosemite Elementary, located in a rapidly growing section of the county, was dramatically impacted by increasing student enrollments. In 1989 the district had an enrollment of 4,520 students and consisted of seven elementary schools with an eighth school scheduled to open in the winter of 1990. In the 1988–89 school year Yosemite had 750 kindergarten through sixth grade students enrolled in a four track year-round school. The student body consisted of students from a wide range of family backgrounds from upper-middle class to unskilled migrant workers. Of all of the schools in the study, Yosemite had the highest socioeconomic index (2.47) and the lowest per cent of Aid to Families with Dependent Children (2 per cent). It should be noted that the low per cent of AFDC recipients may be due to the fact that many immigrant families (especially undocumented aliens) do not claim AFDC because of fear of jeopardizing their immigration status.

Students falling into each parent occupation category, as reported on the 1988 sixth grade California Assessment Program Report was as follows: professional — 42 per cent, semiprofessional — 23 per cent, skilled/semiskilled — 14 per cent and unskilled — 15 per cent. Since 1983, there was a steady increase from 24 per cent to 42 per cent in the number of students whose parents fell in the professional category. This shift paralleled the rising house prices in the area. Approximately 12 per cent of the students were non-English speaking.

The school was built in the 1950s and the physical plant consisted of twenty-seven regular classrooms, two classrooms used for special education, a media/library center, and a room for the resource specialist. There were thirty-one certificated teachers, two of whom were special education teachers. The regular staff was assisted by a part-time mathematics teacher, two full time Miller-Unruh reading specialists, and an aide, who worked in the math and reading lab and served students who scored below the 25th percentile on the Comprehensive Test of Basic Skills (CTBS). The school also had a full-time librarian, the part-time services of a nurse and district psychologist, and two instrumental music teachers. The school had six bilingual teachers and ten classroom assistants. The Gifted and Talented Program served 29 per cent of the students.

The school received categorical funding from a variety of sources, including $46,935 in School Improvement funds. In recent years the school suffered a decline

98

in funds, which greatly impacted the math lab and reading program, reducing the math resource teacher from full time to part time. In the 1989–90 school year even further cutbacks were scheduled because of enrollment shifts and improved test scores for the lowest income group.

In a recent study of effective districts (Chrispeels and Pollack, 1990), Yosemite's district was classified as an effective district. The student population at Yosemite was representative of the district's population as a whole, except that there were fewer children from unskilled parent occupations in the whole district, for example 7 per cent in the district versus 15 per cent at Yosemite. Based on the 1988 results of the California Assessment Program for both third and sixth grades, students from each parent occupation category consistently scored above their counterparts in the state. The district was recognized in the county as outstanding for its curriculum alignment efforts, excellent staff development programs, careful teacher selection procedures, and extensive training provided for administrators. All of these factors have helped this district to achieve both excellence and equity in many of its schools. The one problem area for the district has been meeting the needs of its limited-English speaking students. This problem surfaced in the interviews conducted for the effective district study and in the staff interviews conducted at Yosemite in December 1986. Even though Yosemite was experiencing problems as a result of the four-track schedule, in the interviews in 1989 the bilingual teachers reported that the district was providing more support for the program. This change in perspective was also noted at Pinyon, located in the same district. The difficulty of the district in accepting responsibility for addressing the needs of the limited and non-English speaking students reflected the problems the community had in accepting the Hispanic population. Many of the Hispanics were workers in the regions' flower and vegetable fields or household workers for the affluent population. The issue of meeting the needs of the limited-English speaking students has impacted the program, staff, and students at Yosemite over the last five years.

In the winter of 1989, a new principal was assigned to Yosemite, but during the period of this study, the school was under the leadership of a principal who came to the school in the summer of 1983. The survey and interview results reflect his tenure at the school. Soon after assuming the leadership of the school, the principal asked the county office of education for assistance in conducting an effective schools study. He saw the process as a good way to indentify student needs and focus the efforts of the staff. The principal, teachers, support staff, and parents all completed the Connecticut School Effectiveness instruments (the assessment instruments used when the county initiated its program and before it developed its own). Yosemite was one of the first schools in the county that asked to participate. Compared to other schools in the study, Yosemite's overall achievement results were above the state average in 1983–84, as was indicated in Chapter 2 in Figures 2.5 through 2.8, which presented the five-year trend in achievement data for each of the eight schools. The school exemplified one of the concerns often expressed about voluntary school effectiveness or improvement programs: the schools that most need it never volunteer, and the ones that least need it are always the first to volunteer. However, the principal was very concerned about the instructional program the school offered low-achieving students who, as he described the situation, 'are most in need of high quality professional help and yet were receiving all of their extra help from teaching assistants who

Figure 6.1   Comparison of Mean Scores of teacher responses on the Effective Schools
Surveys completed in 1985 and 1989

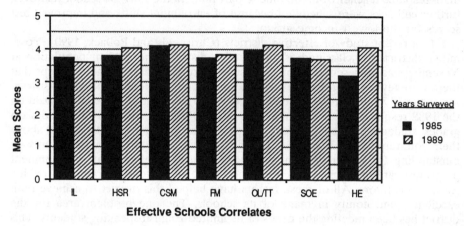

Legend: IL = Instructional Leadership, HSR = Home-School Relations, CSM = Clear School
Mission, FM = Frequent Monitoring, OL/TT = Opportunity to Learn, Time-on-Task, SOE =
Safe Orderly Environment, HE = High Expectations.

had no training in working with children scoring below grade level.' Yosemite
represents a good case study of how deliberate and planned changes in the
transformative process positively enhanced student achievement, and how subsequent changes in response to external environment pressures derailed school
effectiveness efforts and student achievement gains. This case study also adds
insights into the influence of tracking on student achievement.

Figure 6.2   Five-year trend in Yosemite's third grade CAP scores

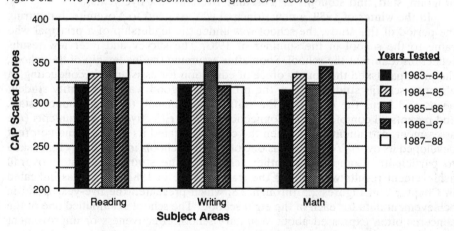

Figure 6.1 presents the results of staff surveys completed in 1985 and 1989
(mean scores for 1983 were no longer available). It shows that there were minor
shifts in opinions both up and down in mean scores. The correlate with the most
significant change, 'high expectations' (HE) rose from a mean of 3.2 in 1985 to

Figure 6.3 Five-year trend in Yosemite's sixth grade CAP scores

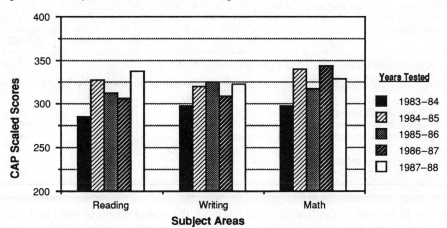

4.01 in 1989. The reason why there was not a more positive shift in survey opinions, as was seen in some of the other case-study schools, will become more obvious as all the dimensions of the transformative process are discussed.

Figure 6.4 Five-year trend in third and sixth grade CAP scores for students from unskilled family backgrounds

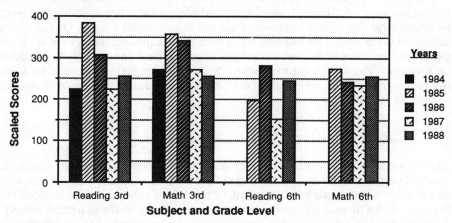

Figures 6.2 and 6.3 present the third and sixth grade CAP results since 1983 in reading, written language, and mathematics. The graph shows that in 1986–7 there was a dip in achievement in reading and written language, but not in mathematics. The results from 1986–87 represent the impact of the implementation of a four track year-round school program in which all gifted students were placed on one track and all limited-English speaking students were placed on another track. Figure 6.4 presents the third and sixth grade CAP achievement results for students from unskilled families before and after the tracking system was implemented. As can be seen, the school achieved significant gains prior to the introduction of the four track year-round schedule, but in the next two years

Table 6.1   Comparison of teacher responses on safe and orderly environment in 1985 and 1989 based on the Connecticut and county Effective Schools Surveys

Survey Item	Per cent Agree	
	1985	1989
• Repairs/alternations responded to in reasonable time*[3]		70%
• There is a positive school spirit	76%	75
• The school buildings are kept in good repair	67	70
• Property of students is secure	67	67
• Students/staff take pride/keep clean and attractive area*		65
• Vandalism by students is not a problem*		55
• Staff enforce student rules consistently/equitably	62	60
• Physical condition of building is pleasant and well kept	53	55
• Few discipline problems are referred to office*		40
• Students respectful/not subject to verbal abuse*		11

its lowest income students slipped. In 1987–88, the scaled scores of third and sixth grade students from unskilled families began to improve, except in third grade math, which again declined. The impact of implementing a segregated four-track schedule on school programs and on staff will be more fully discussed below.

School Culture and Climate

If one word were used to typify the culture of Yosemite and its district, it would be 'competition'. A competitive spirit existed among the schools, with each trying to outperform the others in terms of overall achievement results. Of the seven schools in the district, two had larger and four had smaller percentages of students whose parent occupations were classified as semiskilled and unskilled compared to Yosemite. The staff was proud when its students outperformed students from the four more affluent schools, whether it be on standardized tests or in district sponsored student competitions.

Safe and Orderly Learning Environment

The 1989 staff survey revealed that personal safety was not an issue at Yosemite. Ninety-five per cent of the teachers said they treated students with respect, and 85 per cent said that students were taught the school rules and were responsible for maintaining them. Eighty-five per cent agreed that the staff was treated respectfully and not subjected to verbal abuse. Eighty-five per cent of the teachers also agreed that the administration supported teachers in dealing with discipline matters and that the administration enforced student rules consistently and equitably.

However, the surveys showed that there were a number of issues regarding the school environment that had not been addressed. The overall agreement for the safe and orderly environment correlate was 73 per cent, second lowest among all eight schools. Table 6.1 presents the survey results from 1985 and 1989 and shows which issues remained unaddressed. Four issues stood out as concerns for the staff: vandalism by students (45 per cent felt it was a problem[1]); physical condition of the buildings (45 per cent felt buildings are not well kept[2]); discipline problems being referred to the office (25 per cent felt too many were referred and 35 per cent didn't know); and students verbally abusing each other (74 per cent felt verbal abuse was a problem).

The interviews did not reveal any comments to indicate that discipline or school climate were major concerns. When teachers were asked if there was a systematic process for resolving discipline problems, almost all of them mentioned the time-out room, which had just been instituted by the new principal in 1989. Obviously the newness of the procedure made it foremost in their minds, but it also indicated that before the time-out room was implemented, the only place for teachers to refer students had been to the principal's office. Several of the teachers interviewed thought the procedure was working well, but one commented that there were still some problems that needed to be resolved.

As the faculty at Whitney, the faculty at Yosemite considered verbal abuse by students a problem. The survey data indicated that it was regarded as an area of considerable concern by the majority of the faculty. The staff members interviewed at Yosemite mentioned the problem in terms of increased tension among students in different tracks. In particular they were concerned with the negative perceptions students were developing based upon the track to which they were assigned. The staff was trying to address the problem by teaming classes across tracks and pairing sixth and first grade classes as buddies.

Rewards and Recognition

In 1983 an awards assembly program was initiated to recognize student achievement. In 1984, in response to an open-ended question on the parents' surveys, a number of parents commented on the value of these assemblies. In 1986 when the first interviews of the staff were conducted, all those interviewed commented on the positive role that the assemblies had played in recognizing students for both achievement and behavior. As one teacher commented then, 'The value of the recognition program is that it reinforces student behavior and effort. Students don't work for rewards, but once they get them, it keeps their motivation higher to continue working.' Parents were informed about the awards assemblies and were sent a congratulatory letter.

The 1989 interviews revealed that the awards assemblies were still in place. Several teachers, however, expressed concerns about the assemblies. One commented that like any program, 'It runs its course and then it's time to start a new system. I think we are getting to the point where we need to look at that . . . it's starting to get old.' Another commented that the assemblies were rather perfunctory, and he was not sure that they had much meaning for the students. A third teacher found it very hard to nominate only three or four students. 'I tell the kids I don't like to give these things out. It is really hard. Suppose some kids come up with 90 or 100 every day in math, but another kid is making great leaps and bounds, but is not up there in the 100 per cent range. You have to be really careful about that. It's a fine line. To me that is a weak spot in the awards.' At the end of each year, this teacher had a particularly difficult time, because he felt his whole class deserved recognition for their achievements. Whitney had addressed some of these concerns by the variety of awards given and the number of awards that focused on each academic areas.

The awards assemblies were organized by track. While this procedure made sense, it also reinforced the track grouping as opposed to a whole-school concept.

The tracks at Yosemite created barriers and divided the school in much same way that the lofts had at Sierra.

Based on teacher interviews conducted in 1986, teacher recognition was identified as a strong point at Yosemite. Interestingly, the principal felt he did not do enough to recognize teachers. Yet compared to teacher recognition at the least effective schools, teachers' perceptions at Yosemite were corroborated. Teachers were recognized publicly at the student awards assemblies; there was recognition in the PTA newsletter; birthday cards were given to teachers; and there was districtwide recognition, especially through the mentor teacher program. Each faculty meeting started with sharing 'What's Good at Yosemite'. This sharing was usually initiated by the principal mentioning an instructional practice he had observed in one of the classrooms. Other teachers then chimed in with observations and comments of their own, recognizing achievements of each other, such as good teaching strategies, special projects, and so forth. These practices were mentioned again in the interviews conducted in 1989. Unlike teachers at most of the other schools, teachers at Yosemite felt they received recognition for their efforts. They felt appreciated by the principal and they appreciated each other.

High Expectations

The lack of high expectations for all students surfaced as an issue at Yosemite just as it had at the three other school's described. The overall agreement on the high expectations correlate was 51 per cent in 1984 and 53 per cent in 1985. The staff focused on expectations as an area for improvement. The primary staff-development activity that was undertaken to address this issue was training in TESA (Teacher Expectations Student Achievement). Twenty-two of the twenty-nine faculty members volunteered to participate in the training which was held from 6:30 p.m. to 9:30 p.m. once a month over a seven-month period. In addition, as part of the training, teachers were released during the day to observe each others' classrooms. In the interviews conducted in December 1986, TESA was frequently mentioned as one of the best strategies to raise achievement of low-achieving students. When asked how they had changed as a result of the effective schools process, TESA training was mentioned by all as being a powerful program in changing their perceptions of low-achieving students and showing teachers how to engage them more effectively in the learning process.

The impact of the TESA was revealed in the 1989 effective schools surveys, where the overall agreement with the high expectations correlate had risen to 82 per cent. While the overall perceptions regarding this correlate had moved in a positive direction, concerns were expressed by a couple of teachers during the 1989 interviews that many of the new teachers had not been trained in TESA. They felt that there was a need for renewal in this area. This points up one of the ongoing problems of staff development — how to maintain the impact of training both for those who have been trained and for new staff who come to the school. Table 6.2 summarizes the responses to several key questions on the surveys completed in 1985 and 1989 and shows where perceptions had changed.

A significant issue impacting expectations that surfaced in the interviews in 1987, which was more prominent in 1989, was the concern about the way the children had been grouped in the four tracks. When the school changed from a year-round and a traditional track to a four track year-round school in the summer

Table 6.2 Comparison of teacher responses on high expectations in 1985 and 1989 based on the Connecticut and county Effective Schools Surveys

Survey Item	Per cent Agree	
	1985	1989
• 90–100% of students expected to master basic skills	95%	95%
• Teachers responsible for students learning basic skills	81	100
• Teachers hold consistently high expectations for students	67	100
• All students are expected to be successful in school work	67	100
• Low income/high income students retained proportionately	53	21[4]
• Low achieving students given same opportunity to answer	43	90
• Students achieve identified standards regardless of home	43	43
• Teachers expect over 95% will graduate from high school	39	55
• In math, initial instruction presented to whole class	10	65

of 1986, all of the gifted students were placed on one track and all of the limited-English speaking students were placed on another. A third track was perceived as the average track and a fourth track was designated for new arrivals to the school. When the interviews were conducted in 1987 the track system had been in place only six months. Even at this point, teachers were raising concerns about the tracking. They were frustrated because it was now harder to find time for all teachers to work together. By 1989, the tracking system emerged as a major issue in all of the interviews. Every teacher was concerned about it and the impact it was having on the students and staff. The staff not assigned to the gifted track intimated they were second class citizens. The bilingual teachers felt especially short-changed, because they had the neediest children and the largest class sizes. The kindergarten bilingual teacher had 37 children in her class, because there was no other option for their placement. The teachers also expressed concern about the segregation of the students and the impact that was having on their attitudes towards each other and towards their ability. The principal commented that much of his time was spent dealing with parent complaints about the placement of their children. One teacher commented that parents were vying to get their child designated as a gifted student so he or she could be assigned to the gifted track.

Compared to other school in the study, there were much wider disparities among students' home background at Yosemite and at Pinyon, the other school in the study located in this same district. The tracking served to highlight the differences. These disparities also helped to show that in spite of the TESA training, the teachers' perception of the impact of home background on student achievement had not been changed. (In contrast to Yosemite, Pinyon by 1989 had moved to implement fairly extensive heterogeneous grouping of students).

During the interview, the former principal reflected sadly on the decision he had made to organize the tracks. At the time, he had thought it was the best way to maximize the benefits of a limited number of bilingual teachers for the limited- and non-English speaking students. A strong well-organized parent lobby was another factor that pushed toward the decision for formation of a gifted track. Many of the most active parents on the PTA and on the School Site Council, whose children were also participants in the gifted program, organized and requested that their children be placed on the same track. The parental pressure, combined with the district policy requiring clustering of gifted students, made the principal feel he had no choice but to put them all on the same track. In retrospect, and from his present perspective as principal of another school, he realized that the formation of the separate gifted and bilingual tracks was a serious mistake.

In July 1988, the principal, after repeated complaints from the staff, realized he had to address the problem and to raise sagging staff morale. A tracking committee was formed with representatives from all tracks. The goal of the committee was to identify ways of linking the tracks and bringing children in contact with each other across the tracks. One idea that was implemented was a Big Buddy Program, in which a sixth grade class adopted a kindergarten or first grade class. Several teachers commented that this had worked well. Younger and older students shared reading and writing time together and enjoyed field trips and holiday parties together. A team-teaching subcommittee was created that presented a staff inservice on strategies for team teaching and types of activities that lent themselves to teaming. As a result of their efforts, several other teachers and classes were paired across the tracks to do some team teaching. While these efforts helped, the staff perception was that they were stopgap measures that did not address the fundamental problem of student and staff segregation.

When a new principal was assigned to the school in January 1989, he indicated to the staff a willingness to change the way the tracks were organized. One approach being considered was to increase the number of teachers who were certified to teach gifted classes and then to spread the gifted clusters across all tracks. According to the former principal, parents perceived the GATE teachers as being the most qualified. The result of the track system, he said, had been to undermine the esteem of the many other good teachers who taught in the other tracks. One of the current principal's goals was to encourage all teachers to obtain the additional certification required to teach gifted and talented (GATE) students, thereby eliminating the perception problem that the non-GATE teachers were less qualified. A second approach also being considered was to gradually shift the bilingual classes to other tracks as well. In the interview one teacher commented that they were led to believe that the tracks could not be rearranged.

> We've complained about it for years. Little things were done as I mentioned before, like field trips and PE together, and buddy systems, but it didn't really change the isolation of the bilingual and GATE tracks. We made the best of what we had, but we believed, because we had been told, that it really couldn't be changed.

She went on the to say that the new principal was showing them that the student composition of the tracks could be changed and made more integrated. 'It is a difference in philosophy and approach, but I would hope that if we had to do it over again that would be the approach from the very beginning.' The former principal was in full agreement with this teacher and there was no doubt that he would not make this mistake again.

Home-School Relations

When the initial survey was administered in 1983, home-school relations were identified as an area that the staff wanted to address. The overall agreement with the home-school relations correlate rose from 71 per cent in 1983, to 77 per cent in 1985, to 80 per cent agreement in 1989. Based on the surveys in 1983, the staff felt they needed to communicate with parents more about the instructional program and to encourage more school visits by parents.

The 1984–85 school effectiveness plan focused on several strategies for strengthening home-school communications. Teachers were encouraged to send at least two communications a month to parents about classroom activities. Two teachers agreed to experiment with sending home weekly lesson plans as a way of helping parents know what was going on in the classroom. In January 1985, the school initiated a Parent/Community visitation program. In small groups, parents were invited to come to school during the day to learn more about school programs, the curriculum, and test scores, to have an opportunity to ask questions about the school, and to visit classrooms. Based on comments of parents on the open-ended questions on the parent effective schools survey, completed by parents in December 1985, it was clear that the efforts to communicate with them and to invite them to the school were appreciated. A typical comment was, 'There is now more communication between teacher and parent as to what the class is doing via weekly or monthly letters.' Another parent commented, 'I personally know what subjects were being stressed more than others, and how I could help my child in subjects she was failing.' A third parent stressed the value of the visitation program:

> Parents get periodic invitations, not only to come to school to help with teacher work, but also to visit the child's classroom and observe for a half hour to an hour an academic activity or activities such as math or reading or spelling, etc. This does not have to be often, but a parent can more effectively assess both teacher and school if the parent has been in the classroom actually having observed first-hand a class experience or activity. My child likes the school and the teacher in general.

In the interviews in 1986 and in 1989, the teachers stated that they felt they had excellent parent support. Many parents volunteered and there was an active Parent Teacher Association (PTA) and School Site Council (SSC). The teachers commented on the push that had been made to increase communications with parents. A comparison of the survey results in 1985 with those in 1989 on the home-school relations correlate shows the positive shift in teachers' opinions. Table 6.3 (see p. 108) presents the results from the two sets of surveys.

These results show that there had been a positive shift in opinion on almost every item, except for the completion of assigned homework and the teachers' perceptions of parents' rating of the school. The school community with its many highly educated parents had parents who were supportive and involved, but also quite critical of the school. In addition, the tracking system had undermined staff confidence as well as their perceptions of parental support.

The needs of Hispanic parents were a concern of the school staff, especially of the bilingual resource teacher. From 1984–86, the bilingual resource teacher undertook an initiative to expand the Biligual Advisory Committee, to make sure that every meeting helped the parents understand the educational program, and to create a welcoming environment for Hispanic parents. Even though the bilingual resource teacher left the school in 1987, the bilingual teachers remained in contact with Hispanic parents. The bilingual kindergarten teacher reported that only three of her parents were unable to attend parent-teacher conferences. She thought

Table 6.3 *Comparison of teacher responses on home-school relations in 1985 and 1989 based on the Connecticut and county Effective Schools Surveys*

Survey Item	Per cent Agree 1985	1989
• Teachers communicate with parents in many ways	90%	100%
• Parent-teacher conferences relate to student achievement	90	100
• 90% to 100% parents attend scheduled parent-teacher conferences	67	100
• There is an active parent group	81	95
• Teacher and parents are aware of homework policy	100	100
• Activities of the parent group support school's goals	62	95
• Parents and or community members are frequent volunteers	76	85
• Parents frequently initiate contacts with classroom teachers	78	90
• Teachers contact parents on a regular basis	100	95
• Cooperation between parents teachers re homework monitoring	72	90
• Teachers invite parents to observe instructional program	48	65
• Almost all students complete assigned homework	57	55
• Most parents would rate this school superior	62	50

the high attendance rate was a result of her ability to speak Spanish. The bilingual track, however, did not have the same level of parent involvement as the other tracks, especially compared to track C which had all of the Gifted and Talented program participants. Few of the Hispanic parents were free to volunteer during the day. The problem of less parent involvement was not confined to the bilingual track. The former principal acknowledged that when the gifted track was on vacation, there were fewer parent activities and far fewer volunteers. Also the PTA and SSC were composed predominantly of parents whose children were on the gifted track. The school had not made an effort to bridge the parent language barriers and integrate the PTA or SSC as was done at Sierra.

Thus, the tracking system impacted home-school relations as well as high expectations negatively. One of the unintended consequences for the principal was that he had to spend an ever-increasing amount of time placating parents and answering complaints about the track on which their child had been placed. In fact, so much time was spent with parents, the principal reported that it drastically affected the time available for classroom observations and visitations, further distancing him from the teachers.

Shared Mission

At Yosemite, 'clear school mission' was identified as a strength in 1985 and remained so in 1989. In 1983–84, the staff, principal, parents and aides participated in a 'We Agree' process similar to the one conducted at Whitney. In 1984, the staff refined the school goals and sent the following goals to parents:

- To continue to provide a quality education for each child
- To respect the individual student's worth and dignity
- To continue to strengthen teaching skills
- To promote a positive image of Yosemite School
- To encourage active parent participation in the educational process
- To continue to improve test scores on standardized tests (CAP, CTBS)

- To continue to participate in the Effective Schools Program
- To continue to support PTA and School Site Council
- To continue to participate in the Adopt-A-School Program.

The goals were then used to develop a specific plan of action. These goals were vigorously implemented between 1984 and 1986. When the four track year-round school program was implemented, the school lost some of its goal focus. During the interviews conducted in 1989, each staff member articulated a similar formulation of the mission, but the segregation by tracks seemed to be undermining the shared vision.

Norms of Collegiality

The norms of collegiality were another casualty of the implementation of the four track year-round schedule. In the early days of the school effectiveness process, a strong sense of collaboration existed among teachers. The 'We Agree' process conducted in 1983 and again in 1984 had helped to unite the faculty around common goals. Participation in the TESA training, coupled with the follow-up classroom observations, was another uniting force. The teaming of teachers to research and report on effective instructional strategies at faculty meeting, as well as actions by the principal and resource teachers to model effective teaching, all helped to build a culture of teachers as professional colleagues. These norms were fractured by the implementation of the four track schedule. It became nearly impossible to bring the staff together at the same time for staff meetings, let alone for staff development. The strengths of the norms of collegiality, however, did persist in spite of the fragmentation. Through team-teaching efforts, teachers made efforts to continue the cooperation with their colleagues. Grade-level teams did continue to meet, even if less frequently. *Ad hoc* committees were once again convened to try to address the problems caused by the year-round schedule. The experiences of Yosemite offer insights into the strategies and actions of teachers and principals that help to build a professional and collegial culture and barriers that can interfere and inhibit the development of norms of collegiality.

School Technology: Curriculum and Instruction

The curriculum and instruction at Yosemite was strongly influenced by district directives and district-organized staff development. The interviews in 1987 and 1989 revealed that the teachers felt they had a say in the curriculum development through teacher participation on district curriculum committees and participation in selecting new textbooks. These committees also served as vehicles for addressing curriculum concerns. One teacher commented that once, when there were problems with the math program and a number of teachers communicated their concerns through the committee, the problem was then addressed by district administrators. The small size of the district helped teachers feel they had a direct influence on district curriculum decisions. These same positive views about participation and impact on district curriculum committees were not reflected in the opinions of the teachers at Tahoe. The larger size of Tahoe's district clearly makes a difference.

As with all districts in California, the district curriculum was being shaped by the state curriculum frameworks. For example, one teacher explained that the district previously had a heavy emphasis on phonics and had been adamant in this approach. The new state framework in language arts, however, was stressing the use of a 'whole language' approach to reading and the use of literature in the basic reading program. According to this teacher the 'district is jumping on the bandwagon', through the adoption of a new reading series that encompasses the 'whole language' and literature approach. The teacher continued, 'That's really daring and really different from the past.'

Use of Test Results

The interviews in 1987 and 1989 revealed that test scores were reviewed annually with the staff. The teachers were made aware of specific skills their students had or had not mastered. The third and sixth grade teachers received the printout of the individual Comprehensive Test of Basic Skills test results from the previous grade and knew the areas of strength and weakness for both groups of children and for individual children. Based on the analysis, areas for focus or improvement were identified. The principal and teachers did diagnostic work to pinpoint problems by grade level or for individual students. For example, the principal pointed out that one year students scored very low in proper nouns at third grade. He knew that the teachers were introducing proper nouns to students and that the students did not have trouble learning that concept. After careful review, the staff discovered that proper nouns were introduced at the beginning of the school year and mastered by the students, but not reviewed during the year. Therefore, the staff selected several additional in-class and homework assignments that could be given throughout the year to reinforce the concept. This ability of the staff to carefully analyze test results and survey data and set a corrective course of action was similar to the practices of the staff at Whitney, but an ability that was much less developed among the staff members of Sierra and Tahoe.

The interviews of district staff conducted in 1987–88 revealed that the district also placed an emphasis on test analysis and use of test results. Each year the district reviewed the scores of all schools and worked with each principal to see that weaknesses were addressed. In addition, the district organized staff development or acquired new materials to meet specific identified needs that all or several schools seemed to have in common.

Table 6.4 compares the results of the 1985 and 1989 survey results in the area of review and use of test results. There were some discrepancies between comments made during the interviews and staff responses on the survey. The survey data indicate that most of the faculty agreed that results were reviewed. Only half of the faculty felt, however, that they were used to modify the instructional program. In contrast, all of those interviewed indicated that results were used to modify the instructional program. The discrepancy in responses may be due to interpretation of the questions. In other words, in the teachers' minds the instructional program was not modified or changed. They still taught the same

Table 6.4 *Comparison of teacher responses on items related to use of test results in 1985 and 1989 based on the Connecticut and county Effective Schools Surveys*

Survey Item	Per cent Agree	
	1985 Connecticut	1989 County
• Principal reviews and interprets test results with the faculty	72%	84%
• Principal emphasizes meaning and use of standardized test results	58	55
• Principal initiates test results to modify/change instructional program	67	53
• Test results are used to diagnose student strengths/weaknesses	67	95
• Test results are used to plan for reteaching	76	90
• Test results are reviewed and used to modify instructional programs	53	35
• CAP is an accurate/valid measure of the basic skills curriculum	29	15

skills, but the emphasis given to a particular skill may have been different from one year to another based on test results. In the 1989 interviews, one teacher said, 'A couple of years ago we came up with really poor spelling results. . . . We put more emphasis but did not change the program.' Also, a kindergarten teacher pointed out that if they were using test results to modify the instructional program, they would have used more ditto sheets to reinforce punctuation, rather than spending time on teaching writing. This teacher stressed that the testing program was not in alignment with the state framework, a comment that surfaced in the interviews at most schools.

The 1989 survey results confirmed that the test results at Yosemite were used more systematically to diagnose students' strengths and weaknesses and to plan for reteaching. The survey results on these two items were consistent with the interview data. It is interesting to note that the staff at Yosemite, like the staff at Sierra and Tahoe, felt that CAP was not an accurate and valid measure of the basic skills curriculum. The staff at Yosemite also had concerns about how well the CAP test measures their instructional program, but not to the same degree as in the other three schools. When a school is performing well across all income groups, as was the case at Whitney, it is easier for the teachers to accept the validity of the test.

The principal and teachers at Yosemite felt that there was too much emphasis on test scores. The sense of competition in the district and the communitywide comparison created pressures on the staff to see that students performed well. This was an issue that Whitney had not had to face in the last few years; therefore, it again may have been easier for Whitney staff to accept CAP than it was for the staff at Yosemite.

The staff at Yosemite, unlike the staff at Whitney, had not played an active role in curriculum alignment at the school site. This task was performed by the district administrative staff with involvement of teachers at the district level. Extensive curriculum objectives were established for each curriculum area. These objectives were aligned with the state and other standardized tests. Materials were selected that supported these objectives, and teachers were given training by the district in effective instructional strategies designed to implement the curriculum. The active involvement of the teaching staff at Whitney in the alignment process may have been another reason why the staff felt more comfortable with CAP than did the staff at Yosemite.

Academic Focus

Similar to Whitney, Yosemite's district leadership played a signficant role in directing the academic focus for each school and for the district based on the test analysis and identified needs. In keeping with the district's focus of improving instruction, the school scheduled a series of professional development activities on instructional strategies and the teaching process. Some of the topics included:

a) *Decision in Teaching*, a video tape on how to increase the probability of learning

b) *Motivation Theory*, a video tape of the principal teaching a lesson in which the staff was to identify the components of motivation used in the lesson

c) Time-on-task training

d) *Extending Their Thinking*, a video tape on how to elicit higher level cognitive skills

e) Lesson analysis

f) Bloom's Taxonomy for the slow learner.

In addition to these schoolwide staff development activities, the staff also used monthly grade-level meetings to maintain the school's focus on instruction by discussing curricular ideas and sharing teaching strategies. Minutes of these meetings were to be turned into the school secretary for typing and posting on the staff bulletin board. This strategy represents an example of enhancing schoolwide communication among groups — a practice that did not exist at Sierra or Tahoe.

In 1985–86, the school continued its focus on instructional strategies through the TESA training, which, although voluntary, involved most of the staff. By focusing on instructional practices, the school developed an overall academic focus rather than a specific subject area focus. This is not to say that specific subject areas did not receive attention. For example, science kits were purchased and inservices held on their use, as a means of strengthening the science program. Math manipulatives were also acquired, and the math resource teacher instructed the staff in their use. The attention paid to instructional practices in the first three years during which the school was involved in the effective schools program may have been one reason why the achievement at the school remained at an overall high level even during the difficult transition to the four track year-round system.

While the staff agreed that the school still had a clear school mission, the interviews beginning in 1987 and again in 1989 revealed that there was not the sense of clear academic focus that there was in these early years. Implementing and administering a four track year-round schools proved a very dificult task demanding considerable time from the principal; consequently, much of the improvement momentum was lost. Staff members were currently being trained in the writing process and in a literature-based approach to reading, but these were individual efforts and not a schoolwide focus, as was found at Whitney and Sierra. The new reading textbook adoption in 1989–1990 meant that language arts will be made a focus for the entire staff; however, at the time of the interviews there was not a school committee or grade level team planning how the staff would implement the new directive, as was the case at Whitney.

Frequent Monitoring

Frequent monitoring occurred at the school in several ways. First, progress was monitored through test results. Second, the principal monitored through formal and informal observations. Third, the reading and math programs were monitored by the math and reading resource teachers. Fourth, individual pupil progress was closely monitored by teachers. It was clear from interviews of both school site staff and district personnel that test results were used to monitor and adjust school programs.

The district in which Tahoe and Sierra were located was now in the process of training teachers and principals in a clinical teaching/supervision model. This type of training had been occurring in Yosemite's district since 1983; consequently, monitoring through observations was an important monitoring strategy used by the principal. During the interview conducted in 1989, the principal admitted that in the last couple of years, monitoring through observations had not been as systematic throughout the school as was previously the case. The observations had focused most on new teachers, on teachers who were experiencing difficulty, and on teachers who seemed to want feedback. The principal had chosen not to spend time observing teachers who he felt were good teachers but not open to feedback. As mentioned above, more and more of the principal's time was pulled away from the classroom and spent on dealing with administrative issues. As a result, in the last two years monitoring through informal observations was much less prevalent.

The reading and math specialists played a critical role in monitoring implementation of their specific programs. In addition to helping individual students in the reading and math labs, these specialists spent time each day in teacher classrooms giving demonstration lessons or observing the instructional program. In the interviews conducted in 1987, most of the staff mentioned positively the monitoring role of these specialists. In the interviews conducted in 1989, only one teacher mentioned monitoring by the reading teacher from time to time. She concluded by saying, 'I'm not using *Caterpillar Capers* in my classroom and no one really cares. The reading specialist we have now doesn't care.' No doubt the loss of funding for the full-time math specialist cut into time that was available for direct work with classroom teachers.

Finally, teachers at Yosemite had effective systems for tracking individual pupil progress. The coordinated curriculum and specified objectives helped each teacher to know what they were to cover. The monitoring helped them to know how well students had mastered the skills, and reteaching and remediation were an important part of the instructional process. In summary, during the past five years, use of tests for individual teacher monitoring of students was a common practice. However, monitoring of school programs had slipped and was perceived to be less effective than in 1987.

Opportunity to Learn and Time-on-Task

Through classroom management training and attention paid to instructional issues, Yosemite maximized learning time and provided opportunities to learn for all students. The overall agreement for this correlate on the 1985 survey was

82 per cent and in 1989 was 86 per cent. On the 1989 effective schools staff survey 100 per cent of the faculty agreed that:

- a variety of teaching strategies were used in the classroom
- homework was regularly assigned
- there were fifty minutes or more for math each day and two hours or more for reading and language arts
- the school had a written homework policy
- class started promptly
- students learned to the end of the period
- students practiced new skills in group and individual settings
- practice work was planned so students could be successful
- activities for all learning modalities were provided
- alternate teaching was provided for students having difficulty with a skill.

The responses on these questions are similar to those from Whitney. They also reflect the strong development in instructional strategies that had been pursued by the staff at Yosemite. Similar to the other schools in this study, the teachers still felt that learning time was lost through interruptions by the administration, for maintenance of school facilities, or to discipline students. Only 55 per cent of the staff agreed that students received immediate feedback and suggestions on homework, and only 10 per cent agreed that pull-out programs didn't disrupt basic skills instruction.

Staff Development

The pattern of staff development was similar to that found at Whitney. The district organized most of the staff development for all teachers and these activities were offered at the district level rather than at the site. The district had offered extensive training in the Madeline Hunter clinical teaching and supervision model. All teachers were trained and some refreshers have been offered at the site. Effective-teaching practices were a major focus of district inservices. As a result of the effective schools survey, the principal at Yosemite took the initiative to organize the TESA training. Staff members from other schools were invited to participate in the TESA training, but the largest proportion of participants came from Yosemite. The interviews conducted in 1987 revealed that this program had considerable impact on the staff.

When the county's Effective Schools Surveys were developed in 1986, a number of staff development questions were added to the instructional leadership correlate. Therefore there are no comparative data for the survey completed by the Yosemite staff in 1984 and 1985. The responses to the questions in 1989 did shed some light on how the school perceived staff development issues. Table 6.5 compares the responses to the staff development questions from Yosemite and the other three case-study schools.

The results from Table 6.5 show that the responses to these items do not correlate with overall achievement results. Whitney and Yosemite had far higher achievement results, yet the staff did not indicate higher levels of agreement in those items.

Table 6.5 Comparison of teacher responses from Whitney, Sierra, Tahoe and Yosemite on staff development in 1989 based on the county Effective Schools Survey

Survey Item	Per cent Agree			
	Whitney	Sierra	Tahoe	Yosemite
• Principal emphasizes participation in staff development activities	100%	92%	90%	80%
• Principal active in promoting staff development	90	96	85	70
• There is a staff-development program based on school goals	75	86	90	55
• Principal and staff plan the staff-development program	65	78	55	30
• Primary focus of staff development — increase knowledge of topic	90	100	95	80
• Primary focus of staff development — acquisition of new skills	75	93	75	75
• Primary focus of staff-development — application of knowledge and skills	85	89	85	80
• There is follow-up assistance by administration to support staff development skills	65	89	53	55
• Staff development evaluated on evidence of use in classroom	40	61	40	70

Table 6.5 shows that the principals at all four schools emphasized participation in staff-development activities. The data also show that the teachers at Sierra expressed the most positive views toward staff-development and the principal's role in the process. Reasons for this were documented in the Sierra case study which showed that staff development was a major focus for the past three years. The principal and staff at Sierra planned and carried out many staff development activities, as confirmed by the Sierra staff having the highest agreement with the survey statement that the principal and staff plan staff-development activities together. Whitney's staff is the next highest in expressing agreement with this statement. A significant part of the staff development provided for Whitney was organized by the district. This was also true for Yosemite. Tahoe planned some staff development, especially the school-based training in the writing process.

The very low agreement (30 per cent) at Yosemite indicated that there was little staff development at the school in the last year. If these questions had been asked on the 1985 survey, there might have been a higher percentage of agreement, because in the first three years of the effective schools process the staff was far more active in organizing and leading site-based staff-development activities as well as participating in district inservices. Like some of the other effective schools efforts, staff development, too, seemed to have slipped at Yosemite with the implementation of the four track year-round school.

In 1988–89, training in the writing process was offered in the district, and teachers, including some from Yosemite, participated. Similar training had also been provided in cooperative learning strategies. From the interviews it was not possible to determine the degree of participation in these programs. It is important to note that when asked which strategies were helping to raise achievement for low achieving students, only one person at Yosemite mentioned the writing process or cooperative learning. This is in sharp contrast to the responses given at Whitney, Sierra, and several other of the most effective schools, where almost every teacher mentioned the impact of these programs on helping lower achieving students be more successful. Two years before, the staff at Yosemite was eagerly discussing the impact of TESA. There was no such excitement expressed in 1989 about any staff development activity.

Organizational Structures and Procedures

In reviewing data from the last five years at Yosemite, it is easy to see the impact of changes in organizational structures and procedures on the school. When the school first initiated the effective schools process, students attended either a traditional school year track or a year-round track. While this arrangement meant there were two groups of teachers, it was possible to get everyone together most of the time for faculty or grade level meetings or for staff development. In 1986 when the four track year-round schedule was implemented, the school suffered a set-back to its improvement momentum and efforts. The impact on staff morale as a result of segregating students by ability and language on tracks has been discussed above. The operation of four tracks also impacted the three key variables of shared decision-making and collaboration, problem-solving, and communication.

Shared Decision-Making and Collaboration

In 1983–84 the school staff voted to participate in the effective schools process. After completion of the effective schools surveys, the whole staff had an opportunity to hear the results. The entire teaching staff, several parents, and classroom assistants participated in a 'We Agree' process to define school goals. The goal-setting process was repeated by the entire staff in 1984–85. A school effectiveness steering committee was selected to guide the school's improvement efforts. Subcommittees were established to work on particular needs that had been identified. Monthly grade level meetings were held, that had as their focus the sharing of instructional strategies as well as problem-solving and identification of issues to be addressed by the whole faculty. At faculty meetings, teams of teachers took responsibility for researching and sharing information on effective-teaching strategies for their colleagues.

From 1983 to 1986 there was a real sense of shared purpose and action on issues that the staff felt were important, based on what they had learned from the effective schools surveys. This strong sense of shared purpose was not as prevalent in the interviews conducted in 1989. The school effectiveness steering committee was no longer meeting. The principal stated that, if he could retrace his steps, one action he would do differently would be to maintain the school effectiveness committee. He felt that by disbanding the group much momentum had been lost. As a result of the four track year-round schedule, far fewer grade level meetings were held in 1987–89, and there was a lack of focus and attention being given to improvement efforts.

Collaboration and shared decision-making suffered in the difficult transition years when the four track year-round schedule was being implemented, because of the administrative time absorbed in managing the new organizational structure. In the fall of 1988, the principal recognized that the segregation issue had to be addressed and he established a school committee to brainstorm possible solutions. The solutions developed by the staff resulted in more team-teaching and collaboration across tracks. While these collaborative efforts helped, the interviews in 1989 revealed that a sense of segregation and isolation existed that negatively impacted collaborative efforts in ways that had not been present in 1986.

In the interviews conducted in 1986, when asked what role teachers have in making instructional decisions, 80 per cent of the teachers replied they have an important role in their classroom in determining how they teach and how they motivate students to learn. All stated that the curriculum was determined for them at the district level through the grade level expectancies and the textbook adoptions. They explained, however, that teachers were involved on the district curriculum committees. Similar responses were expressed in the interviews conducted in 1989. One teacher summed up the situation this way: 'A younger, inexperienced teacher will be dictated by the curriculum simply because he or she is inexperienced. The experienced teacher will use the curriculum in the best way that suits his or her teaching abilities. You will look through the book and pick out the best and work up other material to fill in the holes.' At Yosemite there was not a committee ready to go through a new text as a whole school to 'pick out the best and fill in the holes' as the staff at Whitney had done with their new math textbook.

Problem Solving

When asked if there was a systematic process for resolving both instructional and discipline problems, all staff members interviewed in 1986 said 'yes'. They cited the role of committees, grade level teams, faculty meetings and the important individual role played by the principal. In 1989, the answers to this questions were far more negative and vague. The inability to satisfactorily resolve the segregation of students had undermined the sense of efficacy in solving problems that permeated the school in 1986. The surveys reflected the loss of efficacy somewhat, but not as strongly as the interviews. In response to the question 'Can the principal and staff solve most problems?' in 1985, 86 per cent of the staff agreed. In 1989, the agreement with this statement had dropped to 75 per cent. It is important to keep in mind that the teachers interviewed in 1989 were veteran teachers who had been on the staff when the school initiated the effective schools process, and several had actively participated on the steering committee. Thus, these teachers had experienced the full changes in organizational structures and procedures over the last five years and had consistently expressed concerns about and had struggled with the tracking and segregation issue.

Communication

Communication surfaced as one of the most difficult problems resulting from the four track year-round school schedule. As one teacher said, 'There is no time when we are all together. One quarter of the staff is always on vacation; therefore, when you have meetings or staff-development activities, someone is always missing.' When the organizational problem of communicating across the four tracks was overlaid with tensions caused by the segregation among tracks, communications became even more difficult. By the fall of 1988, the situation had reached a crisis point, and the principal organized a staff meeting in November that was held away from the site to discuss the tracking issue. While no fundamental changes were made, this was an important first step in bringing the staff together to communicate about the problem. The new principal, who assumed the leadership position in January 1988, made it clear that one of his priorities was to alter the segregation of students on the tracks.

While it is possible to trace the problems that the four track year-round school had imposed on the faculty of Yosemite and how it had impacted staff collaboration, shared decision-making, problem-solving, and communication, it is critical to point out that there was more total staff involvement and participation on committees at Yosemite than was found at Tahoe. Establishing a schoolwide committee to address a problem was a more familiar response at Yosemite than was found at Sierra. The lessons from Yosemite are clear, however: an external environmental change, such as the need to implement four tracks instead of two to accommodate student enrollment growth, can derail the improvement process. There was a period of readjustment and refinement necessary to find new ways of working together given the separation caused by the tracks. These changes along with other variables, negatively impacted test scores. Two other schools in the study found themselves in similar situations of having to change configurations because of growth in students enrollment and had the same consequences in terms of impact on organizational structures and procedures and on student outcomes.

Instructional Leadership

In both the 1986 and 1989 interviews, observing classrooms was identified as one of the most significant roles the principal played in guiding instruction and making instructional decisions at the school. In 1986 one teacher described the process this way:

> The principal sets the tone and where the emphasis should be. He follows through with this emphasis in the classroom through observations. There are four [observations] per year with a post conference follow-up session. One is isolated as a teacher. It is great to get the positive feedback from the principal.

Several other teachers commented on the helpfulness of the positive notes that were left by the principal when he observed the classroom. Another strong point was the principal's willingness to teach lessons, to have himself video-taped doing a lesson and to have the lesson critiqued by teachers as part of a faculty meeting. His teaching skills were highly regarded by the staff, thus they had confidence in his ability to give them guidance in their lessons and to learn from his comments. One teacher summarized the principal's instructional skills this way:

The principal thought like a teacher. When someone is the boss they [sic] sometimes forget what the job is all about and that's true of teaching too. It's easy to write up programs for this and that and they [sic] forget what it's like to implement and carry them out. The [principal] is the kind of guy who could just come right in and take over your job as a teacher and nothing gets lost because he's thinking like a teacher. Consequently, his support was always directed at teaching so that makes him much more effective.

In the interviews in 1986, several other important roles were also mentioned, such as organizing staff development, monitoring the implementation of district curriculum, focusing staff meetings on instructional issues, utilizing the skills of the resource teachers to work in the classroom, making presentations to the staff, analyzing test results, and selecting new staff members.

In 1989, the responses were less inclusive. The principal had the disadvantage of being a lame duck principal. The staff knew he was leaving and so did he; therefore, many issues went unresolved in the intervening months. The principal himself commented that so much of his time was consumed with dealing with community concerns about the year-round school, that in the last two years the amount of time he spent in the classroom had greatly diminished. The principal and the staff acknowledged that his leadership was less visible and active in the last two years in terms of instructional issues. Table 6.6 compares of the survey results in 1985 and 1989 and shows where there had been changes in teachers' perceptions regarding the instructional leadership role of the principal. Overall, the results show that there was a slight negative trend in opinions with less agreement on some of the items. A significant change that surfaced and that was corroborated by the principal's own statements is that he was less available and visible throughout the school in 1989 than he was in 1985–86.

Table 6.6   Comparison of teacher responses on items related to instructional leadership in 1985 and 1989 based on the Connecticut and county Effective Schools Surveys

Survey Item	Per cent Agree 1985	1989
• Following formal observation, principal discusses observation with teacher	100%	95%
• Classroom observation by principal focused on improving instruction	81	80
• Principal is accessible to discuss instructional matters	95	85
• Principal and faculty can solve most problems	86	75
• Principal encourages teachers to accept responsibility for student achievement	71	85
• Principal seeks ideas and suggestions from staff	53	85
• Principal makes several formal classroom observations each year	75	70
• After formal observation teacher and principal develop instruct improvement plan	85	70
• Principal initiates effective coordination of instructional program	86	65
• Principal is highly visible throughout the school	86	53
• Principal makes frequent contacts with students and teachers	96	65
• Instructional leadership from the principal is clear, strong and central	62	65
• Principal gives feedback to teachers re instructional techniques	71	45
• Instructional issues frequently the focus of staff meetings	48	35

The principal's leadership in the instructional area was significant in helping the school launch an effective schools efforts and to bring about a significant increase in achievement for students from the two lowest income groups. When the four track year-round system was implemented, the principal found his energies consumed by addressing administrative issues and community concerns for placement. In 1986 one teacher said, 'This is a strong staff and it could run the school by itself.' He was correct in recognizing that Yosemite had instructionally strong teachers and an excellent overall level of achievement. Unfortunately, the students from low income families suffered, and their achievement fell below comparable groups in the state when the principal's instructional leadership was diverted to administrative and community matters. The principal, however, had planted the seed that 'equality of outcomes' needed to be a goal, the school staff had experienced achieving that goal, and now the staff was working to recover from this temporary set-back by diminishing, and hopefully in the near future, eliminating the impact of tracking students by ability or language.

Summary and Conclusions

This case study is significant in illustrating the close interrelationship among inputs, the transformative process, and students outcomes. Based on Coleman *et al.*'s (1966) findings about the power of family background factors in determining student outcomes, the demographic shift at Yosemite of from 24 to 42 per cent professional families could be expected to lead to increases in overall student achievement without changes in the transformative process. However, changes were made in these processes as a means of meeting the needs of the school's small (11 per cent) lower income Hispanic population. The result was a dramatic improvement in the CAP scores of the two lowest income groups — the groups that most benefit from well-designed school improvement. When Yosemite had to make organizational/ structural changes to accommodate a large increase in enrollment (even though the enrollment increase was largely of professional families), this had a significant effect on the achievement of the lowest income group.

Several important transformative changes and their subsequent reversal need to be highlighted. First, the implementation of the effective schools process between 1983 and 1986 altered the climate and culture of Yosemite to one that resembled the culture of learning and achievement that had evolved at Whitney. Unlike Whitney, Yosemite had no major safety issues to address before changes in the school's technology could be undertaken. The school did implement a schoolwide discipline plan, which Rosenholtz's (1989) study has shown helps to support effective classroom practices. Rewards and recognition programs were implemented for students and teachers. The problem of raising expectations for low income students was tackled directly by undertaking an extensive training program in TESA. Considerable efforts were made to strengthen home-school relations by focusing on teacher-parent communication, especially in regard to school and grade level goals and objectives and classroom activities. Special efforts were made to reach the Hispanic families and involve them in school life. Through participation in the 'We Agree' process a shared sense of mission was developed by the staff and community representatives and actively shared with the community. Strong norms of collegiality were developed through sharing at staff meetings, through organizational structures that brought teachers together to solve problems, and through staff-development activities.

Second, changes were also made in the school's technology. Particularly important was the reallocation of state School Improvement Funds (SIP) to hire professional staff to work with students who were below grade level. The aim was to catch these students up with their classmates, not just to remediate. The difference is subtle but significant. It is the kind of difference in attitude toward low-income, low-achieving students that evolved at Whitney, but was absent at Sierra and Tahoe. Another significant change in the school's technology was the focus on instructional strategies in both the district and site staff-development programs. The staff accepted that the curriculum, in large measure, was predetermined. Their professional role lay in developing their knowledge and skills in how to teach effectively and in how children learn. The ability of the school to focus so strongly on instructional strategies was due to the skills of the principal. Principals in this district were selected for their instructional skills and these skills were continually reinforced in district administrative training. (The principal of Pinyon, also located in this district, was similarly acknowledged by the staff as being instructionally strong and able to model different teaching strategies — a sharp contrast to a staff comment about the principal at Tahoe). Another change in the technology that may help to account for growth in student achievement was the use of resource teachers not just to teach low-achieving students, a practice common in most schools, but also to conduct demonstration lessons and work actively with teachers to gain skills in implementing new instructional strategies. These teachers, along with the principal also played an important monitoring role.

Third, in the area of organizational structures and procedures, there were small but important changes. A school effectiveness group was established to guide and oversee the change process. Strong grade level teams that had problem-solving functions were also established. Faculty meetings shifted from just addressing management issues to being a time to focus on instruction, involving teachers in their own growth and development. These changes closely paralleled those made at Whitney, but were less in evidence at Sierra and Tahoe. The major organizational change came after 1986, when the school implemented a four track year-round school schedule. This change had negative impacts on the previous organizational changes as well as on all other aspects of the transformative process.

Finally, it should be noted that the above changes were accomplished by the coordinated leadership of the principal, vice principal, math, reading, and bilingual resource teachers, the librarian, and key teachers on the grade level teams and on the school effectiveness team. It should also be noted that even though this was a high SES school, during the period 1983–1986, the principal spent considerable time on instructional and organizational issues. Hallinger and Murphy (1986) reported that in high SES schools, principals spent more time on community relations and less on instructional issues compared to principals in low SES schools. At Yosemite this was not the case. This is important to note, because when Yosemite had to implement the four track year-round schedule, and the principal's attention was drawn away from instruction to handling community relations, many of the improvement efforts were derailed and student achievement suffered as a result. Although there were strong norms of collegiality and shared leadership, these were not sufficient to overcome the loss of principal leadership.

Between 1983–1986, Yosemite represented a model of institutional development that Fullan Bennett and Rolheiser-Bennett (1990) has said is so necessary for genuine school improvement. By 1988–89, the multitude of changes that had been undertaken in the transformative process were greatly undermined. Several lessons about institutional development emerge from the experiences of Yosemite. First, a structural change of the magnitude of implementing a four track year-round schedule is likely to have profound impacts on all aspects of organizational life. Without care and consideration to how such a change is implemented, previous improvement efforts and effective working patterns can be disrupted in ways that negatively impact student outcomes. Second, structural barriers that separate teachers can undermine norms of collegiality, opportunities for shared decision-making and problem-solving, communication, and collaboration among teachers. All of these factors have been shown to be essential to altering the transformative process in ways that lead to institutional development and enhanced student outcomes. Third, when too much of the principal's time is consumed by other issues (in this case, handling community concerns, in the case of Sierra, addressing district or countywide issues), there is likely to be insufficient time to lead the school instructionally and to guide and sustain changes in the transformative process. Fourth, teachers and principals can learn from their mistakes. Taking corrective action will not always be easy, but a tradition of analyzing data and solving problems can enable a staff to begin working towards a solution. This is precisely what the new principal and staff of Yosemite were doing.

Notes

1 It should be noted that the elementary school was located across the street from a high school, which may account for some of the vandalism problems that the faculty felt existed.
2 The continuous use of the small campus by so many students was no doubt impacting building maintenance.
3 Questions with asterisks were not asked on the Connecticut School Effectiveness Questionnaire, but were added when the County Effective Schools Surveys were developed in 1986.
4 While the 21 per cent agreement on this item in 1989 looks like there has been slippage, it is important to note that on the 1985 survey, 34 per cent disagreed with this questions and 14 per cent said they didn't know, in 1989, only 5 per cent disagreed with the question, and 74 per cent said they didn't know. The placing of the low-income bilingual students all on one track may be the reason that the majority of teachers now reported they did not know about retention practices.

Chapter 7

Increasing School Effectiveness: Lessons from the Eight Case Studies

In Chapter 1, an interactive model of the transformative process of school effect-iveness and improvement was presented (Figure 1.4). The model has four major components: school culture and climate; school technology: curriculum and in-struction; organizational structures and procedures; and instructional leadership. They were used as frames of reference for analyzing the data and presenting the case studies. It is through leadership by the principal and in conjunction with school staff that changes occurred in the other three components to bring about school improvement and increased effectiveness at the classroom level. This chapter summarizes the key findings from the eight schools in relationship to the four components of the model, examining the components separately and in re-lationship to each other. Conclusions will be drawn regarding the developmental nature of the school effectiveness and improvement process.

School Culture and Climate

The variables that comprise this component — safety and order of the learning environment, rewards and recognition, sense of a shared mission, norms of collegiality, high expectations, and home-school relations — create the ethos of the school which Rutter, *et al.* (1979) and Mortimore, *et al.* (1988) found to be significant in contributing to a school's overall effectiveness. School improvement programs often seem to turn to this component first as a place to initiate the change process. The schools involved in this study tended to follow this pattern. The changes often involved symbols, such as initiating reward and recognition programs, refurbishing school facilities, or implementing schoolwide discipline plans. For several of the schools involved in this study, these were important first steps and usually had an immediate impact on the school environment and teacher morale. Other aspects of the culture, such as norms of collegiality, expectations for student achievement, especially by children from low-income families, and teacher attitudes toward families that shaped home-school relations, involved deep-seated norms and beliefs that were usually reinforced by organizational structures and procedures and the school's technology. They proved much more difficult to change. When changes were achieved, they again were usually found to be preceded by changes in other aspects of the transformative process.

Safety and Order

Although four of the eight schools in the study served urban populations in terms of SES and ethnic diversity of the students, none of the schools in the study had safety issues comparable to inner city schools in Chicago, Detroit, or New York. After analyzing the data across the eight schools, several points appear to be significant in regard to safety and order. First, Whitney, the school with the greatest third grade achievement gains, had the greatest change in per cent agreement among teachers on the safe and orderly correlate. Second, Tahoe, the least effective school, improved in this correlate, but remained well below the other schools in total agreement by staff with the survey items. Third, Yosemite and Lassen, two schools in the more effective category, had lower percentage scores than several less effective schools, indicating that there may be a threshold level. Once the threshold is reached, improvements in the safety, order, or appearance of the school may not significantly impact student achievement. Once a reasonable climate has been created and little teaching time is lost to student misbehavior in the classroom, vigilance in maintaining a safe and orderly learning environment will increase or reinforce staff morale, but it is less likely to raise test scores.

Conclusion: Improvements in the safety and order of the learning environment were often one of the first activities to be undertaken. While these improvements may be necessary and important, they are not sufficient to achieve increased school effectiveness.

Rewards and Recognition

Implementing student reward and recognition programs often accompanied improvements in the safety and order of the learning environment. By 1986, all eight schools had recognition programs in place; however, there was some variability among reward programs. First, Sierra, one of the two least effective schools, focused its recognition program more on behavior than on academic achievement. In addition, the recognition was primarily centered in the lofts or classrooms rather than schoolwide. Tahoe, the other least effective school, had a schoolwide recognition program, but compared to the other schools, it was fairly new and still developing. Third, only Whitney had developed a comprehensive recognition program that focused on improvement and achievements in every academic area. The extent and the breadth of the recognition program appeared to contribute to the academic focus of the school, a stress on achievement, and increased expectations. Fourth, the staff at Yosemite, one of the first schools to initiate the effective schools process, felt that its recognition program had become stale and doubted that it was having the same impact on students as it had initially. This is an important insight that highlights the difficulty of maintaining the impact of innovations over time if there is not constant review and renewal. Finally, the student recognition programs were important in linking schools and families. Yosemite and Whitney not only invited parents, but the principal also sent letters home expressing appreciation for parental support that enhanced student achievement. The recognition program was used very effectively at Whitney to help embed high expectations in the community. This aspect seemed to be less prevalent in the other schools, and especially at Sierra and Tahoe.

A second aspect of recognition explored in this study was teacher recognition. This topic has not been addressed in the effective schools literature. In the most effective schools, most of the staff felt that teachers were recognized for both extra efforts and instructional effectiveness. This was not the case in the three least effective schools. At both Pinyon and Sequoia, significant numbers of staff members (nine at each site) had been recognized as mentor teachers. Pinyon, Yosemite, Lassen and Sequoia had designated time during faculty meetings to recognize instructional practices, classroom successes, and innovative projects. The faculty at Whitney and Sequoia were recognized through plaques, name plates, pins, paper weights, community events and staff bulletins. At Whitney, in particular, the recognition for staff, as for students, centered around achievement gains. It can be inferred from the information gained in the interviews that teacher recognition, especially recognition that focused on successful instructional strategies and gains in students achievement, may be as important as student recognition in creating an academic and achievement orientation among staff members. Based on the interviews, staff recognition appeared to be an area that could use more attention. Recognition serves both symbolic and real functions in reinforcing the school's mission (Deal, 1984a). Recognizing teacher efforts in student achievement on standardized tests may be especially significant, given that many teachers felt the tests were not a valid measure of the curriculum they taught.

Conclusion: Well-developed recognition programs that focused on all aspects of academic achievement and rewarded both students and teachers appeared to contribute to increased school effectiveness. The programs, however, need to be reviewed and renewed if they are to continue to have an impact.

Shared Mission

Deal and Kennedy (1982) in their book *Corporate Culture* discussed the important role that a strong, cohesive culture plays in the economic success and viability of corporations. They asserted that 'we need to remember that people make businesses work. And we need to relearn old lessons about how culture ties people together and gives meaning and purpose to their day-to-day lives.' (p. 5) One could argue that most schools have strong cultures because of the enduring practices that persist in schools, even if they have long ago ceased to be effective in educating today's students. Even if the cultures of schools are strong, however, they often are not cohesive. A major reason for the lack of cohesion is that schools serve diverse constituencies, which have dictated a multitude of purposes for schools: custodial care for the young, academic achievement and student mastery of a set curriculum, physical development and well being, citizenship development, and a sorting and socialization function channeling students into appropriate roles. These diverse purposes and expectations frequently have made it difficult for schools to develop a shared vision, mission, and/or cohesive sense of purpose.

All of the schools in this study had a written mission statement. The evidence from the interviews, however, indicated that not all staff members shared the mission, and in some cases, they were unable to articulate the mission. The staff at Whitney, Yosemite, and Pinyon articulated most clearly a common sense of purpose. The staff at Whitney and Pinyon were clearest in articulating an effective schools' goal that included mastery of basic skills by all children. In contrast, as was pointed out in the case studies, a shared mission did not exist at Tahoe and Sierra, the two least effective schools. Their written statements were never given significant meaning through the daily actions of the principal and staff.

Conclusion: In the most effective schools, the teachers clearly understood, shared, and could articulate the mission of the school. The shared mission was given meaning and reinforced by actions in all other aspects of the transformative process.

High Expectations

One of the cultural norms identified in the effective schools literature is high expectations. Expectations or beliefs about students are difficult to alter, because one is required to change attitudes and beliefs. A comparison of Japanese and American educational systems (Stevenson, Lee, and Stigler, 1986) has pointed out that American school staff and families believe that success in school is determined by ability, which teachers frequently view as unalterable and linked to family background. Japanese families and schools, on the other hand, believe that student success in school is dependent upon hard work. These differences in how success in school is perceived are related to the high expectations correlate. To hold high expectations that all children can master the intended curriculum if instructional effectiveness is increased is more akin to the Japanese view than to the current American view of student ability as the determinant of school success. Thus, implementation of an effective schools model requires altering beliefs about the mission of the school and developing instructional practices that enable all students to learn.

Expectations for student success varied in the eight schools. The teachers at Whitney, Yosemite, Pinyon, and Shasta were the most optimistic about their ability to teach all students regardless of home background. They also expressed positive views about their students' ability to do well in school. The staff at each of the four most effective schools, Whitney, Yosemite, Pinyon and Lassen, expected their students would do well on standardized tests. This view was held by far fewer staff members at the other schools. One indication of how hard it is to change beliefs was revealed when analysis of the survey results showed that many of the same items addressing high expectations were rated the lowest at all eight schools (e.g., 95 per cent of the student will graduate from high school, the same proportion of high and low income students are retained, teachers expect that 90 per cent of the children will achieve identified standards, and all students can achieve identified standards regardless of home background). The differentiating factor among the schools was the number of staff members who agreed with each statement. The agreement was much higher in the more effective schools and lower in the less effective schools.

Pinyon and Yosemite present interesting examples of efforts to alter beliefs. Both schools served relatively high SES communities. This meant that for many students high expectations were held by their parents, and the school primarily reinforced these expectations. Both schools also served 15 per cent to 30 per cent low SES students. When the initial effective schools surveys were completed, they revealed that the staff held low expectations for low SES students. Both schools addressed the problem through TESA training (most systematically at Yosemite) and through staff discussion of the impact of tracking and homogeneous grouping at Pinyon. The consequences of these actions, coupled with changes in curriculum and instructional practices, resulted in improved achievement for the lowest SES groups. As the case-study at Yosemite showed, however, gains were quickly lost by reverting to practices that segregated students, undermined expectations, and distracted the school from its academic focus. At Whitney, expectations were raised, not through TESA training, but through curriculum alignment that brought quick achievement gains and helped teachers to see that they could be successful in teaching low-income students. In addition, as discussed above, the rewards and recognition programs for both students and staff helped to raise expectations both at school and in the community.

Holding high expectations did not directly translate into higher achievement for Shasta. The staff at Shasta had one of the highest per cent agreements with the survey items dealing with high expectations, yet its overall achievement placed in the less effective category. Many of the staff members at Shasta had received training in TESA; therefore, they were aware of practices that limited or enhanced low-income students' learning opportunities. Shasta's staff over the years of its improvement efforts had experienced some significant achievement gains by its largely poor and Hispanic student population. In 1989, the staff still expressed the belief that they could help all children learn, even though at this time they were experiencing difficulty in translating beliefs into action, especially at the sixth grade level. The high expectations at Whitney, Yosemite, Pinyon, Shasta, and Lassen seemed to confirm Scheerens' and Creemers' (1989) assertion that increasing achievement causes high expectations for the future. They have argued that the expectations-achievement correlation needs to be seen as reciprocal rather than as causal.

Conclusion: Training programs helped to raise teachers' expectations. To sustain the effect of the training, however, it needed to be ongoing and supported by other changes in the transformative process. In other words, expectations rose more quickly when teachers saw gains in achievement through curriculum alignment and instructional strategies that increased the achievement of the lowest income students.

Home-School Relations

This correlate is closely linked with high expectations. High expectations are not likely if the staff blames families for poor achievement. The per cent agreement on the home-school relations correlate was the only one of the correlates, with an almost one-to-one correspondence between overall levels of achievement and the agreement. The exception was Lassen, which met the criteria as one of the more effective schools, yet had one of the lower per cent agreements on this correlate. First, Lassen, like Tahoe, was one of the only schools not to target home-school relations as an area for improvement. Teachers reported that little had changed in their relations with parents. Second, Lassen's staff, like the staff at Sierra and Tahoe, saw low-income parents as one of the biggest barriers to increased student achievement. Third, although Lassen met the effectiveness criteria, the level of achievement remained well below that of Whitney's, a school serving a similar population. Lassen's gains in student achievement seemed to have been attained through changes in district issued curriculum guidelines, well defined grade level objectives that were closely aligned to the state and district testing program, as well as use of instructional strategies such as clinical teaching, cooperative learning, and a primary program called Workshop Way. Although Lassen had an active parent group and parent volunteers who were highly regarded, the staff was not working to embed high expectations in the community or making extra efforts to communicate and work with the the lowest income parents, as they were at Whitney and Pinyon, and as they had at Yosemite. In the case of Lassen two questions regarding home-school relations remain to be answered:

1 If student achievement continues to improve through instructional strategies or curriculum changes, will staff attitudes eventually become more positive — both in terms of high expectations and home-school relations?
2 Will changes in attitudes toward expectations for students' success and relations toward parents need to change if Lassen is to attain the same level of achievement results as Whitney?

The work done at Sierra to improve home-school relations may offer another important perspective about home-school relations. Although many schoolwide activities were carried out to improve home-school relations (e.g., initiation of a school newsletter, hosting of numerous parent workshops in English and Spanish, active recruitment of parent volunteers and genuine involvement of parents in school decision-making), the actions did not appear to have contributed to improved overall achievement, as measured by standardized test scores and as some of the parent involvement literature suggests it might (Henderson, 1981, 1987). While many of the parent activities created a feeling of openness toward parents, and parent surveys indicated positive parental opinions about the school, teacher attitudes about parents did not seem to change. The interviews revealed that teachers saw lack of parent concern as a major barrier to improved achievement. This was in sharp contrast to the attitudes expressed at Whitney and Pinyon. One of the reasons for these more negative views toward parents may be that the staff had not experienced any gains in student achievement. Teachers felt frustrated in their efforts to raise test scores, and dysfunctional families became an easy scapegoat. Work by Johnson, Brookover and Farrell (1989b) has indicated that teachers' lower expectations for parents may also negatively affect students' perceptions of themselves and their ability to do work. In contrast, the staff at Whitney, Pinyon and Yosemite developed more positive views toward parents over the last five years, espcially low-income and Hispanic parents. The achievement gains reinforced initial teacher efforts to communicate more with parents. The case of Sierra illustrates how difficult the improvement process is and the complexity of the interrelationships among school effectiveness components.

Conclusion: Low teacher expectations for students seemed to translate into low expectations for parents, which hindered positive teacher-parent collaboration. Initial gains in student achievement contributed to improved home-school relations. Strong involvement of parents at a schoolwide level did not seem to lead to improved student outcomes, especially for low-income students whose parents remained uninvolved.

School Technology: Curriculum and Instruction

Creating a culture of achievement and changing beliefs about the educability of all children are more likely to occur if achievement begins to increase. It is changes in the school's technology component that will most quickly bring about increased acheivement. Test data analysis and curriculum alignment are two important elements that comprise this component and often shape the academic focus for the school. Staff development which addresses curriculum and instructional issues, frequent monitoring and time-on-task are also essential elements. Curriculum and instruction are the heart of the school and of each classroom. It is through them that the essential mission of the school is achieved. Based on the interviews, it was clear that all of the schools were directly impacted by state level curriculum changes in language arts, mathematics, science, and social studies. The staff at all eight schools were working to implement many of the approaches suggested in the state curriculum frameworks.

Most of the schools had introduced more math manipulatives into their curriculum, and there was a greater focus on problem solving. Three of the most effective schools — Whitney, Yosemite, Pinyon — had implemented a hands-on, experimental science curriculum. All of the schools, while at different stages, were teaching writing as a process and undertaking a more wholistic approach to reading and language arts. They were moving to implement a reading program that used literature as well as or in place of the basic reading series. Almost all staff members interviewed were excited about the greater use of literature, which they felt was having a profound impact on the curriculum. Some teachers at each school, however, expressed concern that the shift in methods and materials would result in lower standardized test scores, because there was an insufficient match between the new curriculum framework and the state test. Because of these shifts in curriculum, many teachers indicated they did not feel the CAP test was a valid measure of the curriculum. A comparison of the surveys completed in 1987 and in 1989 showed a decrease in the percentage of staff agreeing with this item in all schools, except Whitney. Thus curriculum alignment — the match between what is taught and what is tested — emerged as a significant issue in the improvement process.

Curriculum Alignment

Lassen, Yosemite, Pinyon, and Sequoia were assisted in their improvement efforts by districtwide curriculum alignment. The principal at Whitney, as described earlier, worked with his own staff to align the school's curriculum to the CAP test. The experience and training the staff at Whitney had in aligning its curriculum may be the reason that there was an increase rather than a decrease in the number of staff members who felt that the CAP test was a valid measure of the curriculum. Shasta, Tahoe, and Sierra, all in the same district, were not assisted in curriculum alignment until very recently, when the district adopted a new mathematics text-book. Only the staff at Shasta seemed to have developed some skills in this area — at least in identifying objectives tested on CAP that were not covered in the textbook and in developing or ordering needed materials.

Conclusion: In the more effective schools, there was alignment of the curriculum with the material covered on standardized tests. The alignment was made by either the district or the principal and staff committees at the site. The process of training the staff to align the curriculum seemed to have an empowering effect on the staff, and gave them a sense of control over the curriculum and the teaching and learning process. Curriculum alignment led to better results on standardized tests which, in turn, increased the confidence of teachers in their ability to teach all students.

Use of Test Results

Curriculum alignment in large measure depends on the ability to analyze and use test data. Most staff members in all eight schools indicated that the principal reviewed and analyzed test results and stressed their importance. Whitney appeared to be the only school whose staff members were trained to review and analyze the test data.

Three patterns emerged in response to how test data were used:

1 Use of test data to modify the instructional program. Almost all staff members at Whitney, Sequoia, Lassen, and Shasta said that test results were used to modify the instructional program. Only a third to one half of the staff at Yosemite, Pinyon, Sierra and Tahoe said test results were used to modify the curriculum. One explanation for why teachers said that test data were not use to modify the curriculum might be that teachers felt the curriculum was set by district directives and the textbooks. This view was especially predominant in the interviews at Yosemite and Pinyon — schools in a district with a strong, centralized curriculum.

2 Use of standardized test results to provide feedback to individual teachers. Staff members at Pinyon and Yosemite reported that test results were discussed individually with teachers, and they were expected to modify their instructional program to address deficiencies. Two district programs provided feedback to individual teachers: the monitoring system at Sequoia (called RMS, Reading Management System, and MMS, Mathematics Monitoring System), and the district testing program at Lassen, which was aligned to CAP. In contrast, at Whitney, the principal did not focus on individual teachers, but discussed test results in the context of grade level teams.

3 Minimal use and rationalization of test results. This pattern was mentioned most often by staff members interviewed at Tahoe and Sierra.

Conclusion: While all schools reviewed test results, the more effective schools used the results to assist them in curriculum alignment, to modify the curriculum, and to alter the academic emphasis of individual teachers. Even though most teachers recognized the importance placed on test results, they did not regard the

California Assessment Program as a valid measure of student achievement. Experience in analyzing test data and aligning curriculum led to greater acceptance of the validity of the test.

Academic Focus

Results from the CAP test were often used to help determine the improvement areas on which the school would focus. If problem-solving was determined to be weak, or math scores were down in general, extra effort would be devoted to that area. Staff members at Sierra and Tahoe mentioned that they chose to have staff development in the San Diego Writing Project as a result of analyzing their test data and as a result of the recommendation of the School Improvement Review Team. Test data, however, were not used exclusively to set the foci. Even when an academic area did not require attention, textbook adoption cycles dictated that staff time and inservices be devoted to the new adoption. Similarly, the requirement to address all academic areas in the School Improvement Plan required that areas that had not been addressed in the previous year or two had to become the academic foci for the current year. Managing the pressures to address a variety of academic issues did not always prove an easy task for the schools.

The staff members at Pinyon, Yosemite, Whitney, and Sequoia were assisted in setting a focus by their district through the districts' staff development programs. For example, in the case of Whitney, the major staff development focus in the district was, for two years, in the area of hands-on science, another year it was math manipulatives. In addition, because these schools are located in relatively small districts, the entire school staff usually was required to attend the inservices. As a result the district academic focus was more easily transferred to the site and became its focus. The staff development program for the district in which Sierra, Shasta, and Tahoe were located did not center around one or two topics and, therefore, did not contribute to the academic focus at the school sites.

Although all eight schools had these competing academic demands, the interviews revealed that the more effective schools tended to be more academically focused, especially in areas of critical need determined by the staff. The academic focus was enhanced at Whitney, Yosemite, Pinyon, Sequoia, and Lassen through frequent monitoring, and because the district staff development was more curriculum oriented than seemed to be the case for Sierra, Tahoe, and Shasta.

Conclusion: The interview data indicated that the more effective schools had a stronger and clearer academic focus that was supported by staff development activities and reinforced through monitoring by the principal and by curriculum committees. In addition, the more effective schools were assisted by their districts in setting an academic focus and were better able to manage competing academic foci.

Frequent Monitoring

All of the schools were dealing with new programs, textbooks, instructional strategies, and constantly changing student populations. Monitoring all of these changes represented a challenging task. The interviews and surveys identified three major monitoring mechanisms: tests, grade level teams and curriculum committees, and principal observations and other monitoring actions. The use of test results to monitor, as discussed above, was used more systematically by the more effective schools and less so by the two least effective schools. In addition to the standardized tests, Sequoia had an individual monitoring system for reading and mathematics called RMS and MMS, respectively. These programs allowed teachers to track individual pupil progress. The staff at Lassen had the assistance of a districtwide testing program that allowed teachers to administer and score pre and post tests at the site.

Strong grade level teams and curriculum committees, which relate to school structures and organizational procedures (discussed below), played a critical monitoring role at Whitney, Pinyon, Sequoia, and Shasta. Lassen's grade level teams were involved more in monitoring after the adoption of the district curriculum guidelines. Lassen did not have the strong curriculum committees that existed in the other schools. Yosemite had strong committees and grade-level teams in place prior to the shift to four-track year round. These groups played a significant role in pushing the improvement efforts and monitoring progress, especially for the low income students. Sierra, as discussed in the case study, had strong loft teams that monitored activities in the third-fourth and fifth-sixth grade lofts. However, the staff felt there was little monitoring of the entire school program and there were no schoolwide curriculum committees to assist in the process. The school site council did meet quarterly to monitor implementation of the school improvement plan. The monitoring seemed to be more in the form of 'Did we do what we said we would do?' rather than 'Is what we did working to increase student achievement?'

The principal's role in monitoring progress was weakest at the three least effective schools. The district had placed a new emphasis on classroom observations using a clinical supervision model. The principals at Shasta, Sierra, and Tahoe were in the process of implementing these observations during the last year of the study. The staff at Sierra expressed appreciation for the principal's knowledge and skill in this area and felt that it was helpful. The observations, however, did not focus on other aspects of the program or other instructional strategies. The principals at Whitney, Yosemite, Pinyon, and Sequoia had been conducting clinical observations since the inception of their school effectiveness programs. The principal at Whitney, as a result of the effective schools surveys, increased the number of formal observations, with one observation per year on the school's area of academic focus. The principal at Lassen conducted less formal observations; however, the staff indicated that he frequently dropped into the classrooms and provided feedback to teachers. In the early phase of the school effectiveness process, Yosemite's principal had monitored closely the implementation of changes and had conducted many classroom observations, as had his resource teachers. The principal's monitoring decreased significantly as a result of the implementation of the four track year-round schedule. This lack of monitoring was noted by both the principal and the teachers and seemed to have had an impact on both the strength of the academic focus of the school and the implementation of new instructional strategies.

Conclusion: In the more effective schools, the principal and curriculum committees played a more active role in monitoring the implementation of staff development training, the school improvement plan, and student achievement gains. Principals can be distracted from the monitoring process by other school management issues or district demands on their time. The consequences of less monitoring appeared to be diminished implementation of staff development programs and weaker academic press or focus.

Instructional Strategies and Staff Development

As a result of both site and district staff development programs, new instructional strategies were being implemented in all eight schools. The major difference was in the degree and uniformity of implementation and the length of time such practices had been in place. For example, the staff at Whitney, Sequoia, Lassen, Pinyon, and Yosemite had all been trained in a clinical teaching-supervision model through districtwide staff development. The training had generally occurred between 1985 and 1987. New staff members were required to participate in clinical teaching inservices during their first year of employment. In contrast, at Shasta, Sierra, and Tahoe training of some staff members in the Essential Elements of Instruction (EEI) had begun only as recently as 1987–88. During the next two years, the principals and trained staff members were to train the rest of the staff members at their site. The staff at Sierra, which had developed an extensive staff development program, were pleased with the model and seemed to be looking forward to being trained by their own staff members. In contrast, some staff members interviewed at Tahoe expressed hostility toward the EEI model and the expectation that teachers were to change teaching behaviors.

A similar pattern was found in the training on how to use math manipulatives, hands-on science, and cooperative learning. Training in teaching writing as a process did not fit the same model. The entire staff at Sierra, one of the less effective schools, was one of the first among the eight schools to be extensively trained in the Writing Project. In contrast, the staff at Whitney had received only one workshop in the writing process. Teachers at Yosemite and Pinyon were being trained in 1987–88 through a series of district workshops. As mentioned in the Tahoe case study, training in teaching writing as a process was the first schoolwide staff development experience for the school.

Staff development and school improvement are closely linked. Teachers cannot improve their instructional practices unless they are given time and opportunities to learn and practice new skills. There was high agreement across all schools that principals encouraged participation in staff development and promoted staff development activities. Almost all teachers also agreed that the staff development activities helped them acquire new knowledge and skills and to apply them in the classroom. Again most teachers in most schools agreed (with the exceptions of Lassen where 64 per cent agreed and Yosemite where 52 per cent agreed), that staff development was based on school goals.

Two problems regarding staff development surfaced in the surveys and interviews: First, most teachers in more effective and less effective schools agreed that staff development was not evaluated on the basis of use in the classroom. Second, a number of staff members felt that there was a lack of sufficient training in new programs or instructional strategies and lack of follow-through during the implementation phase. This problem was identified in research on implementation of change (Fullan, 1982; Fullan and Pomfret, 1977; Hall and Hord, 1987;

Huberman, 1983; Huberman and Miles, 1984). It is a problem that can be especially acute in a school engaging in school improvement, because several changes are being implemented at once. The staff at Sequoia, a school that showed marked improvement in student achievement in the last three years, felt that their staff development program had improved in three ways. First, staff development tended to be more focused, with several sessions being held on a single topic, so that skills could be better learned. Second, they felt there was more follow-through, because they were discussing implementation strategies and problems in staff meetings or grade level teams. Third, they felt that staff development activities were showing them how to integrate the curriculum and address the multiplicity of skills and subjects that they were required to teach.

As the case study of Whitney showed, the principal addressed the issue of follow-through after staff development by monitoring lesson plans and collection of class work. In the case of Pinyon, Yosemite, Whitney, Lassen, and Sequoia, follow-through was monitored through classroom observations. In the early days of Yosemite's improvement process, much emphasis was placed on increasing teachers' repertoire of instructional strategies. The mathematics and reading resource teachers, as well as the principal, played critical roles in assisting teachers in implementing new teaching strategies in their classrooms. The staff at Sierra and Tahoe, the two least effective schools, expressed frustration that often there was no follow-through nor sufficient refresher courses so that new skills could become internalized.

Mentor teachers or teachers who had received special training in a particular instructional strategy proved helpful in reinforcing and sustaining the implementation of staff development activities. This role for mentors was part of the original intention of the California mentor program, but one that has not always been realized (Little, 1989). The staff at Sequoia, Pinyon and Whitney expressed appreciation for having the 'experts' on their site who were able to assist them.

Although Shasta had difficulty is sustaining the same level of achievement growth as some of the other more effective schools, the staff efforts to improve oral language skills represented an interesting model. The staff, by and large, fit Fullan, Bennett, Rolheiser-Bennett's (1990) description of teacher as learner. Efforts made to improve oral language skills illustrate the interplay of the four key components of teacher as learner identified by Fullan and his colleagues: technical, reflective, researcher, and collaborator. The teachers had to learn through inservices and readings the technical knowledge needed to improve the development of oral language skills. To develop materials and implement the program, staff members met frequently. These regular meetings brought them together in collaborative work groups. The school had undertaken other collaborative efforts in the past so that the norm of collegiality existed and facilitated their cooperative effort. The program implementation involved experimentation and action research. After the first year, the staff reconvened to reflect on what had occurred and to modify the program in ways that would strengthen it and increase its impact on students. According to the teachers interviewed, the effort had resulted in the development of better oral language skills. Since oral language is not directly tested on the CAP test, the benefits of the staff's labor were not shown in higher test scores, especially in the short time frame of this study. The approach represents a model of staff development and improvement that, applied to other areas, has the potential of greatly enhanced student achievement. (Fullan 1990;

Fullan, Bennett, Rolheiser-Bennett, 1990; Joyce and Showers, 1988; Rosenholtz, 1989).

The staff at Sierra and Tahoe, schools that also served large percentages of limited or non-English speaking students, stated in the interviews that they needed a much more systematic approach to teaching oral language; yet they lacked the organizational structures to implement the needed staff development. Furthermore, the norms of collegiality to develop a kindergarten through sixth grade program did not exist.

The results from this study tend to confirm that site-based staff development, frequently led by teachers within the school, was an effective method for improving staff skills and was more likely to have a lasting impact. In the smaller districts, district-led staff development was effective because, in most cases, the entire staff from each school was involved in the training programs. The effectivenss was also enhanced if it was supported by site-based experts who provided on-going coaching. In the larger district, district-conducted staff development did not appear to be as effective because a potpourri of workshops were offered to teachers that frequently had little relation to perceived site needs. In addition, usually only a few members from a site were trained, and there were no provisions for them to become trainers at their own site.

To address some of these problems, the larger district was trying a two-tiered model to train staff in the Essential Elements of Instruction (i.e., the principal and a core of staff members from each site were being trained; they then had the responsibility to train the rest of the staff). This model seemed to offer a more effective approach for staff development in a large district. With a cadre trained at each site, coaching and follow-up, two essential elements for implementation of an innovation (Joyce and Showers, 1988; Little, 1982, 1989), were possible. Sierra's extensive site-based staff development program (discussed in the case study), combined with this model, had the potential of becoming, in Fullan's words, 'an overall strategy for professional and institutional reform' (Fullan, *et al.*, 1990, p. 16). Sierra, however, illustrated the close interaction of the four major components of the effective schools model. The staff development component's potential impact was limited by organizational structures and procedures, other curriculum and instructional issues, and cultural norms that prevented cross grade level collaboration.

Conclusion: Staff development in the more effective schools contributed significantly to increased achievement, because it was of sufficient duration, involved large numbers of staff members, provided time for coaching and sharing of strategies, and the implementation of new skills were monitored by the principal or curriculum committees. School structures, such as team-teaching, classroom observation opportunities, curriculum committees, grade level teams, or lofts, appeared to be important means of reinforcing staff development training. Strong norms of collegiality also tended to reinforce the impact of staff development programs.

Organizational Structures and Procedures

Reports from the Carnegie Forum, *A Nation Prepared: Teachers for the 21st Century* (1886), the Holmes Group, *Tomorrow's Teachers* (1986), the current emphasis on restructuring, and the research of Little (1982, 1989), and Rosenholtz (1989), have all stressed the need for greater roles for teachers in influencing school decisions, playing active leadership roles, and engaging in collaborative professional development. The existence of structures and organizational conditions that support school improvement are essential elements of an effective schools model. Supportive organizational procedures include such aspects as time for joint planning, encouragement of team-teaching, policies that support site-based staff development, and school improvement norms that engage the staff in self-examination and reflection about teaching practices. Supportive structures include grade-level team meetings, curriculum committee, staff meetings that focus on instructional issues, and a school site council or steering committee that has responsibility for developing and monitoring a plan for improvement. Based on interview and survey data, there appeared to be a close link between the existence of collaborative structures and the successful implementation of changes in either school technology or school culture. It proved difficult for the schools in this study to evolve a shared sense of mission, develop norms of collegiality, establish a coordinated curriculum, and sustain high expectations without the existence of collaborative structures to bring teachers together not only in their grade level, but across grade levels and as a whole school.

Committee Structures that Fostered Collaboration

The structures in each school that promoted or inhibited teachers working together can be related to Hargreaves' (cited in Fullan, 1990) typology of school cultures: fragmented individualism, Balkanization[1], contrived collegiality, and collaborative cultures. The two least effective schools had fewer organizational structures that contributed to developing a collaborative culture. At Tahoe, fragmented individualism was the dominate interaction pattern. There was also the danger of some Balkanization among teachers who had been in the school for many years versus the newcomers who were serving on the newly formed principal's core curriculum committee. The loft arrangement at Sierra created a working arrangement that is more typical of the Balkanization found among secondary school departments. Two of the three lofts represented very strong working teams that indeed demonstrated considerable collaborative efforts in planning lessons and team-teaching. Compounding the Balkanization, in the third loft and among the self-contained classrooms there was individual fragmentation. Except for four yearly staff meetings, Sierra did not have committees that cut across grade levels or that involved the staff in collaborative curriculum planning. The staff felt that barriers were being broken through the schoolwide staff development programs, but without other structures that would enable them to share and practice what was being learned, they felt that the unity created through the staff development program was being undermined.

In contrast, there seemed to be much stronger norms of professional collegiality and collaboration in evidence at Whitney, Yosemite, Pinyon, Lassen, Sequoia, and Shasta. All used grade level teams, curriculum committees, school site councils, and regular staff meetings as vehicles for teacher involvement. Teachers in these schools also indicated that informal time in the teachers' lounge at lunch and recess were often devoted to planning and discussion of curriculum and instructional issues. At Sierra, teachers also used their lunch time for planning, but again, they were isolated in their lofts. In the case of Whitney, Pinyon, Yosemite, and Lassen, teachers were frequently involved at the district level on district curriculum committees which were perceived as genuine opportunities for shaping decisions that affected their schools. No doubt the smaller size of these districts contributed to opportunities to impact decisions.

As discussed in the case study of Yosemite, in the early stages of its improvement efforts, the school developed a strong committee structure, and staff members assumed significant roles by researching and sharing new instructional strategies. The extent of their efforts to improve instructional delivery was unique among the study schools. The movement to four track year-round schedule, however, undermined the team efforts, showing fragility of the new working relationships. The days of sharing were replaced by teachers Balkanized into four tracks, with those teaching the bilingual track feeling most isolated and segregated. In addition, there seemed to be a pattern of contrived collegiality emerging as the principal made efforts to bring teachers together across the tracks for specific projects or events but which were not seen as solving the fundamental segregation problem.

Conclusion: The more effective schools had organizational structures such as regular grade level meetings, curriculum committees, and staff meetings that focused on curriculum and instruction. These structures facilitated communication among teachers, helped to build professional collegiality, enabled the faculty to work together, and created a sense of the school as a whole. The less effective schools that lacked these structures had more difficulty implementing and sustaining the changes they were making in other aspects of the transformative process.

Opportunities for Shared Decision-Making

If structures exist for collaboration, a second critical issue is on what topics can teachers collaborate and make decisions. Teachers at all schools were involved in writing the school improvement plan. Only at Tahoe was there some concern about how the new plan being developed by the core curriculum committee would be integrated with the existing school improvement plan on which everyone had worked. In addition, the teachers interviewed at Tahoe felt they had not had a significant role in decision-making in terms of the new plan or other district-made decisions that they were being forced to implement.

The teachers at Lassen, Whitney, Sequoia, Yosemite, and Pinyon taught a prescribed district curriculum. Within that framework, teachers felt they had leeway in applying instructional strategies within their own classroom. Teachers at Lassen and Whitney, in particular, mentioned that they were supported by their administrator to try new approaches. As one teacher at Whitney said, 'There was freedom as long as they met their achievement goal.' The teachers did not indicate disagreement with the curriculum. In fact, at Lassen the teachers felt the district curriculum guide had made a significant impact on helping the school to improve. More significantly, several Lassen teachers stated that the curriculum guide had served as a focal point for grade level discussions. Teachers were now sharing strategies and plans for meeting curriculum objectives. Shasta, Sierra, and Tahoe did not operate with closely prescribed curriculum objectives. One could argue that these teachers had more potential for meaningful involvement in site-level curriculum planning. As cited earlier, the staff at Shasta had been extensively involved in developing an oral language curriculum. This was not the case, however, at Sierra and Tahoe because there were neither the structures nor the time for schoolwide curriculum planning.

Conclusion: Teachers in the more effective schools had clear curriculum guidelines. They felt the guidelines gave the school and themselves needed direction. They felt empowered to shape the instructional processes within their own schools and classrooms. In terms of other aspects of school life teachers expressed the view that they had adequate opportunities to help make decisions. There were strong norms of professional collegiality and structures that enabled teachers to work together.

Instructional Leadership

The term 'instructional leadership', relatively new to educational literature, originated from effective schools research. The term is intended to differentiate between actions of principals needed for school improvement, and the more traditional roles principals fulfill as administrator, building manager, and community relations specialist. The term implies that a principal who is an instructional leader is more actively engaged in instructional issues. In a review of eight effective schools studies, Sweeney (1982) identified six instructional leadership behaviors of principals that were fairly consistent across the studies. These behaviors were:

1 Coordinated instructional programs
2 Emphasized achievement
3 Evaluated pupil progress frequently
4 Established an orderly atmosphere
5 Defined instructional strategies
6 Supported teachers (p. 349)

The studies reviewed by Sweeney were focused primarily on describing schools in low SES communities. More recent studies (Hallinger and Murphy, 1985b; Rowan and Denk, 1984; Teddlie, Falkowski, Stringfield, Desselle, and Garvue, 1984) have compared the behaviors of principals in effective schools in high and low SES communities. Hallinger and Murphy (1989) have characterized the actions of the instructional leader in an effective low SES school in the following way:

> Faced with the task of turning a school around, the principals in effective low SES schools appear more directive and forceful in setting high standards for students and teachers (Hallinger and Murphy, 1985b; Rowan and Denk, 1984). They buffer their schools from the environment and attempt to create a learning climate that communicates high expectations and that rewards students for the desired behavior. (p. 14)

In contrast, in high SES effective schools, their description of the behavior of principals had far less to do with instruction and more to do with community relations.

These principals tend to exert less direct control over the internal operations of the school. The high visibility of parents in and around the school represented a form of environmental control over internal processes. Thus, their role involves maintaining a consensus over the school's direction, mediating the demands and expectations of the community, and smoothing relations between teachers and parents. (Hallinger and Murphy, 1989, p. 15)

These descriptions illustrate two important points. First, the term instructional leadership has remained undefined (Rost, 1987; Scheerens and Creemers, 1989; Van de Grift, 1990). Second, the effort to define the term by describing behaviors may be problematic, because behaviors that are appropriate in one context may not be appropriate in another. In a recent article, Van de Grift (1990) highlighted the difficulties of a behavioral definition of instructional leadership in his critique of several studies of instructional leadership. First, he questioned the validity and reliability of the assessment instruments used in a number of studies to evaluate the principal's instructional leadership. Second, he pointed out that the correlations between the instructional leadership score and student achievement were weak or negative on more than half of the instructional leadership behaviors assessed. Third, he criticized the researchers for not reporting, except in the appendices, areas in which there was a negative correlation or in which principals in more and less effective schools behaved similarly.

Van de Grift also discussed the work of Andrews and Bamburg (1989), which was based on a valid and reliable assessment tool; it showed a significant correlation between the teacher assessment of a principal as being a strong instructional leader and high student achievement. While Van de Grift did not dispute their findings when he conducted a similar study in The Netherlands using teacher assessments of Dutch principals, he did not find the same strong positive correlation with student achievement. In this study, a similar approach to the one used by Andrews and Bamburg in assessing teachers' perceptions of the principal's instructional leadership was employed. However, the measure of effectiveness was aggregated grade level achievement gains at third and sixth grade over four years, not individual pupil gains over two years. While the assessment instrument was similar and has been tested for reliability and construct validity, the items do not describe exactly the same behaviors as either the Washington (Andrews and Bamburg, 1989) Effective Schools survey or the instrument used in the Dutch studies.

The findings from the eight schools involved in this study tend to confirm those of Van de Grift. There was not a significant correlation between the survey results and student achievement. In other words, three schools, Yosemite, Pinyon, and Lassen, which met the criteria of effectiveness, had lower overall mean scores on the instructional leadership correlate than did Shasta and Sierra, Schools which were less effective. This does not mean that instructional leadership was not occurring. Rather the problem may lie in trying to define instructional leadership by specific behaviors in widely varying contexts, using different assessment instruments, and different standards or criteria for determining effectiveness. Foster (1986) has asserted that there is a need to allow the study of leadership 'to be conceptualized differently: it must allow for historical and hermeneutic approaches; it must abandon the search for quantified rigour; it must lose the reductionist and uncritical mentality of orthodox social science.' (p. 9)

Moving a school to greater effectiveness calls for leadership, because it requires a transformation of the school. In the context of this study, leadership is defined as an influence relationship among principal, school staff, students, community, and district staff intended to bring about changes in the culture, school technology, and organization of the school so that there are significant and equitable achievement gains for all ethnic and income groups. Based on this definition, effective schools leadership encompasses four broad dimensions: shared vision or mission, shared leadership, shared learning, and a commitment to change. Based on data from this study and the work of others (Bennis and Nanus, 1985; Fullan, *et al.*, 1990; Rosenholtz, 1989; Rosow and Zager; 1989; Rossman, Corbett, and Firestone, 1988), these dimensions of leadership are more likely to bring about long lasting change that transforms the school to an institution where all children are enabled to master the basic curriculum and to develop as learners.

Shared Vision

As discussed above, the staff in the more effective schools were able to articulate a more consistent and coherent statement of the school's mission. In the two least effective schools a shared mission was not expressed. The principal at Tahoe had a sense of what he wanted to accomplish. His vision was a transforming one. He clearly wanted to raise achievement levels and increase the academic success rate of his largely poor and limited-English speaking students. By the conclusion of this study, he had not yet developed a shared vision with his staff. At Sierra, the staff shared a common social goal for students, but there was not a shared vision in regard to academic achievement goals.

The shared visions at the more effective schools were continually evolving. Rost (1987) has stressed that 'purpose is usually not static but is constantly changing as leaders and followers come and go, as the influence process works its effects on both leaders and followers, and as circumstances, environment, and wants and needs impact on the relationship.' (p. 3) One of the influencing and mediating factors in both sets of schools was student gains or lack thereof on standardized tests. As student achievement rose, it appears that the staff in the more effective schools developed a stronger academic mission and began to believe that all children could learn the intended curriculum. In the most effective schools the vision was jointly created and recreated by principal and staff; it was not mandated by the leader. For example, at Whitney in the first few years, safety and order was the primary mission. In time, as achievement began to rise, a clear academic focus emerged. In contrast, as long as Sierra and Tahoe continued to have no achievement gains, it was difficult to develop a shared vision that focused on academic achievement. The district's vision of increased test scores was not shared by the schools.

Commitment to Change

Vision has been defined as *what can and should be*. Thus by definition if a school staff has a shared vision, there is a commitment to change. To increase a school's effectiveness requires vision, commitment to change, and a significant transformation. It requires developing fundamentally different assumptions about the function of schools, the achievement of students, and the distribution of educational benefits. Traditional beliefs about schools, especially beliefs in the sanctity of the bell-shaped curve, grouping practices, and A to F grades, are hard to change. It is no wonder that the term 'maverick' is frequently used to describe leaders in the early descriptions of inner city effective schools.

Like vision, the commitment to change seemed much more prevalent among staff members in the more effective schools than in the less effective schools. One possible explanation for this willingness to change is that early changes in some aspects of the transformative process — such as implementing a schoolwide discipline code, establishing a rewards or recognition program, aligning the curriculum, or creating a math lab produced desired results. Consequently, teachers were then more willing to engage in continued change efforts. The less effective schools, on the other hand, had not been as successful in seeing their change efforts achieve the desired results — an improvement in test scores. This led the staff to look elsewhere for explanations of why they had not improved and diminished their enthusiasm for additional changes. At both Sierra and Tahoe the staff expressed frustrations at the changes in the community and wished that parents would change and behave more like middle-class white parents, or in one case, like middle-class Filipino parents. As one teacher at Sierra said, 'We are doing all we can do.' In contrast, teachers at Whitney talked about wanting to get all students to the ninetieth percentile. The principal at Tahoe knew he had not reached his goal, and he was committed to continued efforts by himself and his staff. Unfortunately, the staff that were interviewed did not believe the goal was possible and were not fully part of the change effort; they therefore did not share the same commitment to change.

Shared Leadership

The early effective schools studies identified strong instructional leadership, especially by the principal, as one of the components of an effective school. (See the lists of characteristics of Purkey and Smith, 1983, Figure 1.2, and Murphy, Hallinger and Mesa, 1985, Figure 1.3, presented in Chapter 1). A thesis presented in this book is that leadership is not merely a component of an effective school but is the overarching and driving force that unites the school culture, school technology and organizational structures in such a way as to bring about enhanced student achievement. A second major thesis is that leadership is shared. These concepts were depicted in Figure 1.4 in Chapter 1. Fullan, Bennett, and Rolheiser-Bennett (1990) in their model of school improvement articulated a similar view regarding leadership. Leadership was eliminated as a separate component and was identified as one of two key factors that drove their school improvement framework.

> The second driving force for change is leadership and mobilization. We explicitly rejected the idea that leadership be a particular component of the framework. Leadership can, does, and must come from a variety of different sources. Any framework must allow for the fact that leadership

critical for success comes from different sources in different situations (and different sources in the same situation over time). Leadership for success variously comes from the principal, key teachers, the super-intendent, parents, trustees, curriculum consultants, governments, universities, etc. As the list reveals, the driving force for change can initially come from inside or outside the school, and from a variety of different roles. Once the model is fully functioning, leadership does indeed come from multiple sources simultaneously. Certainly the principal, for example, is key, but leadership must be mobilized on multiple fronts for long term development to occur. (Fullan, 1990, p. 16)

Fullan's, *et al.* (1990) assertion that leadership can be exercised by numerous players both inside and outside the school, was confirmed in this study. It was clear in the cases of Whitney, Yosemite, Pinyon, Sequoia, and Lassen that district leadership played a role in several key instances (e.g., curriculum alignment, test analysis, staff development) that enabled the more effective schools to change faster than was possible in the less effective schools. State leadership dramatically affected curriculum, especially in the area of language arts and mathematics.

At the school site level, Hord, Stiegelbauer and Hall (1984) also found that in more effective schools, principals did not lead by themselves. There were often one or two other change agents who played critical roles. Andrews when interviewed by Brandt (1987) stated that in his analysis of principal leadership, principals who were perceived as strong leaders by teachers were also the most active in nurturing leadership in others, especially teachers. It is through shared leadership that a group can be mobilized for action. As was discussed at several points in the four case-studies, teachers were actively involved in leadership roles. This was especially true in the most effective schools. The principals at Pinyon and Sequoia had a talented pool of mentor teachers on which to draw for instructional leadership. The principals at Whitney and Yosemite trained and supported teacher leaders. In contrast, in the less effective schools, collaborative leadership was not the norm. At Sierra, there were loft leaders, but the loft structure inhibited them from becoming schoolwide leaders. At Tahoe, the principal had made some beginning efforts to develop leadership by establishing the core curriculum committee. However, by the conclusion of this study, it had not been in operation for a sufficient period of time to assess its impact on the school and on student achievement.

This study tends to confirm that leadership by principals, teachers, and district and state officials is both central and essential to school transformation and enhanced student effectiveness. The data from this study suggest that the transformation of Whitney, Pinyon, Yosemite, and Lassen and Sequoia into more effective schools occurred because the principal and staff led the school to a new place through a comprehensive approach that altered and integrated the school's culture, technology and organizational structures in ways that better supported student learning. The data from Whitney strongly indicated that the principal engaged in significant leadership acts, perhaps the most important being the conscious development of teacher leadership. The data from Yosemite clearly support the need for both principal and staff leadership. The Yosemite staff found that when the principal's leadership in the instructional and improvement roles was withdrawn, it was difficult for teacher leadership to sustain itself in these areas as well. Equally important are the observations from Tahoe and

Sierra, the least effective schools, that in the absence of mechanisms that develop or encourage schoolwide shared leadership, the leadership role of the principal appears to be made more difficult.

Shared Learning

A unique contribution of the Fullan, Bennett, and Rolheiser-Bennett (1990) model of school improvement and institutional development is the central place they have given to *teacher as learner*. The term teacher in their model is broadly conceived as 'anybody at the school level who is a professional educator, for example, classroom teachers, teacher leaders, head teachers, vice-principals, and principals' (p. 15). They conceive the *teacher as learner* to be the bridge that links school improvement to classroom improvement. The point that is not as clearly made in this model is that the *teacher as learner* is also central to leadership. If leadership is conceived as an influence relationship, then learning and teaching among adults at the school must be key features of the influence process. If leadership is bringing about 'real intended change' (Rost, 1987), continuous learning is absolutely essential. Without a critical diagnosis of the present status and vigorous exploration of ways to move from the current to the desired condition, change is not likely to occur. Perhaps one of the most significant paradoxes of leadership is the need for vision and direction and at the same time the need and willingness to reshape the vision and direction through the process of continuous learning.

The interviews with the principals revealed that the principals in all eight schools were learners. They had not all been equally successful in achieving the goals they had intended, but all were reflective and thoughtful about the processes in which they and the staff had been engaged. Also, they all encouraged learning by their staff. The excitement expressed by staff members in all eight schools regarding their use of cooperative learning or of literature in their reading program attested to the learning they had done in the last four years. Even though Sierra had not had student achievement gains to celebrate, the staff was genuinely pleased and excited by the staff development they had undertaken. They all felt that they were better teachers as a result. Only Tahoe had failed to develop a strong learning culture. While not all principals and their staff had been successful in transforming their schools into achievement cultures, all but one had been successful in establishing a learning culture and moving closer to the model of *teacher as learner*.

In summary, in all eight schools leadership was taking place. Like many of the other dimensions of effectiveness, the differences were in degree. The more effective schools exhibited higher levels of shared vision, commitment to change, shared leadership, and shared learning.

Conclusion: Analyzing and assessing specific behaviors of principals and other leaders may be helpful, especially in guiding actions that will increase effectiveness in particular contexts; however, these specific behaviors may not capture the essence of leadership. A broader definition of leadership as an influence relationship among principal, staff, community, and district, that focuses on shared leadership, shared vision, commitment to change, and shared learning helps to explain the way leadership serves as the driving force in school improvement and brings about changes in the other three components so that the outcome is improved achievement for all students.

Summary and Conclusions

This chapter has drawn together the data from the eight schools involved in this study. As was outlined in Chapter 2, there are important differences among these schools — in size, in demographics, in age of the school, in yearly school schedules, in length of time involved in the school effectiveness efforts, in the district context, and in the school culture that has evolved over the years. All of these schools are similar in one important aspect: the principal and staff were engaged in efforts to increase student achievement. Understanding how their improvement efforts unfolded — the recurring themes, the stumbling blocks, and the factors that enhanced the process — has been the purpose of the in-depth case-studies presented in chapters 3–6 and this chapter's cross-case analysis.

Using the open systems model (Figure 1.1) presented in Chapter 1, it is possible to see the impact of changing inputs on the transformative process. The two most significant were growth in student enrollments and changes in principalships. How these input changes were handled in the transformative process affected the school's overall efforts to improve. This study has confirmed that schools can make a difference in enhancing the achievement of students from ethnically diverse, low-income families. The case studies indicate that the challenges to raise that achievement, however, are considerable, especially if low-income students are the predominant group.

Figure 1.1 also tried to capture the embedded nature of schools and their systems. As the case-studies illustrated, the school is shaped by the district in which it is located. Some district actions proved helpful and essential to the school-site efforts to improve; other actions appeared to be counterproductive. Community pressures and district policies were significant environmental forces in the decision of Yosemite's principal to institute a gifted and bilingual track as the four track year-round schedule was established. The case-study data also showed the impact of the California Department of Education inputs. Each school's curriculum was being altered through the new curriculum frameworks. The new state test to assess students' writing would also soon be impacting the instructional program. The teachers, on the whole, at each school did not view the state input changes negatively. Nevertheless, each district and school was faced with the challenges of staff training and development which would translate the rhetoric and theory of the frameworks into practice. Depending on factors in the transformative process, the schools differed in how rapidly and successfully they were achieving this translation.

Schools, in large measure, do not have control over inputs or other environmental perturbations that buffet and effect their operation. In most of the current efforts to restructure schools (e.g., Rochester, NY; Dade County, FL; San Diego, CA), inputs have remained largely unchanged. Only schools of choice that are proposed in some restructuring schemes will have more say over student inputs. Therefore, it is the transformative process of schooling over which the staff has control and through which changes are made that will lead to different student outcomes. Figure 4.1 in Chapter 1 depicts the transformative process that has been the central focus of this study. The four components presented (Climate and Culture, School Technology, Organizational Structures and Procedures, and Leadership) have served as the framework for examining the transformative process. The case studies have attempted to document the changes that occurred in each component and the interrelationships among the components. For the case-studies and cross-case analysis, several overall conclusions can be drawn that seem to indicate why some schools were able to achieve a higher level of effectiveness than others. First, creating organizational structures that bring the staff together and that support the change efforts appeared to be crucial to changes in outcomes. The structures needed to provide multiple opportunities for participation so that the whole staff was involved. The structures needed to be both horizontal and vertical in design so that all aspects of school life were brought together. Without these structures, the schools seemed to lack the scaffolding on which to build and sustain other improvements.

Second, while climate and school environment changes often needed to be a first step in the improvement process, it was changes in the school technology that were more likely to lead to increased student achievement. However, implementing changes in the teaching and learning process were far more difficult to carry out, especially if they required thoughtful and time-consuming staff development. Some of the case-study schools developed models for staff development and teacher growth that were helping them to succeed in this challenging area.

Third, the beliefs about students' abilities to learn, the power and role of family background in student learning, the relationship between hard work and natural ability in student achievement, and teachers' beliefs in their competency to teach all children are deeply held beliefs and norms that are difficult to change. Changes in these beliefs began to emerge only when there was sufficient data that showed a link between teacher efforts and student achievement gains.

Fourth, the case-study data indicate that leadership is needed at all levels — state, district and school site — and among all participants — state and district administrators, principals, and teachers in order to achieve and sustain school improvement and effectiveness. The case-study data also suggest that effective schools leadership is more that instructional leadership. All aspects of the transformative process will need to be addressed, guided, and coordinated to achieve improved outcomes for students.

The next chapter returns to the data gathered from teachers in the case-study schools and presents teacher views on school improvement. In the school improvement and restructuring literature there is much talk about the need for teacher leadership and for enhanced roles for teachers. It seems that there is a need to talk with teachers who have been involved in trying to improve their schools to see what guidance they would give on how schools can be improved. The topic is one that needs much more exploration than is possible in this brief chapter, but the views of the teachers involved in the case-study schools can provide a place to begin.

Finally, Chapter 9 draws together the data from this and other school effectiveness studies to see what lessons might be learned that will be helpful to schools involved in restructuring. Much has been learned about the processes of improvement in the last twenty years, it is important for that information to be used, as schools continue their efforts to help all children learn.

Note

1   The term Balkanization is derived from the breakup of the Balkans after World War I into small, mutually hostile political units.

Chapter 8

Teacher Views on School Improvement

A major thrust of the restructuring movement is the involvement of teachers in school-based management and the development of a professional culture (Lieberman, 1988). The goal is to increase student achievement by giving teachers more voice in decision-making and expanding teacher leadership roles. Rosenholtz (1989) in her book, *Teachers' Workplace*, provided data that showed the significance of teacher collaboration, decision-making, shared goals, team-teaching and involvement on teacher commitment to the profession and student achievement. Teachers' certainty about their craft and their skills were enhanced when teachers had time to talk and work with each other. As the case-studies and cross-case analysis in this study revealed, extensive involvement by staff in decision-making and structures that facilitated collaboration were hallmarks of the most effective schools. The purpose of this chapter is to analyze how teachers themselves define an effective school and describe the improvement process necessary to reach their goal. Do teachers in the most effective schools differ in their views about what is an effective school or how to improve schools compared to teachers in the least effective schools? How close do teacher views on improvement match empirical data? To answer these questions, teachers in each school were asked the following two questions: 1) If your school was described as an effective school what would that mean to you? 2) Think of yourself as a consultant to another school and based on what you have learned from your experiences in the improvement process, what would you recommend other schools do, what should be done differently? (See Appendix B).

Teachers responded quickly and succinctly to the first question, but found the second one to be a challenge. Most of the teachers could not talk about improvement in the abstract, but continued to talk about their own school. The responses to the questions, however, are enlightening. First, there were consistent responses across all schools about what an effective school meant to these teachers. Second, as will be seen, the responses indicate that teachers have important knowledge about the improvement process. The recommendations the teachers made closely paralleled the factors that Lieberman (1986, 1988), Little (1986), Rosenholtz (1989), this study, and others have found to be most important in enhancing student achievement. In other words, the teachers in these schools, which had been involved in school improvement efforts for over five years, identified many of the factors research has shown essential to school improvement.

Third, teachers in the schools that had made the least progress in terms of student achievement gave recommendations that were similar to their counterparts in the more successful schools. The difference was that the teachers in the least effective schools stated their recommendations in terms of *what should be done that they were not doing*, whereas the teachers in the other schools expressed their recommendations in terms of continuing or refining the successful practices they had already begun. Only one teacher in the least effective school in the sample said 'to just continue what they were doing; it would work if the students were different (meaning more affluent, less non-English speaking students) from the ones they were trying to teach'. Overall, the teachers in the least successful schools knew what needed to be done even if all the forces necessary to move from theory to practice had not coalesced in their own schools.

The questions posed to teachers were open-ended ones, and responses varied within each school, especially in regard to the question on how to improve. Analysis of the responses, however, revealed several important common and reoccurring themes that were addressed by teachers in every school. In response to the first question, the definition of an effective school, three major themes emerged and were mentioned by almost every teacher in every school. The themes were:

1 children would be learning what was expected (the intended curriculum) to their fullest potential;
2 children would be happy and enjoy coming to school;
3 teachers would be working together in a systematic way to bring about improvement.

One or two teachers in six of the schools mentioned that good discipline was essential to the definition. Teachers in three of the highest achieving schools mentioned the importance of equality of outcomes. In the lowest achieving school in the sample, Tahoe, parent involvement was mentioned as an essential aspect of effectiveness by four of the teachers, while it was mentioned only once in two other schools. This response is important because it indicates that the teachers see the potential of increased student achievement as only partially in their control.

In response to the second question regarding how to improve, the themes addressed many of the important aspects of school life described in the case studies. The teachers' responses touched on key aspects of school organizational structures and procedures, school technology, and school culture and climate. Leadership, particularly by the principal, was not discussed directly, but was embedded in some of the comments. For purposes of discussion the issues raised by the teachers have been clustered under these broad headings, however, their responses illustrate the overlapping and interactive nature of organization, culture and technology and the overarching aspect of leadership in creating congruence and wholeness in the school.

Shared Decision-Making and Collaboration

The importance of organizational structures and procedures to foster shared decision-making and collaboration dominated all of the responses. Teachers verified that they thought opportunities for shared decision-making were of paramount importance to school improvement. The teachers' views on the importance of shared decision-making are in line with current calls in the restructuring literature for greater teacher involvement and participation in school decision-making and governance (Barth, 1990; The Carnegie Task Force, 1986; The Holmes Group, 1986; Schlechty, 1990). However, two important points can be gleaned from the teachers' comments that need to be considered seriously in discussions about restructuring and shared decision-making. First, the teachers did not see participation in shared decision-making as an end in itself, but rather as the essential means to reaching their goals of improved student achievement and school effectiveness. Second, the teachers were most concerned about making decisions in regard to curriculum and instructional practices, not on overall school governance, budgetary and administrative matters. In the minimal amount of time available to teachers to participate in shared decision-making, the teachers decision-making seemed to focus primarily on what mattered to them the most — their classrooms, their teaching, and students' learning. The structures that enabled these teachers to participate in making decisions about the issues that mattered to them were grade level team meetings, schoolwide curriculum committees, school site councils, and faculty meetings. The opportunities for shared schoolwide decision-making, however, were greater in the more effective schools than in the less effective schools. In their recommendations to others, teachers in both types of schools stressed the importance of shared decision-making and the need to create structures to facilitate it.

- One of our strengths I'd keep is teacher involvement in instructional decisions, especially on curriculum committees.
- Everyone needs to be involved in writing the school plan, through both curriculum committees and grade level teams.
- Organization is terribly important, the relationship and articulation between staff members and grade levels. There is no end to what can be accomplished by group support.
- Well, obviously I think the strength comes from our cooperation as a team and that teacher input is important in making decisions that effect things that we know most about — the classroom.
- Staff involvement is critical to school improvement. Committees need to be set up in areas of instruction, and there needs to be strong grade level teams to share ideas and work together.

In the least effective school, one teacher's comment was typical of the concern for greater involvement in decision-making.

Don't follow in our footsteps. Do more monitoring of what is going on. Have clear goals about where you want to go. *Have greater involvement of staff in decision-making* (emphasis added). There is a need to build up and support staff, not just monitor in a negative way.

By bringing staff together to make decision, the principals in these schools were fostering collaboration and problem-solving and diminishing the isolation that teachers so frequently feel. The comment of the last teacher reveals the frustration of a teacher cut off from the decision-making process. Involvement in collaborative instructional and curriculum decision-making is crucial for several reasons. First, it empowers and enables teachers in their craft. Rosenholtz found that:

> The degree of teacher collaboration strongly and independently predicts teacher certainty. Teachers who share their ideas, who unabashedly offer and solicit advice and assistance, and who interact substantively with a greater number of colleagues, expand their pedagogical options and minimize their uncertainty. (p. 111, 1989)

Furthermore, in the process of making decisions, Rosenholtz speculates that as teachers make conscious decisions that require them to evaluate strategies, ideas, and materials on behalf of the whole school, they also learn to reflect and modify their own classroom behavior.

Second, shared decision-making creates a schoolwide focus and increases mutual responsibility for outcomes. As Barth (1988) has argued:

> When others are deciding, teachers can resist, lobby, hold out, and in inventive ways attempt to influence a situation to their own advantage. When teachers work for the common good, they may lose a large measure of self-interest in the outcome. With leadership and responsibility comes the need to see others' points of view and act fairly in their eye. (p. 133)

Barth is not sure many teachers are willing to make this trade; however, the teachers in the schools in this study had had enough experience with shared decision-making to be convinced that its benefits outweighed its drawbacks. Third, shared decision-making and collaborative structures provide opportunities for teachers to be leaders. In each school, as committees were established, especially the curriculum committee, teachers had opportunities to volunteer for those areas or topics that most appealed to them or in which they had the most expertise. As teachers working in a particular area became more knowledgeable, they in turn led the staff in inservices or assisted their grade-level team mates. Throughout the interviews, teachers expressed appreciation for the expertise and knowledge of their colleagues.

School Structures Facilitate a School Culture of Open Communication and Shared Goals

In discussing the relationship of communications to shared goals, teachers were linking the importance of structures to climate and culture. The establishment of grade-level teams, curriculum committees, and total staff involvement in the development of their school improvement plans created many opportunities for teachers to communicate and share ideas with each other. The teachers interviewed in all schools expressed the importance of communication to the improvement process.

- Improvement requires openness and time for discussion with colleagues.
- To improve, we need to pull together, talk with each other constantly, talk about ideas, observe others and team together. The principal has a important role in communication through an open-door policy and by building an awareness among staff through discussion of issues, being open and flexible to talk about issues, but not intimidating teachers.
- Our clear focus is getting stronger, because we talk so much with one another and work together.

The critical importance of communication was captured by a teacher at Lassen who had been very active in the improvement process, but who would soon be moving to a new school with the principal. Several of the teachers from Lassen, the principal, and others teachers who had been selected were now meeting monthly to be ready when the new school opened.

I can already see the communication we have here will carry over to the other school. When we left a meeting last night, we were all so excited talking to each other, you kind of spark each other and you can't stop. I couldn't sleep last night; it was all so exciting. So I would really like to see that kind of communication continued. Not in an overly organized way but through good meetings and the open-door policy and access-ibility of the principal.

In the two schools that had not improved significantly, the value of commun-ication was also stressed. Expressed in terms of their own context, teachers in both schools focused on the need to have more total schoolwide communications as a prerequisite to school improvement. Neither of these least effective schools, however, had sufficient schoolwide structures in place to foster the communica-tion the teachers desired and thought necessary for an improvement process to be successful.

Rosenholtz (1989) found that the nature of talk or communication distin-guished schools with high and low levels of goal consensus. In high consensus schools, curriculum and instruction were mentioned as significant topics of discus-sion among teachers. In low consensus schools, social activities and complaints about student behavior were more common topics. While this study did not examine the nature of the talk in the higher achieving and lower achieving schools, the responses to the question in both effective and less effective schools indicated that the teachers were not thinking about communication as idle chatter, but communication about goals, curriculum and instructional practices. Teachers in this study understood the importance of goals and communicating about goals as illustrated by their responses to the question on how to improve.

- The most important thing for the school to do is to establish what is important for them; creating a clear school mission so that what you are doing is going in that direction, so that it's not fragmented.
- The staff needs to develop a shared belief about the potential of children to learn, regardless of their background.
- One of the things we've done already (teacher is moving to a new school), is we've written our SIP (School Improvement Program) plan. We will

not be an SIP school for several years, but we all felt it was important to have a common goal.
- We need to have better communication about what the goals really are.
- The school needs to set new goals regularly and use the 'We Agree' process as a way of sharing ideas and talking to each other to come up with common goals.
- To be effective, we must be willing to work hard as a total staff to accomplish our goals.

Shared goals, an aspect of a school's climate and culture, and effective communication and collaborative structures are closely linked and need to be viewed as an interrelated process. Some of the current literature on organizational development and change stresses the creation of a vision and establishment of a mission and goals as essential acts of leadership necessary to bring about organizational renewal. The vision-creation is usually done by the leader and communicated to followers (Bennis and Nanus, 1985). As Helgesen (1990) has stated, vision is a one-way process. 'A vision may exist alone, in the mind of a single human being — it can still be a vision if it remains uncommunicated.' Helgesen further argued that:

> Vision has become one of the buzz-words of the decade. It can be grand-sounding way of referring to many things: a long-range plan, a particular focus or even just the devising of a corporate slogan. In my speechwriting unit, when floundering at the top led to rampant rumors and mistrust within the company, we speechwriters were charged with printing up plastic vision cards as a way of assuring everyone that management was up to the task of imaginative leadership. (p. 221)

The problem with this notion of vision is that it may or may not lead to shared goals. There may be a need to turn vision on its head. Vision may not be the beginning of the improvement process, but the result of the process if channels for communication and collaboration are developed. McLaughlin and Yee (1988) found in their survey of teachers that informal exchanges with teachers about instructional practices to be far more helpful than formal university courses or district-sponsored staff development. They go on to stress that, 'In schools with low levels of collegial exchange, it is difficult to create shared norms or to build a sense of common purpose for instructional improvement. . . . In more isolated environments, teachers do not often get beyond complaining about difficult kids.' (p. 35) One of the teachers in this study summarized the relationship between collegiality and developing a shared vision this way: 'A staff must be cohesive, grow together, feel comfortable with change. Once this is in place they can start assessing, identifying weak spots, set goals, develop an improvement plan, develop strategies and then evaluate.'

A feminist perspective may be helpful in giving insight into the relationship between collegiality and shared goals. Helgesen found that the women leaders she studied emphasized 'the role of voice over that of vision. The woman leader's voice is a means both for presenting herself and what she knows about the world, and for eliciting a response' (1990, pp. 223–224). McLaughlin and Yee (1988) spoke of a similar kind of leadership voice when they quoted one of the teachers in their study who said:

The current principal works so hard and is so visible that teachers are motived to work harder, too. Also, she talks to teachers as equals, not down to them. She says things like "what are *we* going to do," "*we* have a problem," "this is what *we* need to do, I can't do it myself". "This is something *we* have to live with." (Italics in the original, p. 32)

The teachers in the effective schools in this study were brought together not so much by a common vision, but rather through dialogue and communication that gave them opportunities to express their voices both formally and informally. The research on women's ways of knowing and perceiving (Belenky, Clinchy, Goldberger, and Tarule, 1989) has documented the importance to women of interconnectedness with both others and information established through dialogue. Given that the majority of teachers in these schools were women, it is not surprising that the women saw the close link between communication and goal development. The implications for school improvement are significant: school improvement will be enhanced by leaders who establish collegial structures that facilitate dialogue and the development of the teachers' voice as the means for developing school goals and vision. Visions of an effective school or a restructured school will emerge over time as part of the process if there are ample opportunities for teachers to express their voice.

Linking School Culture and School Technology

The climate and cultural frame and school technology frame are brought together through teacher discussions of a need for a schoolwide focus. Teachers in all schools expressed the need for activities and actions that would bring the total school together. Improvement is not just in the hands of the individual teacher. It requires the involvement of all staff and the focus on all children. Areas for schoolwide focus that were mentioned by some of the teachers were a well-integrated kindergarten-sixth grade curriculum, schoolwide discipline, student recognition, staff development, and involvement in writing the school improvement plan. Some of the comments addressing these issues were:

- I would bring about a uniform program K-6.
- Having clear objectives K-6 is essential.
- A tight schoolwide discipline plan is essential.
- Establishing a schoolwide discipline plan really helped.
- Be sure there is a good discipline plan adhered to throughout the school.
- Students need more schoolwide recognition. It needs to come from the principal — that is different from getting recognition from me. There needs to be more schoolwide involvement and the top has to play a more active role in pulling us together.

Rosenholtz found in her study a close relationship between schoolwide discipline plans, development of shared goals, and increased teacher commitment. 'For its part, the extent to which student conduct is choreographed schoolwide seems a necessary prerequisite for goal consensus, as teachers and principals remove those obstacles that stand in the way of instructional goals' (1989, p. 27). Teacher commitment to teaching was greatly undermined, if discipline in the classroom was an unresolved issue. Without a schoolwide discipline plan, teachers felt isolated and did not tend to turn to their colleagues for support and help. The teachers in these schools understood Rosenholtz's observations. In fact, instituting a schoolwide discipline plan was not only one of the first improvement acts in most of these schools, but also was one of the first activities that brought teachers together in a collegial relationship. Another area of collaboration for teachers had been in the development of the school improvement plan. If they had not been involved, they knew they should have been.

- The development of the school improvement plan has to involve everyone.
- I would like to bring about a uniform program K-6. It seems in K-3 we have a very strong program, motivated teachers that will stand on their heads to get the job done. Somehow we cross that line at 4th grade.
- I think the emphasis should be on a cohesive staff. I know this isn't going to be easy, but if you have teachers working together for the good of all kids, not only are they (the staff) going to be friendly and supportive, but the children are going to feel that support, too.
- There was a real effort to involve all teachers in the beginning. . . . This is now more difficult with four tracks. The problem with the four tracks is that someone is always missing the meeting, always missing a piece of what has been decided.
- Be willing to work as a total staff to accomplish our goals.

A final critical area that teachers recognized as essential to developing a unified culture was the provision of schoolwide staff development, especially on topics that dealt with curriculum and instructional practices. As was illustrated in the case studies and cross-case analysis, staff development was most effective when it was school based, or if not held at the school, was an inservice in which all or most staff participated and was linked to identified school needs. The benefits of such learning opportunities were not lost upon these teachers.

- To improve, a school needs to support improvement with schoolwide inservices that unite the staff and create a common language.
- Whole school staff development is essential.
- We need to keep the inservices, especially where the total staff is involved.

Assessment and Monitoring of School and Student Progress

A critical aspect of the curriculum and instructional component is using test data to monitor student progress and assessing the effectiveness of school programs. While it was not as frequently mentioned as some of the topics discussed above, two or more teachers interviewed in each school mentioned the need to closely monitor student progress, to review programs, and makes changes that were indicated by assessment data. The teacher responses indicate that on the whole these schools, in Rosenholtz' terms, were *learning enriched* schools (Rosenholtz, 1989, p. 80). The teachers understand not only the importance of continued staff development, but also the learning potential from reflecting on their own efforts to improve.

- To improve, we need to look at ourselves honestly, collect self-evaluative data and reflect on it. We need to look to see if the quality criteria are in place, and be fully aware of the state frameworks.
- Self-study is critical; be true. Don't assume anything, and make sure what you expect is really there. Keep what is effective and see how you can improve on it. See what is weak and get busy improving it. Visit other schools to see how we might do things better.
- Use the effective schools process to collect data. Constantly review the school program. Where are we going? Are we being effective?
- One thing that has been really helpful is sitting down with other teachers and talking about things that we think we need to do to improve the school. . . . Then we addressed what needed to be done and actually formed a committee that spent some time to develop a plan.
- Focus in on curriculum and assess more frequently.
- Pay attention to what makes a difference, especially in curriculum.
- Everyone needs to become more familiar with the Program Quality Review process as a way of monitoring and reviewing school programs.
- Monitoring of children's progress is essential.

All of these schools have benefited from having several monitoring tools at their disposal: the school effectiveness surveys, test data analysis that was done either by the district or the school itself, and the Program Quality Review Process, which involves both an internal and external review of school programs at least once every three years. The teachers and principals in these schools, on the whole, understood the power of data to drive the school improvement process.

The School's Culture, Home-School Relations and Student Achievement

The community in which the school is located is one of the external factors affecting the school's student inputs. The research of Coleman, *et al.* (1966) confirmed the significance of family background to student achievement. The data from this study indicate that how the school staff reacts to family background factors is influenced by the transformative process. All teachers felt that family background influenced student achievement. However, as changes were made in the school's curriculum and instructional practices, in organizational structures and procedures, and in the school's cultural attributes, teachers in the most effective schools felt more empowered to teach all students more successfully. As a result, student family background factors began to be seen as not the only determinant of a student's school success. Teachers' practices combined with actions to strengthen home-school relations and parental support were seen to be means to increase student achievement.

At least one or two teachers in each school mentioned parent involvement as a component in the improvement process. The schools which had the highest SES parents expressed the view that strong parent support had been key in the improvement process. Parents were viewed as partners, and structures existed to facilitate their involvement and participation. Teachers in schools which served many more students from lower SES families, spoke in terms of the need to bring parents into the school and to find more ways to involve them. Comments from these schools were:

- Try everything you can to bring parents in to be allies and have more parent meetings.
- The last area of change would be parent involvement. That's a key. Making education important to parents so they can make it important to the kids.
- So really strong parent involvement is something we're working on to make it a more effective school.
- What is needed is more parent involvement; finding ways to get parents more involved formally in the system, because that's where I see the changes really having to come from, at least a lot of them.
- More parent involvement is needed, and we need to have more classes for them.

The schools that had strong parent support expressed confidence in their parents and in themselves. 'Staff working together is like the relationship between parents and teachers working together. There is no end to what can be accomplished.' Rosenholtz (1989) identified a similar finding in her study:

> Parent involvement in their children's learning is yet another direct, independent contributor to teacher certainty. Schools that enable parents to help their child at home, to participate in teachers' instructional programs and to become better informed about their children's progress increase teachers' certainty about a technical culture and their own instructional practice. (p. 114)

Lacking parent support, there is a tendency to feel isolated from the community and to blame parents for school failures, as was seen in the pattern formed by some of the case-studies of teachers in the least effective schools. The expressions of the desire for more parent involvement as part of the improvement process on the part of the lowest SES schools seem to fit Rosenholtz's (1989) description of moderately moving schools; teachers recognized there was a gap between home and school, but did not have any concrete plans to close the gap.

Leadership by Principal and Teachers

Given the open-ended nature of the interview questions, leadership, especially by the principal, was not explicitly addressed in many of the teacher responses; yet, it was implied in many. The strong theme of collaboration and cooperation that ran through the responses indicated that shared leadership was seen as a major factor that was contributing to each school's improvement. Leadership was also deemed essential if a school was to improve. The principal's role in facilitating and initiating collaborative leadership was implied, but not explicitly discussed.

In the two least effective schools, more of the responses conveyed a negative tone reflecting what they felt was not happening in their schools. The implication was that there needed to be more leadership by the principal, especially in bringing the staff together to work on schoolwide issues. One teacher stated that there was a need for 'real leadership'. Another said there needed to be more modeling from the top. In contrast, in the more effective schools, the openness and role of the principal as a factor in bringing about school change and facilitating teacher participation was emphasized. Two teachers phrased it this way.

- The principal must be willing to be open and flexible, to talk about issues, but not intimidate teachers ... to build the self-esteem of teachers and students.
- The principal plays a critical role in creating a strong culture, capitalizing on teacher strengths and following through with staff decisions.

As schools begin to restructure, there is a need to clarify roles and responsibilities of both teachers and principals. It was clear from the interviews in this study that teachers saw the critical need to leave their own classroom and to be involved with schoolwide issues. They recognized the significance of the grade-level team meetings, curriculum committees, school site council, and faculty meetings as vehicles for bringing about change both at the school level and in their own classrooms. They also recognized the principal's role in facilitating teachers' leadership and collaboration. How they perceived their own leadership and the principal's and the interplay between the two, however, was not fully explored in this study. This is an area that needs more attention, especially if schools are to successfully negotiate the new relationships implied in the push to restructure schools.

Summary and Conclusions

The data presented in this chapter showed that teachers in these schools had developed a consistent view of what an effective school ought to be. They accepted the responsibility for both the academic growth as well as the emotional-social growth of children. Significantly, they also understood that teacher cooperation and collaboration were necessary to achieve their goal of improved student achievement. They wanted their schools to be a happy place for children, and they recognized that the best way for that to occur was for the school to be a good place for teachers to work. None of these schools can be regarded as *stuck* schools that Rosenholtz (1989) found in her study. The movement in some had been more moderate than in others, but all were moving.

An important explanation for why none of these schools was truly *stuck* is that through the conscientious, if not always successful, efforts to improve, teachers in each school had come to understand some of the qualities necessary for organizational growth and renewal. In other words, important teacher-learning was occurring not only about curriculum and instructional practices, but also about organizational life — the need for structures to support collaboration and shared decision-making and the need for a culture that created a schoolwide focus. Responses to the question about how schools should improve fell into six major categories: 1) shared decision-making and collaboration; 2) communication and shared goals; 3) activities and actions that established a schoolwide focus or orientation; 4) assessment of school and student progress toward goals; 5) and home-school relations; and 6) leadership, by principal and teachers. Teachers in the most effective schools talked largely in terms of continuing or refining their own current practices in each of these areas, whereas teachers in the least effective schools presented recommendations in terms of what should be done, especially in their schools. The teacher responses revealed that teachers have much to share about school improvement. The lesson contained in this chapter is that teachers in improving schools may be valuable consultants and resources to other schools that are also working to improve. The benefit to tapping this teacher talent is likely to be twofold: the teachers will provide valuable assistance to their sister schools and at the same time will more likely redouble their efforts to improve their own school.

Chapter 9

Purposeful Restructuring: Lessons from Effective Schools Research and Practice

The purpose of this chapter is to examine the lessons learned from effective schools research and practice and to discuss how they could be helpful in guiding current efforts to restructure schools. As discussed earlier, effective schools programs and restructuring are similar, because they both focus on the transformative process of schooling in relation to outputs. This is not to say that inputs are not important. Studies have documented that principals and staff in more effective schools play an active role in securing additional resources as well as asserting more authority in school site personnel decisions than do their colleagues in less effective schools (Venezky and Winfield, 1979; Glenn, 1981; Leithwood and Montgomery, 1982; Hallinger and Murphy, 1987b; Rosenholtz, 1989). Restructuring proposals frequently call for more autonomy in staff selection and for additional resources that will allow more release time for staff to participate in learning opportunities, planning and curriculum development. Restructuring plans built on the concept of parental choice through vouchers or magnet schools would radically alter the make-up of student inputs into the transformative process. The essence of effective schools programs and restructuring efforts, however, lies in altering the transformative process. It is in this regard that educators and policy makers pursuing restructuring can benefit from effective schools research and practice. The following sections of this chapter highlight some of the lessons to be learned that could lead to purposeful restructuring in ways that create a climate for learning and achievement in schools.

Improved Student Outcomes: The Impetus for Change

An important and lasting legacy of school effectiveness research is the focus on student outcomes (Murphy, *et al.*, in press). Effective schools research and practice have gone through two phases regarding student outcomes. (Wimpelberg, Teddlie, and Stringfield, 1989). The first phase was concerned with equity in outcomes, whereas the second phase has been driven more by concerns for efficiency in outcomes, that is, increased or improved outcomes for all students to be achieved within the current financial constraints of the school or district. Both of these themes — equity and efficiency — are present in the current calls to restructure schools. Understanding the history and the reasons for the shift from equity to efficiency has implications for restructuring.

The driving force behind effective schools research and school effectiveness programs was the desire to turn equal opportunities into more equitable outcomes for poor students in major urban areas. Researchers, challenged by Coleman's, *et al.* (1966) and Jencks', *et al.* (1972) conclusions that family background was a more powerful determinant of student success than school input variables, set out to find schools where achievement gains were higher than would be expected, given the socioeconomic characteristics of the school's student population (Brookover, Beady, Flood, Schweitzer and Wisenbaker, 1979; Edmonds 1979a and b; Kiltgaard and Hall, 1974; Phi Delta Kappa, 1980; Weber, 1971). The majority of school effectiveness programs established as a result of these early studies were largely centered in urban areas and were driven by equity concerns. As popularity of the effective schools model spread, both research and practice began to focus on schools in more diverse socioeconomic settings. Wimpelberg, Teddlie, and Stringfield (1989) have argued that the change in school context from largely urban elementary schools to suburban and rural elementary and secondary schools produced a second phase of effective schools research that shifted concerns from equity to efficiency.

> Efficiency overshadows equity as a natural value base when researchers move beyond the urban elementary school population and vary the elements of school context within effective school designs. In effect, context-varied studies ask, 'How can we understand the complex configuration of factors that produce higher achievement in *any and all schools*?' (emphasis in original, Wimpelberg, *et al.*, p. 88).

The authors also assert that a second efficiency concern is, given a generally finite and inflexible budget, what makes one school more effective (i.e., efficient) than a comparable school in producing student achievement gains.

As Wimpelberg, *et al.* pointed out, the shift in context from poor urban schools to all schools accounts in large measure for the shift from equity to efficiency as the impetus for change in effective schools research and programs. Another factor is the use of norm-referenced tests as outcome measures which show that middle-class school districts are performing relatively well compared to their urban counterparts. The overall test results eliminate the pressure from these districts to focus on student outcomes since their clientele are relatively satisfied with the outcomes. Middle-class districts that have drawn upon the effective schools research have typically focused on assessing the presence of effective school characteristics as measures of effectiveness rather than student outcomes. In addition, many of these districts and schools are not disaggregating student achievement data or other school outcome variables, such as attendance, discipline infractions, grade distribution, college admissions, by either socioeconomic levels of students or by parental educational levels. A General Accounting Office report prepared for the US House Education and Labor Committee found that fewer than 25 per cent of the school districts which claimed to have implemented effective schools programs had disaggregated student achievement data (1989). In the diverse socioeconomic contexts of most districts, without disaggregated data, the equity focus is quickly lost. Summarizing the findings from ten case studies, Lezotte (1990) stressed the importance of disaggregated data.

These districts [the case study districts that had implemented effective schools programs] emphasized repeatedly the need for disaggregating measured or observed student outcome data. This process differs from place to place, but when it is done and discussed it forces institutional attention to be directed toward the issues of equity. Publication of outcomes makes it difficult to ignore the mission of teaching for learning for all. (Lezotte, p. 199)

The power of disaggregated achievement data in maintaining the focus on equity is shown in the current study in the case-study of Yosemite. When tracking was implemented as an efficiency measure to better meet the resource needs of gifted and bilingual students, the subsequent year's disaggregated test data showed that the action was *ineffective* in terms of outcomes for both high and low income groups. Without the disaggregated data, the full impact of this change would not have been known by the school staff. The point is not that efficiency is antithetical to equity, but rather, within diverse contextual settings, it is important to keep a focus on equity.

The push to restructure schools has emerged during this second efficiency phase of effective schools research and is also occurring in varied school contexts. The efficiency argument is one of several rationales advanced for why schools must be restructured, and has been most strongly put forward by Kearns and Doyle (1988) in their book *Winning the Brain Race*.

The first wave of reform has broken over the nation's public schools, leaving a residue of incremental changes and an outmoded educational structure still firmly in place.

The second wave must produce strategic changes that restructure the way our schools are organized and operate. It must recreate a public school system characterized by accountability and performance. . . .

If current economic and demographic trends continue, American business can expect to spend $25 billion a year in remedial training programs for new employees. Public education has put us at a competitive disadvantage — our workforce doesn't have the skills an information-based economy needs. (Kearns and Doyle, p. 140)

Kearns and Doyle are concerned about the high dropout rate as well as the underachievement of so many students. They recognize the decline in the number of white middle-class students and the need for schools to be far more successful in educating inner city children from diverse backgrounds. Given these demographic changes, equity is of some concern; however, from their perspective, the urgency for restructuring arises primarily from stark economic realities of the need for a well-trained labor force to maintain America's place in a world market. The call for restructured schools is also driven by concern for the underachievement and inefficient achievement of middle-class students. In a recent interview, Albert Shanker President of the American Federation of Teachers, stressed the efficiency argument this way:

I'm convinced by the data from international comparisons. For example, our top group — students who are able to write well, to solve complex mathematical problems, to understand principles of science — is between 2.6 per cent and 6 per cent of our graduating 17-year olds, while every other industrial country in the world does much better than that. It doesn't matter whether you look at British, French, or Dutch schools, there's absolutely no question that between 16 and 30 per cent of their graduates function at that level. . . . The fact is that the most advantaged kids who ever walked the face of the earth aren't learning very much. (Brandt, 1990, p. 11)

Those favoring restructuring argue that given their current structure, schools are not producing the outcomes needed by society. Industry finds itself having to perform the function of the schools: providing basic education. Businesses' conclusion is that piecemeal reforms will no longer suffice; to achieve efficiency in outcomes, a major overhaul is needed.

Efficiency is not the only rationale advanced for restructuring schools. While improved student outcomes are also the ultimate end of two other restructuring proposals, the reasons for restructuring are different. The Carnegie Task Force and both of the national teacher organizations, but especially the American Federation of Teachers, have argued that schools must be restructured in ways that make the workplace a better place for teachers. The argument is as follows: schools are not attractive places to work; therefore, they do not attract the best and the brightest into teaching. Furthermore, the most able teachers do not stay in the profession because of poor working conditions. The best method to increase student achievement is to restructure the work environment for teachers in ways that empower teachers to act professionally. (Brandt, 1990; Carnegie Task Force, 1986; Lieberman, 1988; Elmore and Associates, 1990; Timar, 1989) In other words, the part of the transformative process of schooling that is to be restructured is how teachers work together and their role in governance and decision-making at the school. A third rationale presented for restructuring again sees student outcomes as the ultimate reason for restructuring, but draws on the work of Goodlad (1983) and Sizer and Houston (1987) for ideas of how the transformative process is to be altered. Their studies of schools showed them to be stultifying places for both teachers and students. They have argued that only through fundamentally restructuring the teaching and learning process can student learning be enhanced (Timar, 1989).

Driven by such diverse reasons for restructuring, any change can fall under the rubric of restructuring. The danger is that the term loses its sharpness and meaning. In sorting through the quagmire of reasons for restructuring, data from the effective schools research show that the following points need to be considered. First, the focus on outcomes should not be lost as schools struggle to reshape the transformative process in more radical ways. Second, equity needs to be as great a consideration as efficiency in evaluating outcomes. By disaggregating outcomes, both equity and efficiency concerns can be kept in mind. Third, as the case-studies in this book and as other effective schools research document, all aspects of the transformative process — teacher workplace conditions, teacher-student interaction through curriculum and instruction, and teacher development opportunities — need to be addressed if greatly improved student outcomes are to be achieved. Fourth, while the initial list of school effectiveness characteristics had a linear and rationale appeal, the actual implementation of effective schools research has proved to be messy, nonrational, and nonlinear. There are common themes and threads in the fabric of effective schools, but multiple paths to effectiveness.

School Organizational Structures and Procedures

The very term restructuring implies changes in the structures of schools. Changes in governance, daily schedules, grouping of students, and classroom arrangements that foster team-teaching are all being considered by schools in the process of restructuring. The type of change pursued relates to the rationale driving the restructuring. The teacher empowerment rationale, for example, is more likely to focus on the establishment of governance structures. Restructuring based on the need to alter the relationship between teacher and students, on the other hand, is more likely to focus on teaching strategies and grouping of students within the classroom and in the school. In the case-studies documented here, there was evidence of increased use of team-teaching, experiments with redeployment for reading, and movements toward heterogeneous grouping of students, especially as the schools began to implement a literature-based approach to reading and to use cooperative learning strategies. The case study of Yosemite also provided a clear example of the negative impact of severe ability tracking.

The basic school classroom structure of thirty to thirty-five students assigned to a teacher prevailed in this study and is the dominant arrangement in most case-studies of effective schools. No school in this study had radically changed its daily schedule. Proponents of restructuring argue that school improvement and school effectiveness programs have not gone far enough. They have merely tinkered with incremental changes (Kearns and Doyle, 1988). The evidence from these case studies and others would support this conclusion (Rosenholtz, 1989; Taylor, 1990); however, it is clear that a qualitatively different type of instruction is going on in effective schools and effective classrooms compared to ineffective schools (Teddlie, Kirby, and Stringfield, 1989). These classrooms represent fertile ground for more research into effective practices as well as into the conditions that foster teachers' willingness to experiment and reflect on their practice, a quality that existed in the effective case-study schools and classrooms.

A number of restructuring proposals driven by the teacher empowerment and efficiency rationales have stressed the need to create shared school governance structures and to initiate site-based management (Jenni, 1991; Raywid, 1989; Timar, 1989). The arguments for site-based management are particularly strong in large urban systems such as Dade County, FL, New York City, Chicago, to mention a few. It is argued that the failure of schools to increase student achievement is largely due to oppressive bureaucratic controls imposed by the central administration and the sense of powerlessness to address local issues and concerns that these controls engender in teachers and site administrators. Site-based management (SBM) schemes generally call for personnel, curriculum, and budget decisions to be made by teachers, principal, and in some cases, parents and students (at the secondary level). The assumption is that given opportunities to make decisions, two benefits will accrue. First, teachers will have a greater sense of job satisfaction and professionalism. Second, students will attain higher levels of achievement, because better decisions will be made on their behalf. The problem facing policy makers is that it is difficult to ascertain whether SBM accomplishes these goals, because it is difficult to demonstrate a linear cause and effect relationship between SBM and student outcomes. Research on effective schools has shown that establishing school decision-making structures appears to be central to successful effective schools efforts (Kijai and Norman, 1990; Pollack, *et al.*, 1987; Rosenholtz, 1989; Taylor, 1990). In other words, effective schools have been quietly engaging in school-based management and governance, often with out formal declarations or public fanfare. As more schools move to establish school governance structures, it is important to use the data from these studies as well as research on school councils that was conducted in the 1970s in California, South Carolina and Florida (Chrispeels, 1980; Kijai and Hollingsworth, 1987; Kijai and Norman, 1990; Stanton and Zerchykov, 1979; Zerchekov and Davies, 1980), and recent investigations of site-based management (Casner-Lotto, 1988; Raywid, 1989; Jenni, 1991). These studies contain valuable insights on how to increase opportunities for school governance and decision-making that will avoid some of the pitfalls encountered by the early school councils. The following points summarize some of the useful lessons from previous school council and SBM research.

1. Many school council and school-based management schemes have accomplished far less than expected, because council participants, including administrators, teachers and parents, were not adequately trained to perform these new roles (Stanton and Zerchykov, 1979; Taylor, 1990; Jenni, 1991). In discussing the school effectiveness efforts of his district, the Superintendent of Geary County Schools in Kansas remarked that far more attention should have been given to training staff in how to implement a successful change process (Taylor, 1990).

2. Site-based management can falter if the range and number of decisions the school has to make is greater than the time available to make them (Timar, 1989; Jenni, 1991). The individual schools involved in effective schools efforts cited in this study were not necessarily given more power to make decisions, but they found considerable latitude to actually make site decisions once they started working on how to improve outcomes. The study of maverick effective schools also has shown that schools within the same school system will differ dramatically in the amount of site decision-making that occurs, with the more effective schools taking charge of their own destiny even within the confines of a large bureaucratic system.

3. Site-based management typically devolves decision-making authority to the school. Another approach, suggested by examining individual school improvement efforts, would be for the school staff to request decision-making authority in those areas that it identifies as necessary to meet its students needs.

4. School-based planning and decision-making teams have been a central part of almost all school effectiveness programs (Taylor, 1990). Sometimes these teams have been specially created, other times existing groups took on the function of serving as the school effectiveness planning team. The purpose of these teams was to find ways to enhance student learning. A significant by-product of their creation was the empowerment of teachers. Accomplishing mutually established goals may have been the primary source of teachers' sense of power. Site-based management teams established primarily to give governance opportunities to teachers and parents may not lead to a sense of empowerment unless they make student outcomes their explicit focus and end (Levine and Taylor, 1991).

5. The creation of an SBM team may help some teachers to be empowered,

but it runs the risk of creating a small leadership core leaving the rest of the faculty uninvolved. The evidence from the case-studies in this book demonstrates the benefit of multiple opportunities for decision-making through such structures as grade-level teams, department committees, curriculum committees, and *ad hoc* problem-solving task forces. The creation of these structures was both conscious and evolving as needs arose. The experience of Tahoe, one of the case-study schools, also indicates the danger of establishing two competing groups (i.e., the principal's anointed change group and the regularly elected school-site council).

6. The work of the school council, SBM team, or effective schools planning team needs to be data driven (Pollack *et al.*, 1987; Lezotte, 1990) and focused on student outcomes, not on governance for governance's sake.

7. The establishment of multiple formal and informal structures for teacher and parent participation in problem-solving and decision-making facilitate communication, foster collaboration, and build norms of collegiality (Pollack, *et al.*, 1987). As Rosenholtz' (1989) data showed, shared decision-making structures also change the nature of teacher talk, especially informal talk before, during and after school, from complaints about students to mutual problem-solving strategies to help students.

In summary, addressing organizational structures and procedures will be an essential part of restructuring. The structures schools adopt will depend to some extent on the rationale driving the change process. Research on effective schools shows that school site governance is essential to improvement in student outcomes; however, the governance must be a means to an end, not an end itself.

Curriculum and Instructional Practices

A second major cluster of variables that must be addressed in restructuring are those encompassed under curriculum and instructional practices or the school's technology. This cluster goes to the heart of teaching for learning. The effective schools variables associated with the school technology component, especially the focus on basic skills, direct instruction, and time-on-task, have been criticized the most (Murphy, Hallinger and Mitman, 1983). The primary arguments against considering these as essential correlates of effective schools are that the focus is too narrow, that students need far more than basic skills, that instruction and curriculum will vary with the context of schooling, that there are far better ways to teach students than direct instruction, and that rigidity can routinize instruction and dull students' enthusiasm for learning. All of these arguments have merit, and most practices taken in the extreme prove to be counterproductive. As researchers continue to study effective learning environments, new and more invigorating instructional strategies have been identified. Reviewing the data on effective schools research, however, provides important insights and principles to use in guiding restructuring in these important curricular and instructional areas.

Academic Focus

A frequent variable cited as essential to school effectiveness is academic focus. The early research described the academic focus as centered on the basic skills of reading, writing, and mathematics. This has since been criticized as far too narrow a focus. It is important, however, to examine the context in which the research was conducted to understand the reason for the focus and its implications for restructuring. As mentioned above, one of the major contributions of effective schools research and practice has been to draw attention to student outcomes (Murphy, 1990). The primary tool for assessing outcomes, especially in the early days of effective schools research, was norm-referenced basic skills tests. Since these tests represented a means by which schools could judge their own performance against previous achievement and could compare their results with other schools, it is only natural that greater emphasis was placed on raising basic skills test scores. As Lezotte has frequently commented, 'What gets measured gets done.' If basic skills get measured by norm-referenced tests, it is only natural that basic skills will get taught. Furthermore, it was important for schools to find ways to increase achievement on these important public measures. Without achievement gains, it is unlikely that teachers would come to believe that all children can learn and that their teaching is central in determining the level of learning. An important observation from the case-studies described in this book is that when teachers saw their students gaining mastery in so-called basic skills, they also developed the confidence to take their students to higher levels of learning and to examine and develop other areas of the curriculum. The curricula of the most effective schools included hand-on science, social studies, and art and music integrated with the basic curriculum. The Louisiana effective schools studies similarly confirmed that classrooms in effective schools provided far richer learning environments and more interactive teaching than classrooms in ineffective schools (Teddlie, Kirby, Stringfield, 1989).

Research studies typically occur at a moment in time. This is certainly true of most of the effective schools studies. 'A focus on basic skill' became identified as an essential correlate of an effective school because the research examined schools at one point in time in large urban areas. Over time and in different contexts, a focus just on basic skills has been shown not to be a constant, but a focus on academics continues as a viable effective schools correlate in different contexts. The case-studies and the five-year Louisiana study revealed that there is an evolutionary process that occurs in effective schools and classrooms. The evolution frequently encompasses new innovations and foci that are prevalent in the educational research community. In their comparative description of two schools, one effective the other ineffective, Teddlie, *et al.* (1989) captured the power of an academic focus.

> If the amount of time spent on academics was the most impressive feature of School One, the lack thereof was the unifying characteristic of School Two. A week-long fund-raising event was used as an excuse for the lack of class time spent on actual instruction. There was no attempt to tie the patriotic theme of the fund-raiser into instructional activities. Collecting money in one class period took 35 minutes. The investigators were dismayed at the number of interruptions attributed to such non-academic projects. One member of the research team returned to the school two weeks later. He was unsurprised to find the 'one-week' fund-raiser in its third week. (Teddlie, Kirby and Stringfield, 1989, p. 9)

The lesson that needs to be carried forth is that an academic focus remains essential to school effectiveness and will remain essential in restructured schools, *if the goal is to improve student learning*. This is important because the multiple purposes of schooling usually continue to exist within the school and in the larger community. A recent study by Townsend (1991) showed that only 25 per cent of the parents regarded academic focus as the primary role of the school. Development of self-esteem, social and citizenship development, providing students with skills necessary for employment, development values and responding to the educational needs of the local community were also considered important goals for schools. Mission statements of schools typically reflect these diverse goals. Furthermore, school restructuring, itself, is beset with multiple agendas. Basic skills may no longer be the focus in restructured schools, but the need to understand the critical link between focus and outcome measures remains. Schools engaging in restructuring and wanting to expand the focus or mission of the school need to pay attention to how student progress will be monitored and outcomes assessed. It is no accident that monitoring of student progress and academic focus are two key features of effective schools. In summary, effective schools research indicates that while a focus on basic skills may be too narrow, the need for a clear academic mission remains essential, if increased student achievement is to be the outcome.

Instructional Practices

The attention given to direct instruction is, to some extent, a reflection of the time and context of the effective schools studies. Direct instruction is defined here as an approach in which the teacher presents the learning task to the whole class or group, and leads and controls the learning task. In general direct instruction follows several key instructional principles, such as creating an anticipatory set, specifying what is to be learned, demonstrating the skill or concept to the class or group, providing students with guided practice, providing feedback and reinforcement during the guided practice, and then giving the students opportunity for independent practice. Direct instruction was identified as a teaching strategy that was proving effective in schools serving large numbers of low-income students (Brookover, 1985). Like basic skills, the concept of instructional practices has been greatly expanded to encompass far more than direct instruction, as illustrated in the case-studies. While many of the schools started with a model of effective instruction, similar to the direct instruction model described in the early effective schools studies, these schools were also the first to adopt other innovative teaching strategies, such as cooperative learning, teaching writing as a process, use of literature in the teaching of reading, use of manipulatives in teaching mathematics. Comments from teachers revealed that the training and mastery of one instructional strategy, (i.e., the Elements of Effective Instruction, or the five-step lesson plan) gave them the confidence to try other approaches. The importance of competence has been stressed in other staff development studies (Joyce, with Bennett and Rollheiser-Bennett, 1990).

> Until participants achieved a fairly good degree of control over the content of the training, commitment remained insubstantial but rose as

competence rose. High initial commitment, on the other hand, tends to decline unless competence is achieved. (p. 28)

Second, as teachers came to believe that their instruction had a significant impact on student learning, they were eager to seek new ways of teaching that would further enhance learning.

An analysis of the experiences of the case-study schools suggests several lessons that may be helpful to schools involved in restructuring. First, it seems important for the school staff to have the opportunity to master at least one effective instructional strategy. The strategy mastered may be less important than the actual mastery. (The strategy selected is most likely to reflect current research and practice, as it did with the schools involved in the original effective schools studies.) Through mastery, teachers increase their self-confidence and sense of efficacy. Second, mastery in one area tends to speed mastery in other areas. Third, good instructional practices and effective teaching go hand-in-hand with a clear academic purpose. They are the essential tools for achieving the purpose.

Finally, schools that have incrementally achieved a reasonable degree of effectiveness are much more likely to be ready to engage in major initiatives and innovative restructuring, such as envisioned by Sizer (Sizer and Houston, 1987) or Goodlad (1983, 1987). A school district that is engaging in a restructuring process and plans to proceed without any major personnel changes, would do well to identify the effective schools within its district as the first candidates for further restructuring. In the two schools, cited in the quote above from the work of Teddlie, *et al.* (1989), School One had a strong focus on academics and had in place a significant number of other qualities that distinguished it as an effective school with positive outcomes for students. In contrast, School Two remained, five years after the original study, an ineffective school, in terms of outcomes and lack of effective school characteristics. Upon first review, School Two might seem to be the likely candidate for a major restructuring effort. However, in the absence of replacing the school staff, School Two is unlikely to be able to bring about changes. School One, on the other hand, is in a much better position to implement additional significant changes having already made many incremental changes in the direction of increased effectiveness.

Time-on-Task

Another variable associated with the school technology component is time-on-task. Like basic skills and direct instruction, time-on-task in its original context and form may not now be viewed as an essential correlate of an effective school. Yet, time remains a critical and finite resource for schools (Canady and Hotchkiss, 1985). There are again several lessons from effective schools research and practice that may be helpful to schools engaged in restructuring. First, two themes of restructuring are: 1) changing daily schedules and the ways in which instructional time is allocated, and 2) changing the way teachers and students interact. Before changes are made, the school staff must become aware of the way time is currently used. Time-on-task instruments, both in their current form or in expanded and revised forms, could assist the staff in gaining needed data. Through time-on-task analyses, teachers could see how much time is spent in teacher talk versus student activity. In addition, experiments in expanded blocks of learning time need to be compared with traditional time allocations to gain insights into how the time is being used and its effect on student learning. Second, teachers in the case-study schools, who were trained in collaboration with their colleagues to conduct time-on-task analyses, gained valuable insights into their own teaching. The structured observations served as a tool for encouraging reflection about the practice of teaching and for professional dialogue among teachers. These are two goals frequently mentioned by those who would restructure schools.

Use of Test Results to Assess Student Progress and Program Effectiveness

Three of the important legacies of effective schools research and practice are: 1) the focus on student outcomes, 2) the disaggregation of outcome data to assess the equity of the schooling process, and 3) the use of test data to change schooling practices. Effective schools research has brought to the fore the benefits and limits of standardized, norm-reference testing. Standardized testing allows comparison across schools and districts. Only through comparable test results is it possible to evaluate the impact of one school's transformative process with another. In addition, the effective schools process with its focus on equity in outcomes, not just equality of opportunities, has brought attention to the need to disaggregate test data by gender, income or educational level of the parent, ethnicity, and by language preference. California has been one of the few states to collect and provide such comparative data. Other districts engaged in an effective schools process, have developed systems to disaggregate data by students receiving free or reduced price lunches or by mother's educational level. The critical need for such data has stimulated other states to begin providing similar disaggregated test results. Whatever the outcome measures developed for restructured schools, it will be important to preserve the use of disaggregated data.

The use of norm-referenced tests as the primary student outcome measures by both researchers and practitioners involved in implementing effective schools processes has helped to highlight the limits of such tests. First, by their very definition norm-referenced tests are designed to sort students into two groups, those who are above and those who are below the norm, regardless of what students have learned since entering school. In the short run, a school can bring larger numbers of students above the norm, but in the long run the norm must be re-established so that the bell-shaped curve is maintained. Second, the norms are set by the most advantaged students, who bring to school from home the knowledge-base that underlies most of the test questions. This is especially true since the tests usually measure facts and lower level thinking skills. Thus, the tests help to confirm the economic class and ethnic divisions in society (Carnoy and Levin, 1976). Teachers working in schools in economically deprived neighborhoods become convinced that their students cannot learn or will learn much less, whereas teachers in advantaged neighborhoods are continually reinforced that they are doing a good job. Finally, the heavy reliance on norm-referenced tests has meant that middle-class schools have maintained a self-congratulatory attitude about their achievements. If one's students are already scoring at the 90–99 percentile, what more can one do? Meanwhile, international test data indicate that American students have slipped further and further behind their European and Asian counterparts (Brandt, 1990).

To address the limits of norm-referenced tests, several states and districts involved in effective schools efforts have moved toward creating mastery or criterion-referenced tests. The goal is to match the test to the curriculum being taught to better assess what has been learned. In addition, there is pressure to test far more advanced thinking skills, especially through the direct assessment of writing, as has been implemented in California and Connecticut. Effective schools research and practice has raised a number of questions regarding assessment and measures of student outcomes. Answers to these questions are critical to both effective schools research and restructuring.

1 How do we assess not only what students already know, but also what value the school has added to their knowledge base?
2 How do we assess the full range of human intelligences in ways that are authentic and comparable, and enhance students' and teachers' sense of efficacy and achievement?
3 If schools are encouraged to create diversity of programs to allow parental, student, and teacher choice, how do we assess the diversity in comparable ways that hold schools accountable for outcomes?
4 How do we ensure that outcome measures are disaggregated in ways that help schools to continually address equity and efficiency in outcomes?

In addition to highlighting the limits of measuring student outcomes solely by norm-referenced tests, effective schools research and practice has demonstrated the power of using data to drive the reform process. Teachers can only become reflective practitioners if they have information about their teaching and the impact of particular instructional programs on which to reflect. Most effective schools programs have developed opinion surveys regarding effective schools characteristics and school climate to be administered to parents, students, and staff. Data on other important variables are also collected, such as student absences, discipline infractions, number of tardy students, number of homework assignments given and their return rate, number of books read by students, number of parents involved and their type of involvement. Critical to the self-renewal process is the use of data for ongoing program and performance evaluation. As schools plow new ground through restructuring, it will be important to capitalize on the effective schools' legacy of data collection and analysis. District administrators can play a critical role in assisting schools to develop simple and useful data collection systems. Both teachers and students should be encouraged to become action researchers. Portfolio assessment systems that are being considered by a number of schools and districts involved in restructuring offer unique potential to involve both students and parents in assessing their progress. If the relationship between teacher and student is to be altered, then changing the types of assessments as well as widening the circle to include students and parents in the evaluative process would appear to be essential. Effective schools' efforts have shown the value of using data to set school goals. Using assessment data to help students and their families set growth goals as well is a logical next step.

Staff Development

Shanker (1990) has argued that restructured schools must be places where both students and teachers are learners. Unfortunately most schools have minimal budgets for staff development and are allocated even less time for carrying out staff development activities, especially those that would lead to institutional development. Schools involved in the California School Improvement Program, which now encompasses almost all elementary schools, can request up to eight days for staff development. Yet few districts allow the full amount. The primary reason for failure to utilize the days which are available is the concern for public outcry that the school is not fulfilling its custodial function.

Again, effective schools research offers insights in achieving the goal of creating a learning community. One of the significant findings from the research is that if the school is a rich learning environment for students, it is also likely to provide learning opportunities for the staff (Austin, 1981; Glenn, 1981; Hallinger and Murphy, 1985a; Mortimore *et al.*, 1988; Pollack *et al.*, 1987; Rosenholtz, 1989). Staff development in effective schools is usually school-based, addresses school improvement priorities, and is ongoing rather than a single, occasional workshop (Levine and Lezotte, 1990).

Joyce and Showers (1988) and Stallings (1989) have documented the qualities of effective staff development programs. Of particular importance are the observation — practice — feedback — modification loop. Little (1986) has identified the importance of staff development that pays as much attention to implementation as to training. In addition, she documented the following four aspects as essential to successful implementation of staff development programs: 1) a critical mass of teachers from each school site to be involved in the training; 2) ongoing opportunities for the teachers and trainer to work together during the implementation phase; 3) a three-year commitment which involves weekly inservice and curriculum planning sessions; and 4) active participation by the principal in both training and implementation phases. Teachers in this study, even when they had participated in multiple staff development sessions on a given topic, expressed the need for continued training and discussion to refresh their memories and keep the innovation in place. Similiar to Little's (1986) findings, data collected for this study showed that if staff development was not site-based, the majority of teachers from the school had to participate, and they had to perceive that the district staff development addressed critical site-diagnosed needs. By meeting site-based needs that had been identified by the staff, the motivation for participation and use of the innovation was much higher (Joyce, Bennett and Rolheiser-Bennett, 1990). Other studies of effective schools have confirmed these findings (Levine and Lezotte, 1990). In their review of effective school studies, Levine and Lezotte also pointed out that:

> Within this emphasis on practical, ongoing inservice training at the site, much of the staff development at unusually effective elementary schools has taken the form of both intra-grade and cross-grade level meetings and planning sessions at which teachers work together to improve coordination of instruction, select key learning objectives for mastery oriented approach to instruction, determine how to improve the performance of individual students with problems, and otherwise

work to attain important schoolwide objectives . . . (Levine and Lezotte, p. 16)

This passage is significant because it shows the close relationship among several key variables such as staff development, school organizational structures, data collection and analyses, and school goals and academic focus. These linkages were borne out in the case study of Tahoe where most instances of staff development did not meet the criteria presented above, and even if they had, the school did not have the infrastructure of grade level teams or curriculum committees to ensure continued implementation and follow-through. What Tahoe lacked was a way to integrate staff development as part of its institutional development in ways that would join both school and classroom improvements (Fullan, 1990).

Another important example of the interactive nature of the components of the system is demonstrated in the relationship between staff development and leadership. Little's 1986 study confirmed that it was not sufficient for the principal to sanction the training and attend some or all of the sessions. The principal also needed to be an active participant during the implementation phase. Active involvement of the principal in follow-up and implementation was observed in the case-studies in the most effective schools. Principals participated by setting aside time in grade-level meetings to prepare hands-on science activities, doing demonstrations and videotapes of lessons for critique by teachers, and by monitoring implementation through lesson plans and staff meeting discussions. Given the radical nature of change envisioned by those writing about restructuring, the lessons regarding staff development, especially the relationships among staff development, school organization, and leadership, are critical for schools involved in the restructuring process. Only by approaching staff development as a component of the total organization and recognizing its links with other components will it contribute to the institutional development of the school that Fullan (1990) has argued is essential for school improvement and revitalization.

School Climate and Culture

The culture of an organization *is* the organization. A school's culture is the most important variable for bringing about school effectiveness or restructuring. Yet, it is the most difficult variable to describe and to alter. The contributions of effective schools research in understanding the type of culture that fosters student learning and achievement have been considerable. Murphy (1991) in a recent review of the legacies of effective schools research argued that there are three key cultural beliefs that need to be carried forth from the research to new attempts to restructure and improve schools. One of these principles or beliefs has already been discussed: the belief in the importance of measurable student outcomes as the basis for assessing school effectiveness. Linked to the focus on outcomes are two fundamental beliefs that are essential to achieving effective schools outcomes: the belief in the educability of all students and the belief that the school has primary responsibility in ensuring that each child is educated. These basic beliefs go to the heart of the teaching-learning process. The difficulty in altering the beliefs lies at the center of the challenge in bringing about educational change. Attending to the symbols, rituals, myths, heroes and hero-ines of the organization has been one way that schools attempting to become effective have addressed the beliefs, norms, and values.

The aspects of culture and climate that were examined in this study and are typically associated with effective schools research are: 1) a safe, orderly, and positive learning environment, 2) home-school relations, 3) shared mission and purpose, 4) rewards and recognition of student and staff accomplishments, 5) high expectations for both staff and students, and 6) norms of collegiality. Ob-servations and explorations of school words and actions in each of these areas have helped to reveal the beliefs, values, and norms of a school which, in turn, shape and influence the school's organizational structures and procedures and curriculum and instructional practices. The alignment and attunement between words and actions of the school staff and community reflect the deeper levels of the school's culture.

A Safe, Orderly, and Positive Learning Environment

The most important lesson from effective schools research is that safety and order have to become non-issues. If the school is to become a learning commun-ity (Barth, 1990, Schlechty, 1990), concerns over discipline have to be minimal and the approach has to be one of positive reinforcement rather than of pun-ishment. A second lesson is that changes in instructional practices such as the use of group or cooperative learning strategies and interactive teaching will require different definitions of correct student behavior and discipline. The third lesson is that the learning climate and discipline environment are set at the school level and reinforced at the classroom level, not vice versa (Rosenholtz, 1989).

Home-School Relations

A component of an effective school's culture is the relationship that exists between home and school. The research on effective schools, however, has not been as clear cut in demonstrating the nature of the relationship or its impact on student outcomes. Levine and Lezotte (1990) have discussed three reasons for this. First, the level of parent involvement is 'so highly correlated to SES that controlling for SES in regression studies frequently eliminates its relationships with achievement' (p. 22). Second, parent involvement is a vague and all-encompassing concept that is rarely defined and hard to measure. Third, parent involvement, partly because it is so difficult to measure, is frequently omitted as a variable. Nevertheless, a number of studies have certainly found greater levels of parent involvement in effective schools (Comer, 1987; Glenn, 1981; Levine and Eubanks, 1983; Levine and Stark, 1981, 1982; Mortimore *et al.*, 1988; Pollack *et al.*, 1987; Sizemore, Brossard, and Harrigan, 1983; Stedman, 1987). For guidance on the kinds of parent involvement activities that have the greatest impact on student learning, it is necessary to turn to the summaries of research that deal directly with parent involvement (Henderson, 1981, 1985). However, there are two observations from effective schools research that may be helpful in examining and designing home-school relations in restructured schools. First, teacher attitudes towards parents seem to be critical in shaping teacher expectations and attitudes toward students. Furthermore, teacher attitudes are strongly related to their own sense of efficacy in teaching low-income students (Chrispeels and Pollack, 1990; Johnson, Brookover and Farrell, 1989a; Rosenholtz, 1989). For parent involvement to have maximum effect, even if only indirectly on student achievement, schools need to address those variables that impact teachers' sense of efficacy and the skills they need to teach students from diverse backgrounds. A second observation is that effective schools characteristics exist in many families and communities and help to contribute to student success in school (Chrispeels and Pollack, 1990; Clark, 1983). In high socio-economic communities, many families are likely to engage in effective schools practices such as extending the learning time for their students through supervision of homework, family learning activities, and the use of community learning resources. Families are more likely to reward and recognize their children's efforts even when the school does not. Higher income families and their communities have more resources to provide a safe and orderly environment that is conducive to student learning. Families are likely to have high expectations for students and to communicate these to teachers so that expectations from both home and school become mutually reinforcing. In lower socio-economic communities, some families are engaged in similar practices (Clark, 1983). However, the frequency of the engagement is much less, the pattern of engagement may be less familiar to White middle-class teachers, and there are fewer community and school supports to assist families. If teachers' sense of efficacy has not been addressed, teachers are likely to see the absence, rather than the presence of the characteristics. If the school organizational structures, school technology, and climate variables such as discipline, rewards and recognition, have been altered in ways that increase teacher confidence and efficacy in working with low-income families, it is more likely that teachers will see how to build on family-effectiveness characteristics that exist and to extend and embed them where they are weak or absent. Thus restructuring needs to involve not only restructuring the school within, but restructuring the relationships between home and school. Part of that restructuring, if it is to lead to higher student achievement, must focus on the development of a shared mission that encompasses the belief that all students can learn.

Stated and Shared Mission

A stated and shared sense of purpose and mission about all students' abilities to learn and the staff's ability and responsibility to teach has been found to be a characteristic that permeates highly effective schools. How that belief is developed is less well understood, but it is clear that it involves the interrelationship and interaction of all key organizational components. It reflects much deeper parts of the culture that are shaped through symbols, rituals, words, and actions in regard to the school's technology and organizational structures. The case-study of Yosemite represents a good example of how leadership clearly plays a role in using all parts of the organization to nurture a sense of shared mission, and how alterations and discontinuities in various organizational components can disrupt the sense of shared mission. Two lessons emerge from the effective schools case-study research. First, if the goal of a restructured school is to improve student learning, then that needs to be the heart of the shared mission. Second, there is a tendency in the restructuring process literature to state that the first step in restructuring is to develop a mission statement. This is important in setting out a sense of direction; however, it will only become a shared mission if it is cultivated and jointly developed over time. In addition, the mission, if it is to be a shared belief and not just a statement on the wall, will need to be supported in actions and deeds throughout all organizational components. For example, rewards and recognitions represent one organizational symbol that can be used to reinforce the mission.

Staff and Student Rewards and Recognition

Effective schools research has shown that changing the rewards structure can be an important factor for both students and teachers in reinforcing the belief in all children's ability to learn. There may be contextual differences, depending on the school's neighborhood, as to the number and type of recognition given (Hallinger and Murphy, 1986; Teddlie, Wimpelberg, Kirby, 1987). In higher-income neighborhoods, the recognition and reward may be more prevalent in the home, whereas in lower-income communities systematic recognition and rewards will be initiated by the school. Recognition for learning and achievement from either home or school, however, is essential to both teachers' and children's continued efforts at teaching and learning. Effective schools research has also shown that leadership, especially by the principal, in paying attention to cultural symbols reinforces the belief that all children can learn. Some key symbols are displays of students' academic work, use of faculty meetings to reinforce student achievement and teachers' roles in attaining that achievement, displays of test score results and future growth goals, creation of mottos and slogans about students as successful learners, and use of the intercom to commend student achievements, as opposed to just announcing of events or rules. As schools engage in restructuring, it will be important to pay attention to how the current reward and recognition system supports or undermines restructuring efforts. Some questions that will need answering are:

1 What type of learning does the reward structure recognize and reinforce?
2 How does the reward structure for students and teachers reinforce the purpose and mission of the school?
3 Does the reward structure complement changes in instructional strategies that may be focusing on cooperative as opposed to competitive learning?
4 Does the community understand and support the reward and recognition structure? (This will be particularly important if new assessment measures are introduced. For example, the state of Victoria in Australia has recently implemented a comprehensive new evaluation system for grades eleven and twelve, based on far more diverse assessments of student's accomplishments, including portfolios and research projects as well as traditional essays. The University of Melbourne has refused to accept these new assessment procedures for entrance purposes, which, of course, then causes concerns among parents).
5 Are teachers rewarded and recognized in ways that reinforce the direction

of the restructuring effort? (For example, team-teaching, peer coaching, collaborative grade level committees may be at odds with district or state career or job ladder schemes or differentiated staffing structures.).

In summary, the effective schools research has shown that rewards and recognition are powerful cultural symbols that when altered will, over time, influence practices and beliefs of those in the system. These symbols need to be addressed by those engaged in restructuring schools.

High Expectations for Students and Staff

Knowledge about the relationship of expectations (especially those held by teachers for students) and student performance did not originate with effective schools research; however, high expectations have been a consistent variable identified in almost all effective school studies (Armor, *et al.*, 1976; Brookover and Lezotte, 1979; Levine and Stark, 1985; Mortimore, *et al.*, 1988; Pollack *et al.*, 1987; Stringfield, Teddlie, and Suarez, 1986; Stringfield and Teddlie, 1989; Weber, 1971; Venezky and Winfield, 1979). Effective schools research has shown that the words of high expectations have to be supported by actions in all areas of school life, including organizational structures, school climate, and curriculum and instruction. The case-study data illustrate the close interrelationship of organizational components. When, through leadership, changes were made in organizational structures, school technology, and climate variables such as a safe and orderly learning environment, teachers were actually able to accomplish increased achievement with all their students. Only after these achievement gains were made, did teachers begin to change their expectations and their beliefs about the educability of all children. This leads to the effective schools finding that Murphy (1990) has urged needs to be used to guide future change efforts.

> Perhaps the most powerful and enduring lesson from all the research on effective schools is that the better schools are more tightly linked — structurally, symbolically, and culturally — than less effective ones. They operate more as an organic whole and less as a loose collection of disparate subsystems. (Murphy, 1990, p. 9)

In other words, as individual changes in restructured schools are made, they need to be considered and evaluated in the context of the whole organization. Without attention to all parts, what often begins as a successful reform soon may be abandoned because of a failure to tightly link structures, symbols, and the culture.

Teacher Professionalism and Norms of Collegiality

How do schools move from a loose collection of disparate subsystems to wholeness? The effective schools research indicates that a whole-school view and norms of collegiality begin to emerge when changes are made in organizational structures and the ways teachers work together to address technological changes. Those arguing for restructuring have recognized the need to alter the school's organization in ways that foster greater teacher involvement in decision-making and school governance. Evidence indicates these can be powerful forces in building commitment among staff and altering the culture of the school through increased collaboration and collegiality. (Hopkins, 1990; Rosenholtz 1989). They can also be dismal failures leaving the school largely unchanged and teachers who participated feeling frustrated and betrayed (Conley, Schmidle, and Shedd, 1988). The educational literature is full of descriptions of curriculum and instructional innovations that were greeted with great enthusiasm but never implemented in the classroom. Lack of good will or deliberate attempts to sabotage the change are usually not the causes of failure. More likely, long standing beliefs, norms, and values that comprised the culture of the school blocked real change (Deal, 1984; Sarason, 1971).

While research has documented the importance of collegiality in the change process in effective schools, there is less clear evidence about how it is developed. Obviously leadership and organizational variables, as discussed above, play a role. To understand some of the forces working against increased collegiality in schools, it may be necessary to examine societal cultural forces that have shaped the organization and norms of schools. This is especially important because a number of restructuring proposals stress the need to develop a professional culture in schools, to enhance collegiality, and to fundamentally alter the way teachers interact with teachers and with their students. What is pertinent to the discussion of school restructuring and school culture is understanding school and teacher autonomy and interaction in relation to deep-seated cultural norms about teaching. The metaphor of the factory has been used to describe the current culture, structure, and operation of schools (Kearns and Doyle, 1988; Schlechty, 1988; Seeley, 1981). Such features as the centralized, bureaucratic nature of school districts; the division of labor among administrators, teachers, and support staff; the rigid organization of the school day with subject matter allocated to limited and prespecified time slots; the controlled movement of students from specialist to specialist (especially at the secondary level); and the organization of the curriculum as an assembly line for students that is presented through a service delivery model of instruction, all represent elements of a factory-type organization. Certainly understanding the ways in which industrial efficiency practices have impacted the structure and functioning of American schools is essential to knowing how to change them.

A case can be made, especially at the elementary level, however, that the factory model overlays a more profound set of beliefs, norms, and expectations that have influenced the way schools are organized and have limited both collegiality and professionalism. Without understanding this deeper layer, proposals for restructuring may be less likely to succeed. The metaphor that needs to be explored is that of the school as a household and teaching as parenting. While families have undergone profound changes in their practices and structures, both families and schools still have the major responsibility for the care and upbringing of children in ways that perpetuate society and secure the future. As Evans (1988) has pointed out, 'families, like schools, are where generations meet' (p. 74). Again, while some modest changes have occurred, parenting responsibilities are still primarily divided along gender lines with women bearing major responsibility. Similarly, teaching, for all intense and purposes, is women's work. It is not within the purview of this book to explore the reasons that most teaching is undertaken by women, but certainly inherited ideologies, socialization, reproductive issues and expectations which result in women entering and leaving the workplace, segmentation of the labor market into primary and secondary segments, with teaching seen as secondary, the belief in the primary or family wage earner being male, and the exclusion of women, until recently, from most trade occupations, have all contributed to defining teaching as primarily work for women (Curthoys, 1988 and Sykes, 1990). Since teaching is a feminized occupation that places it in a subordinate status, and as Sykes points out, professional status is largely determined by 'client status, and children have little status in our society' (p. 73). In other words, teaching is a job that fits into the bio-cultural and socially constructed roles for women.

Furthermore, the organization of classrooms is closely akin to the organization of the household — women frequently work in isolation and must depend upon their own resources. In earlier times teachers had not only teaching responsibilities, but also custodial duties of lighting the fire and cleaning the schoolroom. While the scope of duties has changed, the isolation and independence has remained. 'Within the classroom, most teachers are independently responsible for planning, implementing, and evaluating instruction, counseling, and supervisory efforts with little direction, feedback, or assistance from other adults' (Conley *et al.*, 1988, p. 264). While schools are now larger in size and students are sorted by age, the structure of the one-room school house has not been dramatically altered. Most classrooms are still organized on the basis of a single teacher with a group of students. Current school structures can be seen as many one-room schoolhouses joined together by a common parking lot. Women, who have seen their mothers working alone in their home or who have been accustomed to working alone in their home themselves, adjust to working alone in their classroom. The isolation and independence of teachers and the barrier that this norm presents to school change has been noted (Conley *et al.*, 1988; Joyce, 1990; Rosenholtz, 1989). What has not been explored is the cultural foundation for this isolation and what deep-seated, unstated cultural norms would have to be changed.

A second household and parenting norm that has influenced teaching is that of the good mother. The good mother provides continuous care and nurturing for her children (Evans, 1988). This norm has influenced teaching in two significant ways. First, the good teacher stays with her children. Absences are minimized. This view has an effect on schools wishing to involve teachers in more planning and decision-making and in staff development. A frequent complaint of the teachers interviewed for this study was that planning activities and staff development took them away from *their* children. The second influence of the perception of the good mother has been to increase tensions between home and school. As more women enter the work force, they have less time to devote to care of their children and less time to donate to the school. Teachers frequently hold negative views of parents and their children if parents are perceived as not providing proper nurture and care. In the least effective schools in this study, parents who were no longer available to assist the school were seen as a problem and barrier to student success. These perceptions are significant issues that must be addressed in the process of school restructuring.

A third link between home and school is the value given to women's work. Since teaching was and still is, in may respects, considered a continuation of parenting (the nurturing, care, and instruction of children), teachers who first taught America's children were not required to have much training. In rural communities and small towns, many women teachers had little more than a high school education themselves. Some may have attended a two-year normal school before assuming their teaching duties. With only minimal training required, little compensation was needed or given. Since teaching was regarded as a continuation of women's work in the home, the justification for the lack of training required and minimal compensation need to be examined from the perspective of how women's work is evaluated by the larger society. The work of women in the home and on the farm from pre-industrial times through the modern era has not been considered to be of economic or monetary value and has not been computed in the assessment of a nation's wealth (Waring, 1988). According to Waring this devaluation of women's work has had profound influences on national policies that effect women's lives such as child care, healthy working and living conditions, transportation, and pay for women who work in economically recognized jobs. While teachers, of course, are paid employees and counted in the national economy, the lack of professional status of teachers and the generally low pay compared to other professions may well have its roots in how women's work is valued (or more precisely, not valued).

As America became more industrialized, certainly the requirements for becoming a teacher were also extended, but not in ways that would make teaching comparable to the training required for other professions. The first wave of reforms in the 1980s called for again strengthening the professional training of teachers by increasing certification requirements. The restructuring proposals advanced by Kearns and Doyle (1988) and reiterated by groups such as the California Business Roundtable (1989) are interesting in that they call for having teachers complete a regular subject major in a topic such as English, biology, history, and then acquire the educational pedagogy in a fifth year at the school site in an internship. Undergraduate teacher education programs would be eliminated. While the internship focus is somewhat new and has parallels in other professions, the proposal for a fifth year for teacher training has been required for over twenty years in California. There is no clear evidence from California that such an approach adopted nationally will produce the desired results — a much better trained teaching force. To accomplish this goal would probably require training much more comparable to medical, architectural, or legal training, especially given the pedagogical knowledge base now available and the complexity of skills required to teach students from diverse cultural, linguistic, and economic backgrounds. Such a recognition of what it takes to be an excellent teacher would have profound implications culturally, politically, and economically. At this point, it is doubtful that society is ready to acknowledge this reality. The degree to which it is acknowledged in the Kearns and Dolye book (1988) and the Roundtable Report (1989) is to create stratifications within the teaching profession — interns, assistant teachers, adjunct teachers, lead teachers. In this way, lead teachers could be remunerated more equitably for the level of mastery they have attained. While these proposals tangentially address the isolation of teachers by creating the potential for having more than one teacher work with students in a classroom (albeit at different levels), they do not address the strong norm of equality that is present in most schools and that has tended to undermine career ladder proposals (Conley *et al.*, 1988).

Finally, the fourth link between school and home (especially homes of an earlier era), is the relationship of female and male. Most leadership positions in schools are occupied by males. In this study of eight schools, seven of the eight were headed by male principals. During the course of the study, the principalship of one of the schools was assumed by a female. This means that while 75–85 per cent of the teaching staff were female, only 25 per cent of the leadership positions were occupied by females. Evans has commented on the effects of this in terms of both gender role definition for children and in terms of school organization. 'The primary (elementary) school is analogous to the family with the male staff as "fathers" — having less contact, more power, authority and importance — and the female staff as "mothers" — more contact, subordinate and of limited importance' (Evans, 1988, p. 93). Conley, *et al.* (1988) has pointed out that some efforts to involve teachers in decision-making fail because of the authority role of the administration.

> Ad hoc teacher committees, which are established at either the district or school level, are expressly designed to enhance teacher participation in decision making. School faculty meetings allegedly serve a similar purpose. However, such committees and meetings are frequently chaired by administrators and thus do not operate under any independent authority. Teachers are thus constrained to respond to agenda items previously selected by administrators, with the broad course of action already determined by school officials. Teachers, critics claim, are relegated to *filling in the details.* (emphasis in the original. Conley, *et al.*, p. 266).

Certainly more women are being promoted to positions of leadership. In the short term this will not necessarily change authority relationships. In the long run, different cultural norms may begin to develop, as women do seem to have different ways of leading (Helgesen, 1990). If the household metaphor has some validity in giving insights into the culture and organization of schools, it will be important to examine the ways women organize their lives to break down the isolation of the household. Can parallel structures be created in schools that will foster the sharing of knowledge, dialogue and cooperation so desperately needed if schools are to be restructured into learning communities for both students and teachers? Given the female nature of teaching, what findings from recent women's studies need to be brought to bear on the process of restructuring? Given the long tradition of isolation and independence of the classroom teacher, how can schools be restructured to foster teacher collegialty and collaboration? Do the proposed changes in teacher certification go far enough to create a truly professional teaching force?

Summary and Conclusions

This chapter has attempted to tease out some of the lessons from effective schools research and practice that could be used to guide efforts to restructure schools. The focus of the chapter has been on the transformative process and has examined each major organizational component that comprises the process. While each component was explored separately as a means of highlighting key learnings, the theme throughout the chapter has been to show the close interconnectedness between each component. Briefly, the chapter discussed the impetus for restructuring that lies in efficiency concerns for increased school outputs. An important consideration from effective schools research is to keep the focus not only on efficiency, but also on equity, if true achievement gains are to be realized. Disaggregated outcome measures were shown to be essential tools for maintaining a focus on equity as well as efficiency.

A second major area addressed was organizational structures. While the nature of a restructured school remains vague, one aspect that has been delineated is the need to develop shared governance structures that will allow teachers greater decision-making opportunities. The lessons from effective schools research are that unless properly linked to implementing the mission of the school, the governance structures may prove counterproductive both in terms of empowering teachers and in enhancing student learning.

School technology in terms of academic focus, instructional practices, use of time and staff development was the third area explored. Each of these variables are closely intertwined and are at the heart of the teaching and learning process. Effective schools research does not provide precise guidance on the contents of these elements, but rather places them in the framework of district and school level organizational and instruction processes that must be arrived at through data analysis and shared decision-making (Taylor, 1990). The research, however, does show the complementary nature of the school effectiveness and teacher effectiveness research and their critical role in enhanced student learning (Davis and Thomas, 1989; Taylor, 1990).

Finally, this chapter examined school culture and climate as it pertains to school effectiveness and restructuring. It is in the beliefs about student learning and school responsibility for student learning that effective schools research provides an important legacy on which to build restructured schools. Furthermore, effective schools research has shown that organizational structures and technology are reflections of the culture and at the same time are independent components, that if altered over time, can lead to changes in the school culture. The symbols, rites, rituals, heroes and heroines of the school are all tools that have been used to enhance effectiveness and will need to be used in the process of restructuring. This section of the chapter also explored the possibility that two goals of restructuring, increasing the collegiality and professionalism among teachers, may be thwarted if deep-seated and unstated cultural norms that have shaped schools are not understood or addressed. The metaphor of the household was used to help highlight these cultural norms.

Schools, more than any other organization in society, are faced with the almost impossible role of maintaining the past and preparing young people for the future. The history of schooling indicates that schools have been better at maintaining the past than at preparing the next generation for the future (Carnoy and Levin, 1976). Systems theory helps to illustrate why change requires that all components be addressed simultaneously. A change in one component impacts other parts of the system. Because of a system's natural tendency to homeostasis, a change in one area often sets off a reaction in another part in an effort to keep the system in equilibrium. Even to bring about incremental changes, the culture, organizational structures and procedures, and school technology have to be brought into alignment through leadership. Perhaps the most important lesson to be drawn from effective schools research is that a complex view of change is needed to match the complex nature of schools.

Effective schools research has shown that while effective schools have retained a pattern of schooling that remains familiar, there has been within them, at the same time, a fundamental restructuring of beliefs about students, teaching and learning. It remains to be seen whether or not with even more radical restructuring these schools can now help their students attain even higher levels of achievement. The history of the effective schools research bodes well for the future, but also points to the difficulty and challenge of the task of change needed to prepare students for the twenty-first century.

Appendix A

San Diego County Effective Schools Survey

THE SAN DIEGO COUNTY OFFICE OF EDUCATION EFFECTIVE SCHOOLS SURVEY[1]

(Elementary Form)

Adapted From:
Connecticut School Effectiveness Questionnaire
Glendale Effective Schools Assessment Instrument
Items from California AB551, 803, Model Curriculum Standards,
School Improvement Program, and Other Resources

Revised 9/86

Developed by San Diego County Office of Education Effective Schools Cadre

Sally Pollack, Team Leader

Mary Beall	Doyle Knirk
Janet Chrispeels	Carol Leighty
David Homiston	Sammie McCormack
Michael Johnson	Bill Padelford
Lean King	Dan Watson
Rita King	Chris Wilson

1 Permission to reprint granted by the San Diego County Office of Education, San Diego, California

THE SAN DIEGO COUNTY OFFICE OF EDUCATION
EFFECTIVE SCHOOLS SURVEY

Introduction

This survey is one component of the San Diego County Office of Education School Effectiveness Assessment Process. The questions are based on items from the Connecticut School Effectiveness Questionnaire and the Glendale Effective Schools Assessment Instrument. Other items have been included that are based on school and instructional effectiveness research.

INSTRUCTIONS

1. Please **DO NOT MARK** the survey. All responses are to be recorded on a separate answer sheet.

2. All questions have five (5) possible responses. Record your answer by marking the appropriate number on the answer sheet. (Use a #2 pencil.) The response categories for each item are:

    1 = Strongly Disagree

    2 = Disagree

    3 = Don't Know

    4 = Agree

    5 = Strongly Agree

3. Although some questions may seem to warrant a Yes-No response, the response categories permit you to indicate the intensity of your feelings in relation to the item.

4. *Your* perceptions based on *your* experience in this school are important.

5. The person administering this survey is available to answer *procedural* questions, but it is your interpretation of each item that is important.

6. Each item must be read carefully. There is not a time limit. Completion of this survey is expected to take approximately thirty (30) minutes.

SAN DIEGO EFFECTIVE SCHOOLS SURVEY
(Elementary Level)

| **KEY TO ANSWER SHEET** |
| 1 = Strongly Disagree |
| 2 = Disagree |
| 3 = Don't Know |
| 4 = Agree |
| 5 = Strongly Agree |

1. In general, teachers expect almost all of their students to do well on norm-referenced (standardized) tests such as CAP or CTBS.

2. The principal makes frequent informal contacts with students and teachers.

3. The principal regularly gives feedback to teachers regarding their instructional techniques.

4. Students are held accountable for maintaining school rules throughout the year.

5. The results of teacher-made tests or chapter tests are used to diagnose student strengths and weaknesses.

6. Students are encouraged to express themselves through questioning and classroom discussion.

7. Teachers in this school base grading on students' achievement of subject matter rather than students' behavior.

8. Classroom tests are given at the end of each instructional unit.

9. Property of staff members is secure.

10. Vandalism or destruction of school property by students is *not* a problem.

11. Follow-up assistance (materials, coaching, etc.) is provided by the administration for implementing skills learned in staff development activities.

12. Property of students is secure.

13. There is a positive school spirit.

14. Special instructional programs are coordinated with the school curriculum and classroom instruction.

15. Phone calls, newsletters, regular notes, and conferences are ways that most teachers communicate with parents in this school.

16. Textbooks and other materials are selected on the basis of how well they support learning objectives.

17. Teachers in this school believe that all students can achieve basic reading skills.

18. To the best of my knowledge, written standards for language arts exist.

19. The principal emphasizes participation by teachers in staff development activities related to instructional improvement.

SAN DIEGO EFFECTIVE SCHOOLS SURVEY
(Elementary Level)

KEY TO ANSWER SHEET
1 = Strongly Disagree 2 = Disagree 3 = Don't Know 4 = Agree 5 = Strongly Agree

20. Teachers in this school spend more time communicating with parents about the good things students do than about the bad.

21. Students and staff members take pride in the school and help to keep buildings and grounds clean and attractive.

22. Administrative leadership is available to resolve disagreements that develop among staff members.

23. The time set aside for basic skill instruction is free from interruptions (e.g., intercom, messages, assemblies).

24. Teachers in this school believe that all students can achieve basic writing skills.

25. Teachers stress academic achievement as a priority for their students.

26. The principal reviews and interprets test results with the faculty.

27. Students in this school try to succeed in their classes.

28. Reteaching and specific skill remediation are important parts of the teaching process.

29. Many students are acknowledged and rewarded for academic improvements and achievements in this school.

30. Students treat each other respectfully and are not subject to verbal abuse by other students.

31. Parents are encouraged to share ideas for school improvement with administration and staff in this school.

32. This school is a safe and secure place to work during the normal school day.

33. Few discipline problems are referred to the office.

34. The principal is accessible to discuss matters dealing with instruction.

35. Staff members enforce the student rules consistently and equitable.

36. The principal emphasizes the meaning and use of standardized test results.

37. The activities of the parent group support the school's goals.

38. Students are frequently rewarded or praised by faculty and staff for following school rules.

39. Teachers in this school believe that all students can achieve basic math skills.

SAN DIEGO EFFECTIVE SCHOOLS SURVEY
(Elementary Level)

KEY TO ANSWER SHEET
1 = Strongly Disagree
2 = Disagree
3 = Don't Know
4 = Agree
5 = Strongly Agree

40. Parents frequently initiate contacts with classroom teachers.

41. Teachers and the principal thoroughly review and analyze test results to plan instructional program modifications.

42. Teachers hold students accountable for clear and accurate writing regardless of the subject matter.

43. The staff development program is regularly evaluated by the staff.

44. Instructional issues are frequently the focus of faculty meetings.

45. Ninety to one-hundred per cent of my students' parents attend scheduled parent-teacher conferences.

46. A primary focus of staff development activities at our school is the application of knowledge and skills in the classroom.

47. Almost all students complete assigned homework before coming to school.

48. Students must master the essential academic skills being taught before proceeding to the next learning task.

49. Students are given specific feedback on assignments.

50. Time allocated for basic skill instruction is consistently followed in each classroom.

51. Parent-teacher conferences focus on factors directly related to student achievement.

52. The physical condition of this school building is generally pleasant and well kept.

53. To the best of my knowledge, written standards in mathematics exist.

54. Teachers and parents are aware of the homework policy in this school.

55. Students are engaged in learning activities until the end of each instructional period.

56. Students not achieving identified standards are given additional help until standards are achieved.

57. The California Assessment Program is an accurate and valid measure of the basic skills curriculum.

58. Students in my class have frequent opportunities to work cooperatively together in small heterogeneous groups.

SAN DIEGO EFFECTIVE SCHOOLS SURVEY
(Elementary Level)

KEY TO ANSWER SHEET
1 = Strongly Disagree
2 = Disagree
3 = Don't Know
4 = Agree
5 = Strongly Agree

59. Students are offered multiple opportunities to practice new skills in both group and individual settings.

60. In this school, the staff development program is evaluated based on evidence of use in the classroom.

61. Administrators support teachers in dealing with student discipline matters.

62. The principal and staff plan the staff development program.

63. Multiple methods are used to assess student progress (e.g., criterion-referenced tests, work samples, criteria check lists, etc.)

64. Students in my class estimate answers to computations and frequently use mental arithmetic.

65. Alternative teaching strategies are provided to students having difficulty mastering a skill.

66. Homework is regularly assigned.

67. In spite of home background, you feel you can successfully teach 90-95% of your students.

68. Seventy-five percent or more of the parents attend open house or back-to-school night.

69. Parent-teacher conferences seldom result in specific plans for home-school cooperation aimed at improving students' classroom achievement.

70. Staff members are treated respectfully by students and not subject to verbal abuse.

71. Cooperation exists between parents and teachers in regard to homework monitoring.

72. Teachers contact parents in this school on a regular basis.

73. There is an active parent group in this school.

74. Teachers **expect** that over ninety-five percent of students in this school will graduate from high school.

75. A variety of teaching strategies are used in my classroom (e.g., lectures, discussion, cooperative/team learning, etc.).

76. To the best of my knowledge, written standards in fine arts exist.

77. Teachers in all subject areas require students to do reading, writing, listening, and speaking.

SAN DIEGO EFFECTIVE SCHOOLS SURVEY
(Elementary Level)

KEY TO ANSWER SHEET
1 = Strongly Disagree
2 = Disagree
3 = Don't Know
4 = Agree
5 = Strongly Agree

78. In this school, parents are aware of the discipline policy.

79. Practice work following direct instruction is planned so students will be highly successful.

80. Most parents have a clear understanding of the school's goals.

81. The mathematics program in my class includes concepts and activities from: number, measurement, geometry, patterns and functions, statistics and probability, and logic.

82. Learning activities that address all learning modalities (e.g., visual, auditory, kinesthetic/tactile) are provided in my classroom.

83. A primary focus of staff development activities at our school is the acquisition of new skills.

84. The principal is active in promoting staff development activities.

85. Most teachers in this school believe that all students can achieve identified standards in each subject area.

86. Students receive immediate feedback on their homework and are provided with specific suggestions for improvement.

87. In general, teachers expect almost all of their students to do well on teacher prepared tests.

88. Most homework assigned to students is independent practice on what has already been learned in class.

89. This school's written statement of purpose defines academic goals that focus on student learning and achievement as this school's major responsibilities.

90. Classroom instruction is generally free from interruption from outside maintenance. (mowing the lawn, repairs, etc.)

91. Two hours or more are allocated for reading/language arts each day throughout this school.

92. Fifty minutes or more are allocated for mathematics instruction each day.

93. Classroom observations conducted by the principal are focused on improving instruction.

94. Most students in this school are eager and enthusiastic about learning.

95. I consistently hold high academic expectations for all students.

SAN DIEGO EFFECTIVE SCHOOLS SURVEY
(Elementary Level)

KEY TO ANSWER SHEET
1 = Strongly Disagree 2 = Disagree 3 = Don't Know 4 = Agree 5 = Strongly Agree

96. A written statement of purpose exists for this school.

97. Objectives in each subject area are the focal point of instruction in this school.

98. Reteaching and specific skill remediation are important parts of the instructional process in this school.

99. In our school, there is a staff development program based on school goals.

100. Students are taught the school rules.

101. Teachers are held accountable for teaching skills or concepts contained in course outlines.

102. The results of teacher-made tests or chapter tests are used to plan for reteaching.

103. The curriculum, instruction, and assessment are aligned with teaching objectives.

104. In general, administrative leadership is effective in resolving problems concerning the educational program at this school.

105. Most parents rate this school superior.

106. Problem solving is an integral part of almost all activities in my mathematics program.

107. The parent organization at this school is considered important by the administration.

108. Instructional leadership from the principal is clear, strong, and centralized in this school.

109. In this school, over 90 per cent of the students are expected to achieve identified standards.

110. The school buildings are kept in good repair.

111. Class is rarely interrupted to discipline students.

112. Teachers, administrators, parents, and students share responsibility for maintaining discipline in this school.

113. Most parents are aware of the instructional objectives at each grade level and in each subject area.

114. Parents and/or community members are frequent volunteers in this school.

SAN DIEGO EFFECTIVE SCHOOLS SURVEY
(Elementary Level)

KEY TO ANSWER SHEET
1 = Strongly Disagree
2 = Disagree
3 = Don't Know
4 = Agree
5 = Strongly Agree

115. I have social studies materials that are adequate for the students' reading abilities in my classroom.

116. Before a formal observation, the principal and teacher discuss what the principal will observe.

117. Low-achieving students are given the same opportunities to answer questions as often as other students in class.

118. Teachers provide activities that develop critical thinking skills.

119. Students' homework is monitored at home.

120. Daily lessons in my room typically follow this sequence: focusing students on the intended learning, teacher presentation, guided practice, specific feedback, independent work, and evaluation of achievement.

121. Teachers in this school feel they are capable of helping all students achieve identified standards.

122. Students are grouped for instruction based upon diagnosed needs.

123. Written standards for reading are included in course descriptions for all subject areas and grade levels.

124. All students in my class are expected to be successful in their school work.

125. Most parents support school personnel when their child is disciplined for violation of rules.

126. The parent organization at this school is considered important by the teaching staff.

127. In mathematics, most initial instruction is presented to the whole class.

128. The principal initiates effective coordination of the instructional program.

129. This school has a written homework policy.

130. Pull out programs (e.g., Chapter 1, Special Ed., Gifted, etc.) are coordinated with basic skills instruction.

131. Teachers are responsible for helping students reach standards of clear and accurate writing.

132. The principal seeks ideas and suggestions from the staff.

133. After a formal classroom observation, the teacher and principal develop a plan for instructional improvement.

SAN DIEGO EFFECTIVE SCHOOLS SURVEY
(Elementary Level)

KEY TO ANSWER SHEET
1 = Strongly Disagree
2 = Disagree
3 = Don't Know
4 = Agree
5 = Strongly Agree

134. The principal makes several formal classroom observations each year.

135. In general, requests for repairs or alterations to facilities are responded to in a reasonable amount of time.

136. Students generally believe that school rules are reasonable and appropriate.

137. Teachers treat students with respect.

138. Class starts promptly at the beginning of each instructional period.

139. The principal and faculty can solve most problems facing this school.

140. The principal is highly visible throughout the school.

141. Criterion-referenced testing occurs frequently in each subject area.

142. Instructional decisions are based on the school's written statement of purpose.

143. The number of low-income students retained in grade is proportionately equivalent to higher-income students retained in grade.

144. To the best of my knowledge, written standards in social science exist.

145. Classroom test results are used to give specific feedback to students.

146. The principal encourages teachers to accept their responsibilities for student achievement.

147. Following a formal observation, the principal discusses the observation with the teacher.

148. Teachers at this school invite parents to observe the instructional program.

149. Students that achieve identified standards do so regardless of home background.

150. Teachers in this school believe they are responsible for helping students achieve identified standards in each subject area.

151. It is safe to work in this school after students are dismissed.

152. A primary focus of staff development activities at our school is to provide increased knowledge and awareness about a particular topic.

153. The principal initiates the use of test results to modify or change the instructional program.

154. Most initial instruction is presented to the whole class when teaching writing.

Appendix A

SAN DIEGO EFFECTIVE SCHOOLS SURVEY
(Elementary Level)

<table>
<tr><td colspan="2">KEY TO ANSWER SHEET</td></tr>
<tr><td>1 =</td><td>Strongly Disagree</td></tr>
<tr><td>2 =</td><td>Disagree</td></tr>
<tr><td>3 =</td><td>Don't Know</td></tr>
<tr><td>4 =</td><td>Agree</td></tr>
<tr><td>5 =</td><td>Strongly Agree</td></tr>
</table>

155. Parents of students in this school are invited and attend school activities such as sports events, plays, concerts, and awards assemblies.

156. Students must achieve identified standards at each grade level and/or subject area.

157. To the best of my knowledge, written standards in science exist.

158. Administrators enforce the student rules consistently and equitably.

Interview Questions for Effective Schools Study

1. Several years ago this school undertook an effective schools process. In the last couple of years, have achievement scores at (name of school) improved, stayed the same or deceased? How about scores of students from low-income families? Are they making improvement gains? How do you know?

   In your opinion, what might help to explain or account for the achievement results of this school?

2. A new teacher has just arrived at this school. How would you describe the effective schools or school improvement process to him/her?

3. When a new teacher comes to this school, how does he or she learn what this school really cares about?

   In your opinion, what is this school's mission?

   Do parents and students share than mission? If yes, how do you know?

4. Have there been any changes in the way the school is organized since you began the effective schools process? If yes, which changes have had an impact on increasing student achievement — in the school and in your classroom?

5. Is the school addressing the needs of low-achieving students? How?

   Which instructional methods have been effective in meeting the needs of these students?

   How do you know they are effective?

6. What role do the teachers play in making instructional decisions? As a teacher do you feel you have an important role to play? If yes, share an example?

7. Do teachers in this school work together on instructional issues? How?

8. How is school improvement sustained in this school? What additional things could be done in the future to sustain improvement?

9. Are there significant barriers which are preventing you from reaching the achievement levels you'd like?

10. What role do test scores play in making instructional decisions? Do you think there is too much emphasis on test scores? If yes, what outcome measure would you rather have emphasized?

11. Are test score results used to modify the instructional program?

12. What role does the principal play in guiding instruction and making instructional decisions at this school?

13. Do instructional decisions reflect the mission of this school? How?

14. Are instructional decision monitored — at the school level and at the classroom level? How?

15. Describe how instructional changes are evaluated or assessed? What role do teachers play in the evaluation? What role does the principal play?

16. Is there a systematic process for resolving instructional problems in this school? Describe. Discipline problems?

17. Are teachers recognized and rewarded in this school? How?

18. Are students recognized and rewarded in this school? How? Are they rewarded for academic improvements? Do all students receive some recognition for academic growth?

19. Have teacher-parent contacts and relationships changed in any way? If yes, describe.

20. What roles do parents play in helping the school increase student achievement? If they are not involved, why not? Have your expectations for parents changed?

21. If this school was described as an effective school what would that mean to you?

22. Have you changed any of your attitudes or teaching practices as a result of the effective schools process? If yes, describe.

23. Knowing what you know now about school effectiveness and school improvement, what would you do differently, what changes would you make in the improvement process?

References

ANDREWS, R.L. and BAMBURG, J.D. (1989, January) *Teacher and Supervisor Assessment of Principal Leadership and Academic Achievement*, Paper presented at the second annual meeting of the International Congress for School Effectiveness, Rotterdam, The Netherlands.

ANDREWS, R.L., SODER, R. and JACOBY, D. (1986, April) *Principal Roles, Other In-school Variables, and Academic Achievement by Ethnicity and SES*, Paper presented at the Annual Meeting of the American Educational Research Association, San Francisco, CA.

ARMOR, D., CONRY-OSEGUERA, P., COX, M., KING, N., McDONNELL, L., PASCAL, A., PAULY, E. and ZELLMAN, G. (1976) *Analysis of the School Preferred Reading Program in Selected Los Angeles Minority Schools*, Santa Monica, CA: Rand Corporation, Ed130-243.

ARGYRIS, C., PUTNAM, R. and SMITH, D.M. (1987) *Action Science*, San Francisco, CA: Jossey-Bass.

AUSTIN, B.R. (1981) 'Exemplary schools and their identification', *New Directions for Testing and Measurement*, **10**, pp. 31–48.

AUSTIN, G.R. (1978) *Process Evaluation: A Comprehensive Study of Outliers*, Baltimore, MD: Maryland Department of Education (ERIC Document Reproduction Services No. ED-160-644).

AVERCH, H.A., CARROLL, S.J., DONALDSON, T.S., KIESLING, H.J. and PINCUS, J. (1974) *How Effective is Schooling? A Critical Review of Research*, Englewood Cliffs, NJ: Educational Technology Publications.

BALDRIDGE, J.V. and DEAL, T.E. (Eds) (1975) *Managing Change in Educational Organizations: Sociological Perspectives, Strategies, and Case Studies*, Berkeley, CA: McCutchan.

BAMBURG, J.E. and ANDREWS, R.L. (1989, March) *Putting Effective Schools Research to Work: The Process of Change and the Role of the Principal*, Paper presented at the annual meeting of the American Educational Research Association, San Francisco, CA.

BARTH, R.S. (1988) 'School: A community of leaders', in LIEBERMAN, A. (Ed.) *Building a Professional Culture in Schools*, New York, NY: Teachers College Press, pp. 129–47.

BARTH, R.S. (1990) *Improving Schools from Within: Teachers, Parents, and Principals can Make the Difference*, San Francisco, CA: Jossey-Bass.

197

References

BENJAMIN, R. (1980) 'Successful schools: The formula begins with responsibility', in BRUNDAGE, D. (Ed.) *The Journalism Research Fellows Report: What Makes an Effective School?* Washington, DC: George Washington University, Institute for Educational Leadership, pp. 69–104.

BENNIS, W.G., BENNE, K.D. and CHIN, R. (1985) *The Planning of Change*, New York, NY: Holt, Rinehart and Winston.

BENNIS, W.G. and NANUS, B. (1985) *Leaders: The Strategies for Taking Charge*, New York, NY: Harper and Row.

BERLINER, D.C. and ROSENSHINE, B.V. (Eds) (1987) *Talks to Teachers*, New York, NY: Random House.

BERMAN, P. and MCLAUGHLIN, M. (1976) 'Implementation of educational innovation', *Educational Forum*, **40**(3), pp. 345–70.

BERMAN, P. and MCLAUGHLIN, M. (1977) *Factors Affecting Implementation and Continuation* (Vol VII), Santa Monica, CA: Rand Corporation.

BERMAN, P. and MCLAUGHLIN, M. (1978) *Implementing and Sustaining Innovations*, (Vol VIII), Santa Monica, CA: Rand Corporation.

BERMAN, P. and MCLAUGHLIN, M. (1979) *An Exploratory Study of School District Adaptation*, Santa Monica, CA: Rand Corporation.

BERMAN, P. and OTHERS (1988) *Restructuring California Education: A Design for Public Education in the Twenty-First Century. Recommendations to the California Business Roundtable*, Berkeley, CA: Berman, Weiler and Assoc. ED 302-618.

BICKEL, W. (1983) 'Effective schools: Knowledge, dissemination, inquiry', *Educational Researcher*, **12**(4), pp. 3–5.

BLENDINGER, J. and JONES, L.T. (April, 1988) 'Create a healthy school culture: An interview with Terry Deal', *The School Administrator*, pp. 22–24, 26.

BLENKY, M.F. CLINCKY, B.M., GOLDBERGER, N.R. and TARULE, J.M. (1989) *Women's Way of Knowing*, New York, NY: Basic Books.

BLOCK, J.H., EFTHIM, H.E. and BURNS, R.B. (1989) *Building Effective Mastery Learning Schools*, New York, NY: Longman.

BLOOM, B.S. (1984, May) 'The search for methods of group instruction as effective as one-to-one tutoring', *Educational Leadership* **41**, pp. 4–18.

BLUMBERG, A. and GREENFIELD, W. (1980) *The Effective Principal: Perspectives on School Leadership*, Boston, MA: Allyn and Bacon.

BOLMAN, L.G. and DEAL, T.E. (1986) *Modern Approaches to Understanding and Managing Organizations*, San Francisco, CA: Jossey-Bass.

BORGER, J.B., LO, C.L., OH, S.S. and WALBERG, H.J. (1985) 'Effective schools: A quantitative synthesis of constructs', *Journal of Classroom Interaction*, **20**(2), pp. 12–17.

BOSSERT, S.T., DWYER, D.C., ROWAN, B. and LEE, G.V. (1982) 'The instructional management role of the principal', *Educational Administration Quarterly*, **18**(3), pp. 34–64.

BRANDT, R. (1987) 'On leadership and student achievement: A Conversation with Richard Andrews', *Educational Leadership*, **45**(1), pp. 9–16.

BRANDT, R. (1990) 'On restructuring schools: A conversation with Al Shanker', *Educational Leadership*, **47**(7), pp. 11–16.

BRIGGS, J. and PEAT, F.D. (1989) *Turbulent mirror*, New York, NY: Harper and Row.

BROOKOVER, W.G. (1985) 'Can we make schools effective for minority students?', *The Journal of Negro Education*, **54**(3), pp. 257–68.

BROOKOVER, W.G., BEADY, C., FLOOD, P., SCHWEITZER, J. and WISENBAKER, J. (1979) *School Social Systems and Student Achievement: Schools Can Make a Difference*, New York, NY: Praeger.

BROOKOVER, W.B. and LEZOTTE, L.W. (1979) *Changes in School Characteristics Coincident with Changes in Student Achievement*, East Lansing, MI: Michigan State University, The Institute for Research on Teaching. (ERIC Document Reproduction Service No. ED-181-1005).

BROPHY, J. (1982) *Research on the Self-fulfilling Prophecy and Teacher Expectations*, East Lansing, MI: Institute for Research on Teaching, Michigan State University, Research Series, 119.

BURNS, J.M. (1978) *Leadership*. New York, NY: Harper and Row.

CALIFORNIA STATE DEPARTMENT OF EDUCATION (1980) *Report on the Special Studies of Selected ECE Schools with Increasing and Decreasing Reading Scores*, Sacramento, CA: Office of Program Evaluation and Research. (ERIC Document Reproduction Service No. ED-188-106).

CANADY, R.L. and HOTCHKISS, P.R. (1985) 'Scheduling practices and policies associated with increased achievement for low achieving students', *Journal of Negro Education*, **54**(3), pp. 344–55.

CARNEGIE TASK FORCE ON TEACHING AS A PROFESSION (1986) *A Nation Prepared: Teachers for the 21st century*, New York, NY: Carnegie Forum on Education and the Economic.

CARNOY, M. and LEVIN, H.M. (1976) *The Limits of Educational Reform*, New York, NY: Longman.

CASNER-LOTTO, J. (1988) 'Expanding the teacher's role: Hammond's School improvement process', *Phi Delta Kappan*, **69**(5), pp. 349–53.

CHAPMAN, J. (1991, January) *School Effectiveness and Management: The Enmeshment of the Qualitative and Quantitative Concerns of Schooling*, Paper presented at the International Congress of School Effectiveness and Improvement, Cardiff, Wales.

CHRISPEELS, J.A. (1980) 'Evaluation as a compliance strategy: Program reviews in California', in ZERCHYKOV, R. and DAVIES, D. with CHRISPEELS, J. *Leading the Way: State Mandates for School Advisory Councils in California, Florida and South Carolina*, Boston, MA: The Institute for Responsive Education, pp. 41–65.

CHRISPEELS, J.A. and MEANEY, D. (1985) *Building Effective Schools: Assessing, Planning, Implementing*, San Diego, CA: San Diego County Office of Education.

CHRISPEELS, J.A. and POLLACK, S. (1989) 'Equity schools and equity districts', in CREEMERS, B.P.M., PETERS, T. and REYNOLDS, D. (Eds) *School Effectiveness and School Improvement*, Amsterdam, The Netherlands: Swets and Zeitlinger, pp. 295–308.

CHUBB, J.E. and MOE, T.M. (1985) 'Politics, markets, and the organization of schools', paper presented at the Annual Meeting of the American Political Science Association, New Orleans, LA, ED263-674.

CLARK, R. (1983) *Family Life and School Achievement: Why Poor Black Children Succeed or Fail*, Chicago, IL: University of Chicago Press.

CLARK, R. (1987) *Family Life and Student Achievement: Why Some Black Students Succeed and Others Fail*, New York, NY: Harper and Row.

CLARK, T.A. and MCCARTHY, D.P. (1983) 'School improvement in New York City: The evolution of a project', *Educational Researcher*, **12**(4), pp. 17–24.

References

CLIFT, R.T. (1985) 'Some neglected elements of effective schools research: A review of literature', *Journal of Classroom Interaction*, **20**(2), pp. 2–11.

COCH, L. and FRENCH, J. (1948) 'Overcoming resistance to change', *Human Relations*, **4**, pp. 512–32.

COLEMAN, J.S., CAMPBELL, E.O., HOBSON, C.J., McPARTLAND, J., MOOD, A.M., WEINFIELD, F.D. and YORK, R.L. (1966) *Equality of Educational Opportunity*, Washington, DC: US Office of Education, National Center for Educational Statistics.

COMER, J.P. (1987) 'New Haven's school-community connection', *Educational Leadership*, **44**(6), pp. 13–16.

CONLEY, S.C., SCHMIDLE, T. and SHEDD, J.B. (1988) 'Teacher participation in the management of school systems', *Teachers College Record*, **90**(2), pp. 259–280.

CRANDALL, D.P. (1983) 'The teacher's role in school improvement', *Educational Leadership*, **41**(3), pp. 6–13.

CREEMERS, B., PETERS, T. and REYNOLDS, D. (Eds) (1990) *School Effectiveness and School Improvement*, Amsterdam, The Netherlands: Swets & Zeitlinger.

CROHN, L. (1983) *Toward Excellence: Student and Teacher Behaviors as Predictors of School Success: Research Summary Report*, Portland, OR: Northwest Regional Educational Laboratory.

CRUICKSHANK, D. (1981) 'What we know about teachers' problems', *Educational Leadership*, **38**, pp. 402–405.

CUBAN, L. (1983) 'Effective schools: A friendly but cautionary note', *Phi Delta Kappan*, **9**, pp. 695–96.

CUBAN, L. (1984) 'Transforming the frog into a prince: Effective schools research, policy, and practice at the district level', *Harvard Educational Review*, **54**(2), pp. 129–151.

CURTHOYS, A. (1988) *For and Against Feminism*, Sydney, Australia: Allen & Unwin.

DAVIS, G.A. and THOMAS, M.A. (1989) *Effective Schools and Effective Teachers*, Boston, MA: Allyn and Bacon.

DEAL, T.E. (1984a) 'Educational change: Revival tent, tinkertoys, jungle, or carnival?', *Teachers College Record*, **86**(1), pp. 124–137.

DEAL, T.E. (1984b) 'Searching for the wizard: The quest of excellence in education', *Issues in Education*, **2**(1), pp. 56–67.

DEAL, T.E. (1985) 'Cultural change: Opportunity, silent killer, or metamorphosis?', in KILMANN, R., SAXTON, M. and SERPA, R. (Eds) *Gaining Control of the Corporate Culture*, San Francisco, CA: Jossey-Bass, pp. 292–331.

DEAL, T.E. (1987) 'The culture of schools', in SHEIVE, L.T. and SCHOENHEIT, M.B. *Leadership: Examining the Elusive*, Alexandria, VA: Association for Supervision and Curriculum Development, pp. 3–15.

DEAL, T.E. and DERR, C.B. (1978) 'Toward a contingency theory of organizational change in education: Structure, processes, and symbolism', in BENSON C. and STALLINGS, J. *School Finance and Organization*, Washington, DC: National Institute of Education, pp. 91–118.

DEAL, T.E. and KENNEDY, A.A. (1982) *Corporate Cultures: The Rites and Rituals of Corporate Life*, Reading, MA: Addison-Wesley.

DEAL, T.E. and PETERSON, K.D. (1990) *The Principal's Role in Shaping School Culture*, Washington, DC: United States Department of Education.

DE BEVOISE, W. (1984) 'Synthesis of research on the principal as instructional leader', *Instructional Leadership*, **41**(5), pp. 14–20.

DORMAN, G., LIPSITZ, J. and VERNER, P. (1985) 'Improving schools for young adolescents', *Educational Leadership*, **42**(6), pp. 44–9.

DOYLE, D.P. and COOPER, B.S. (1988) *Federal Aid to the Disadvantaged: What Future for Chapter 1?*, London, UK: The Falmer Press.

DOYLE, W.J. (1978) 'A Solution in Search of a Problem: Comprehensive Change and the Jefferson Experimental Schools', in MANN, D. (Ed.) *Making Change Happen?* New York, NY: Teachers College Press, pp. 78–100.

DWYER, D.C. (1984) 'The search for instructional leadership: Routines and subtleties in the principal's role', *Educational Leadership*, **41**(5), pp. 32–7.

EDMONDS, R.R. (1978) 'A discussion of the literature and issues related to effective schooling', paper prepared for the National Conference on Urban Education, St. Louis, MO: CEMREL, Central Midcontinent Regional Educational Laboratory.

EDMONDS, R.R. (1979a) 'Effective schools for the urban poor', *Educational Leadership*, **37**, pp. 15–27.

EDMONDS, R.R. (1979b) 'Some schools work and more can', *Social Policy*, **9**, pp. 28–32.

EDMONDS, R.R. (1984) 'School effects and teacher effects', *Social Policy*, **15**(2), pp. 37–39.

EDMONDS, R.R. and FREDERIKSEN, J.R. (1978) *Search for Effective Schools: The Identification and Analysis of City Schools that are Instructionally Effective for Poor Children*, (ERIC Document Reproduction Service No. ED-170-396).

EISNER, J. (1980) 'Good schools have quality principals', in BRUNNDAGE, D. (Ed.) *The Journalism Research Fellows Report: What Makes an Effective School?* Washington, DC: George Washington University, Institute for Educational Leadership, pp. 57–68.

ELMORE, R.F. and ASSOCIATES (1990) *Restructuring Schools: The Next Generation of Educational Reform*, San Francisco, CA: Jossey-Bass.

EPSTEIN, J.L. (1987) 'Parent involvement: What research says to administrators', *Education and Urban Society*, **19**, pp. 119–36.

EPSTEIN, J.L. and BECKER, H.J. (1982) 'Teachers' reported practices of parent involvement: Problems and possibilities', *Elementary School Journal*, **83**, pp. 103–113.

ESTLER, S. (1985) *Clear Goals, Instructional Leadership and Academic Achievement: Instrumentation and Findings*, paper presented at the annual meeting of the American Educational Research Association, Chicago.

EVANS, T. (1988) *A Gender Agenda: A Sociological Study of Teachers, Parents and Pupils in their Primary Schools*, Sydney, Australia: Allen & Unwin.

EVERTSON, C.M. (1986) 'Do teachers make a difference?' *Education and Urban Society*, **18**, pp. 195–210.

FIRESTONE, W.A. (1980) 'Images of schools and patterns of change', *American Journal of Education*, **88**(4), pp. 459–82.

FIRESTONE, W.A. (1987) 'Meaning in method: The rhetoric of quantitative and qualitative research', *Educational Researcher*, **16**(7), pp. 16–21.

FOSTER, W. (1986) *The Reconstruction of Leadership*. Melbourne, Australia: Deakin University Press.

FOSTER, W. (1988) 'Toward a critical practice of leadership', in SMYTH, J. (Ed.) *Critical Perspectives on Educational Leadership*, London, England: Falmer Press.

FUHRMAN, S., CLUNE, W.H. and ELMORE, R.F. (1988) 'Research on education reform: Lessons on the implementation of policy', *Teachers College Record*, **90**(2), pp. 237–57.

FULLAN, M. (1982) *The Meaning of Educational Change*, New York, NY: Teachers College Press.

FULLAN, M. (1990) 'Staff development, innovation, and institutional development', in JOYCE, B. (Ed.) *Changing School Culture Through Staff Development*, Alexandria, VA: Association for Supervision and Curriculum Development, pp. 3–25.

FULLAN, M., BENNETT, B. and ROLHEISER-BENNETT, C. (1990) 'Linking classroom and school improvement', *Educational Leadership*, **47**(8), pp. 13–19.

FULLAN, M. and POMFRET, A. (1977) 'Research on curriculum and instruction implementation', *Review of Educational Research*, **47**(1), pp. 335–97.

FULLER, B. (1987) 'What school factors raise achievement in the third world?' *Review of Educational Research*, **57**(3), pp. 255–92.

FULLER, F.F. (1969) 'Concerns of teachers: A developmental conceptualization', *American Educational Research Journal*, **6**(2), pp. 207–226.

GAUTHIER, J.W. (1983) *Instructionally Effective Schools: A Model and a Process*, (Monograph Number One) Hartford, CT: Connecticut State Department of Education.

GLASER, B.G. and STRAUSS, A.L. (1967) *The Discovery of Grounded Theory: Strategies for Qualitative Research*, New York, NY: Aldine Publications.

GLATTHORN, A.A. and NEWBERG, N.A. (1984) 'A team approach to instructional leadership', *Educational Leadership*, **41**(5), pp. 60–3.

GLENN B.C. (1981) *What Works? An Examination of Effective Schools for Poor Black Children*, Cambridge, MA: Center for Law and Education, Harvard University.

GOOD, T.L. and BROPHY, J.E. (1986) 'School effects', in WITTROCK, M.C. (Ed.) *Handbook of Research on Teaching*, New York, NY: Macmillan, pp. 570–602.

GOODLAD, J.I. (1975) *The Dynamics of Educational Change: Toward Responsive Schools*, New York, NY: McGraw Hill.

GOODLAD, J.I. (1983) *A Place Called School*. New York, NY: McGraw-Hill.

GOODLAD, J.I. (Ed.) (1987) *The Ecology of School Renewal*, Chicago, IL: University of Chicago Press.

GREENBLATT, R.B., COOPER, B.S. and MUTH, R. (1984) 'Managing for effective teaching', *Educational Leadership*, **41**(5), pp. 57–9.

GROSS, N. (1979) 'Basic issues in the management of educational change efforts', in HERRIOTT, R. and GROSS, N. (Eds) *The Dynamics of Planned Educational Change*, Berkeley, CA: McCutchan.

GROSS, N., GIACQUINTA, J. and BERNSTEIN, M. (1971) *Implementing Organizational Innovations: A Sociological Analysis of Planned Educational Change*, New York, NY: Basic Books.

GUBA, E.G. and LINCOLN, Y.S. (1985) *Effective Evaluation: Improving the Usefulness of Evaluation Results Through Responsive and Naturalistic Approaches*, San Francisco, CA: Jossey-Bass.

HALL, G.E. and HORD, S.M. (1987) *Change in Schools: Facilitating the Process*, New York, NY: State University of New York Press.

HALL, G., RUTHERFORD, W.L., HORD, S.M. and HULING, L.L. (1984) 'Effects of three principal styles on school improvement', *Educational Leadership* **41**(5), pp. 22–29.

HALLINAN, M.T. (1987) *The Social Organization of Schools: New Conceptualizations of the Learning Process*, New York, NY: Plenum Press.

HALLINGER, P. (1989, January) *Developing Instructional Leadership Teams in High Schools*, paper presented at the second annual meeting of the International Congress for School Effectiveness, Rotterdam, The Netherlands.

HALLINGER, P. and MURPHY, J. (1982) 'The superintendent's role in promoting instructional leadership', *Administrator's Notebook*, **30**(6), pp. 1–4.

HALLINGER, P. and MURPHY, J. (1985a) 'Assessing the instructional management behavior of principals', *Elementary School Journal*, **86**, pp. 217–247.

HALLINGER, P. and MURPHY, J. (1985b) 'Instructional leadership and school socioeconomic status: A preliminary investigation', *Administrator's Notebook*, **31**(5), pp. 1–4.

HALLINGER, P. and MURPHY, J. (1986) 'The social context of effective schools', *American Journal of Education*, **94**, pp. 328–355.

HALLINGER, P. and MURPHY, J. (1987a) 'Assessing and developing principal instructional leadership', *Educational Leadership*, **45**(1), pp. 54–61.

HALLINGER, P. and MURPHY, J. (1987b) 'Instructional leadership in the school context', in GREENFIELD, W. (Ed.) *Instructional Leadership: Problems, Issues, and Controversies*, Boston, MA: Allyn and Bacon.

HALLINGER, P. and MURPHY, J. (1989, January) *Social Context Effects on School Effects*, paper presented at the second annual meeting of the International Congress for School Effectiveness, Rotterdam, The Netherlands.

HANDY, C. and AITKEN, R. (1986) *Understanding Schools as Organizations*, Middlesex, England: Penguin Books.

HANNA, D.P. (1988) *Designing Organizations for High Performance*, New York, NY: Addison-Wesley.

HART, A.W. and MURPHY, M.J. (1989, March) *Work Design Where it Happens: Five Comparative Cases of Schools*, paper presented at the annual meeting of the American Educational Research Association, San Francisco, CA.

HAWLEY, W.D. (1978) 'Horses Before Carts: Developing Adaptive Schools and the Limits of Innovation', in MANN, D. (Ed.) *Making Change Happen?* New York, NY: Teachers College Press, pp. 224–60.

HELGESEN, S. (1990) *The Female Advantage: Women's Ways of Leadership*, New York, NY: Doubleday Currency.

HENDERSON, A.T. (Ed.) (1981) *Parent Participation and Student Achievement: The Evidence Grows*, Columbia, MD: National Committee for Citizens in Education.

HENDERSON, A.T. (1985) *Parent Participation and Student Achievement: The Evidence Continues to Grow*, Columbia, MD: National Committee for Citizens in Education.

HENDERSON, A. (Ed.) (1987) *The Evidence Continues to Grow: Parent Involvement Improves Student Achievement*, Columbia, MD: National Committee for Citizens in Education.

HERRIOTT, R.E. and GROSS, N. (Eds) (1979) *The Dynamics of Planned Educational Change: Case Studies and Analyses*, Berkeley, CA: McCutchan.

HERSH, R.H., CARNINE, D., GALL, M., STOCKARD, J., CARMACK, M.A. and GANNON, P. (1981) *The Management of Education Professionals in Instructionally*

Effective Schools: Toward a Research Agenda, Eugene, OR: Center for Educational Policy and Management, University of Oregon.

HIGH, R.M. and ACHILES, C.M. (1986, April) *Principal Influence in Instructionally Effective Schools*, paper presented at the annual meeting of the American Educational Research Association, San Francisco, CA.

THE HOLMES GROUP (1986) *Tomorrow's Teachers: A Report from the Holmes Group*, East Lansing, MI: The Holmes Group.

HOPKINS, D. (1990) 'Integrating staff development and school improvement: A study of teacher personality and school climate', in JOYCE, B. (Ed.) *Changing School Culture Through Staff Development*, Alexandria, VA: Association for Supervision and Curriculum Development, pp. 41–67.

HORD, S.M., STIEGELBAUER, S.M. and HALL, G.E. (1984) 'Principals don't do it alone: Researchers discover second change facilitator active in school improvement efforts', *R&DCTE Review*, **2**(3), pp. 1, 5.

HUBERMAN, A.M. (1983) 'School improvement strategies that work', *Educational Leadership*, **41**(3), pp. 23–7.

HUBERMAN, M. and MILES, M. (1984) *Innovation up Close*, New York: Plenum.

HUFF, S., LAKE, D. and SCHAALMAN, M.L. (1982) *Principal Differences: Excellence in School Leadership and Management*, Boston, MA: McBer and Company.

HUFFMAN-CARPENTER, P., HALL, G.R. and SUMNER, G.C. (1974) *Change in Education: Insights from Performance Contracting*, Cambridge, MA: Ballinger.

HUTCHINS, C.L., GUZZETTI, B.J. and RILEY, A.M. (1984) *Review of the Research of Effective Schools and Effective Teaching*, Aurora, CO: Mid-continent Regional Educational Laboratory.

JENCKS, C.S., SMITH, M., ACKLAND, H., BANE, M.J., COHEN, D., GINTIS, H., HEYNS, B. and MICHELSON, S. (1972) *Inequality: A Reassessment of the Effect of Family and Schooling in America*, New York, NY: Basic Books.

JENNI, R.W. (1991) 'Application of the school based management process development model', *School Effectiveness and School Improvement*, **2**(2), pp. 136–51.

JOHNSON, F.L., BROOKOVER, W.G. and FARRELL, JR., W.C. (1989a, March) 'School perceptions of parents' role, interest and expectations for their children's education and student achievement', paper presented at the annual meeting of the American Educational Research Association, San Francisco, CA.

JOHNSON, F.L., BROOKOVER, W.G. and FARRELL, JR., W.C. (1989b, March) 'School perceptions of parents' role, interest and expectations for their children's education and student academic sense of futility', paper presented at the annual meeting of the American Educational Research Association, San Francisco, CA.

JOYCE, B. and SHOWERS, B. (1988) *Student Achievement Through Staff Development*, New York, NY: Longman.

JOYCE, B. (Ed.) (1990) *Changing School Culture Through Staff Development: The 1990 ASCD Yearbook*, Alexandria, VA: Association for Curriculum and Development.

JOYCE, B., BENNETT, B. and ROLHEISER-BENNETT, C. (1990) 'The self-educating teacher: Empowering teachers through research', in JOYCE, B. *Changing School Culture through Staff Development*, Alexandria, VA: Association for Curriculum and Development, pp. 26–40.

KANTER, R.M. (1983) *The Change Masters*, New York, NY: Simon & Schuster.

KEARNS, D.T. and DOYLE, D.P. (1988) *Winning the Brain Race: A Bold Plan to Make our Schools Competitive*, San Francisco, CA: Institute for Contemporary Studies.

KIJAI, J. and HOLLINGSWORTH, S. (1987) 'School improvement councils: The perceptions of school principals in selected schools in South Carolina', paper presented at the annual meeting of the American Educational Research Association, Washington, DC.

KIJAI, J. and NORMAN, J. (1990) 'School site councils, school effectiveness and student achievement', paper presented at the annual meeting of the American Educational Research Association, Boston, MA.

KILTGAARD, R.E. and HALL, G.R. (1974) 'Are there unusually effective schools?' *Journal of Human Resources*, **74**, pp. 90–106.

KOUZES, J.M. and POSNER, B.Z. (1987) *The Leadership Challenge: How to Get Extraordinary Things Done in Organizations*, San Francisco, CA: Jossey-Bass.

LANE, J.J. and WALBERG, H.J. (Eds) (1987) *Effective School Leadership: Policy and Process*, Berkeley, CA: McCutchan.

LARKIN, M.M. (1985) 'Ingredients of a successful school effectiveness project', *Educational Leadership*, **42**(6), pp. 31–7.

LA ROCQUE, L. and COLEMAN, P. (1987, April) 'Leadership and commitment to change in school districts', paper presented at the annual meeting of the American Educational Research Association, Washington, DC.

LEITHWOOD, K.A. and MONTGOMERY, D.J. (1982) 'The role of the elementary school principal in program improvement', *Review of Educational Research*, **52**(3), pp. 309–39.

LeMAHIEU, P. (1985) 'New challenges to effective schools research', *Journal of Classroom Interaction*, **20**(2), pp. 18–21.

LEVINE, D.U. and EUBANKS, E.E. (1983, April) *Instructional and Organizational Arrangements at an Unusually Effective Inner City Elementary School in Chicago*, paper presented at the annual meeting of the American Educational Research Association, Montreal, Canada.

LEVINE, D.U. and LEZOTTE, L.W. (1990) *Unusually Effective Schools: An Interpretive Review and Analysis of Research and Practice*, Madison, WI: University of Wisconsin Press.

LEVINE, D.U. and STARK, J.C. (1981, August) *Extended Summary and Conclusions: Institutional and Organizational Arrangements and Processes for Improving Academic Achievement in Inner City Elementary Schools*, Kansas City, MO: Center for the Study of Metropolitan Problems in Education, University of Missouri.

LEVINE, D.U. and STARK, J.C. (1982) 'Instructional and organizational arrangements the improve achievement in inner-city schools', *Educational Leadership*, **40**(3), pp. 41–6.

LEZOTTE, L.W. (1980, July) *Documenting Successful Schools: Is There a Better Way?*, paper presented at the American Association of School Administrators, Chicago, IL.

LEZOTTE, L.W. (1984) 'More schools are working, but even more can', *Social Policy*, **15**(2), pp. 46–48.

LEZOTTE, L.W. (1986, April) *School Effectiveness: Reflections and Future Directions*, paper presented at the annual meeting of the American Educational Research Association, San Francisco, CA.

LEZOTTE, L.W. (1990) 'Lessons learned', in TAYLOR, B.O. (Ed.) *Case Studies in Effective Schools Research*, Dubuque, IA: Kendall/Hunt.

LEZOTTE, L.W. and BANCROFT, B.A. (1985a) 'Growing Use of the effective schools model for school improvement', *Educational Leadership*, **42**(6), pp. 23–7.

LEZOTTE, L.W. and BANCROFT, B.A. (1985b, April) *School Improvement Based on Effective Schools Research: A Promising Approach for Economically Disadvantaged and Minority Students*, East Lansing, MI: Michigan State University, (ERIC Document Reproduction Service No. ED-274-046)

LEZOTTE, L.W., EDMONDS, R. and RATNER, G. (1974) *A Final Report: Remedy for School Failure to Equitable Basic School Skills*, East Lansing, MI: Michigan State University, Department of Urban and Metropolitan Studies.

LEZOTTE, L.W. and PASSALACQUA, J. (1978, October) 'Individual school buildings: Accounting for differences in measured pupil performance', *Urban Education*, **13** pp. 283–293.

LIEBERMAN, A. (Ed.) (1986) *Rethinking School Improvement: Research, Craft, and Concept*, New York, NY: Teachers College.

LIEBERMAN, A. (Ed.) (1988) *Building a Professional Culture in Schools,* New York, NY: Teachers College.

LIGHTFOOT, S. (1983) *Good High Schools: Portraits of Character and Culture*, New York, NY: Basic Books.

LIPHAM, J.M., RANKIN, R.E. and HOEH, J.A. JR. (1985) *The Principalship: Concepts, Competencies, and Cases*, New York, NY: Longman.

LITTLE, J.W. (1982) 'Norms of collegiality and experimentation: Workplace conditions of school success', *American Educational Research Journal*, **5**(19), pp. 325–340.

LITTLE, J.W. (1986, April) 'The persistence of privacy: Autonomy and initiative in teachers' professional relations', paper presented at the annual meeting of the American Education Research Association, San Francisco, CA.

LITTLE, J.W. (1988) 'Assessing the prospects for teacher leadership', in LIEBERMAN, A. (Ed.), *Building a Professional Culture in Schools*, New York, NY: Teachers College Press, pp. 78–106.

LITTLE, J.W. (1989) 'District policy choices and teachers' professional development opportunities', *Educational Evaluation and Policy Analysis*, **11**(2), pp. 165–80.

MACKENZIE, D.E. (1983) 'Research for school improvement: An appraisal of some recent trends', *Educational Researcher*, **12**(4), pp. 5–17.

MANN, D. (Ed.) (1978) *Making Change Happen?* New York, NY: Teachers College Press.

MANN, D. (Fall, 1986) 'Authority and school improvement: An essay on "Little King" leadership', *Teachers College Record*, **88**(1), pp. 41–52.

Manasse, A.L. (1984) 'Principals as leaders of high-performing systems', *Educational Leadership*, **41**(5), pp. 42–6.

McCLINTOCK, C.C., BRANNON, D. and MAYNARD-MOODY, S. (1979) 'Applying the logic of sample surveys to qualitative case studies: The case cluster method', *Administrative Science Quarterly*, **24**, pp. 612–29.

McCORMACK-LARKIN, M. (1985a) 'Change in urban schools', *Journal of Negro Education*, **54**(3), pp. 409–15.

McCORMACK-LARKIN, M. (1985b) 'Ingredients of a successful school effectiveness Project', *Educational Leadership*, **42**, pp. 31–7.

McCormack-Larkin, M. and Kritek, W.J. (1982) 'Milwaukee's project RISE', *Educational Leadership*, **40**(3), pp. 16–21.

McEvoy, B. (1987) 'Everyday acts: How principals influence development of their staffs', *Educational Leadership*, **44**(5), pp. 73–7.

McLaughlin, M.W. (1978) 'Implementation as mutual adaptation: Change in Classroom organization', in Mann, D. (Ed.) *Making Change Happen?* New York, NY: Teachers College Press, pp. 19–31.

McLaughlin, M.W. and Yee, S.M. (1988) 'School as a place to have a career', in Lieberman, A. (Ed.) *Building a Professional Culture in Schools*, New York, NY: Teachers College Press, pp. 23–44.

Merriam, S.B. (1988) *Case Study Research in Education: A Qualitative Approach*, San Francisco, CA: Jossey-Bass.

Meyer, J.W. (1987) 'Implications of an institutional view of education for the study of educational effects', in Hallinan, M.T. (Ed.) *The Social Organization of Schools: New Conceptualizations of the Learning Process*, New York: Plenum, pp. 157–75.

Meyers, H.W. (1989, January) *Rural Education School Improvement Strategies: Improving Leadership and Organizational Structure*, Paper presented at the Second Annual Meeting of the International Congress for School Effectiveness, Rotterdam, The Netherlands.

Micks, J. (1989) *Factors Affecting Academic Performance in Elementary Schools Serving Low Socioeconomic White Students*, Unpublished dissertation, Claremont, CA: Claremont Graduate School/San Diego State University.

Miles, M.B. (Ed.) (1964) *Innovation in Education*, New York, NY: Teachers College, Columbia University.

Miles, M.B. (1981) 'Mapping the common properties of schools', in Lehming, R. and Kane, M. (Eds) *Improving Schools*, Beverly Hills, CA: Sage.

Miles, M.B. (1983) 'Unraveling the mystery of institutionalization', *Educational Leadership*, **41**(3), pp. 14–22.

Miles, M.B., Fullan, M. and Taylor, G. (1978) 'Organizational development in schools: The state of the art', *OD Consultants/OD Programs in School Districts* (Vol III), New York, NY: Center for Policy Research.

Miller, S.K., Shelley, R.C. and Sayre, K.A. (1985) 'Significant achievement gains using the effective schools model', *Educational Leadership*, **42**(6), pp. 38–43.

Miller, S.K. and Sayre, K.A. (1986) *Case Studies of Affluent Effective Schools*, Paper presented at the annual meeting of the American Educational Research Association. San Francisco.

Morgan, G. (1986) *Images of Organizations,* Beverly Hills, CA: Sage.

Morrish, I. (1976) *Aspects of Educational Change*, London, England: George Allen & Unwin.

Mortimore, P., Sammons, P., Stoll, L., Lewis, D. and Ecob, R. (1988) *School Matters*, Berkeley, CA: University of California Press.

Murphy, J.F. (1988) 'Methodological, measurement, and conceptual problems in the study of instructional leadership', *Educational Evaluation and Policy Analysis*, **10**, pp. 117–39.

Murphy, J.F. (1990, April) *Effective Schools: Legacy and Future Directions*, Paper presented at the annual meeting of the American Educational Research Association Meeting, Boston, MA.

Murphy, J.F., Evertson, C.M. and Radnofsky, M.L. (in press) 'Restructuring schools: Fourteen elementary and secondary teachers' perspectives on reform', *Elementary School Journal*.

MURPHY, J.F., HALLINGER, P. and MESA, R.P. (1985) 'School effectiveness: Checking progress and assumptions and developing a role for state and federal government', *Teachers College Record*, **86**, pp. 616–41.

MURPHY, J.F., HALLINGER, P. and MITMAN, A. (1983) 'Problems with research on educational leadership: Issues to be addressed', *Educational Evaluation and Policy Analysis*, **5**(3), pp. 297–305.

MURPHY, J.F., PETERSON, K.D. and HALLINGER, P. (1986) 'The administrative control of principals in effective school districts: The supervision and function', *The Urban Review*, **18**(3), pp. 149–75.

NATIONAL CENTER FOR EFFECTIVE SCHOOLS RESEARCH AND DEVELOPMENT (1989) *A Conversation Between James Comer and Ronald Edmonds*, Dubuque, IA: Kendall/Hunt.

NEW YORK STATE DEPARTMENT OF EDUCATION (1974a, March) *Reading Achievement Related to Educational and Environmental Conditions in Twelve New York City Elementary Schools*, Albany, NY: Division of Education and Evaluation.

NEW YORK STATE DEPARTMENT OF EDUCATION (1974b) *School Factors Influencing Reading Achievement: A Case Study of Two Inner City Schools*, Albany, NY: Office of Education Performance Review, (ERIC Document Reproduction Service No. ED-089-211).

NEW YORK STATE DEPARTMENT OF EDUCATION (1976) *Three Strategies for Studying the Effects of School Process*, Albany, NY: Bureau of School Program Evaluation.

OLSON, L. (1986, January 15) 'Effective schools', *Education Week*, pp. 11–22.

O'NEIL, J. (1990) 'Piecing together the restructuring puzzle', *Educational Leadership*, **47**(7), pp. 4–10.

PARISH, R. and AQUILA, F.D. (1983) 'Comments on the school improvement study: The whole is more than the sum of the parts', *Educational Leadership*, **41**(3), pp. 34–36.

PATTERSON, J.L., PURKEY, S.C. and PARKER, J.V. (1986) *Productive School Systems for a Nonrational World*, Alexandria, VA: Association for Supervision and Curriculum Development.

PECHEONE, R. and SHOEMAKER, J. (1984) *An Evaluation of the School Effectiveness Program in Connecticut*, Hartford, CT: Connecticut State Department of Education.

PERROW, C. (1970) *Organizational Analysis: A Sociological View*, Belmont, CA: Wadsworth Publishing.

PERROW, C. (1979, 2nd Edition) *Complex Organizations: A Critical Essay*, Dallas, TX: Scott, Foresman.

PERSELL, C.H., COOKSON, P.W., JR. and LYONS, H. (1982) *Effective Principals: What do we Know from Various Educational Literatures?* Paper presented at the NIE Conference on Principals for Educational Excellence in the 1980s, Washington, DC.

PETERS, T.J. and WATERMAN, R.H., JR. (1982) *In Search of Excellence*, New York: Harper & Row.

PETTIGREW, A. (1990) 'Longitudinal field research on change: Theory and practice', *Organization Science*.

PFEFFER, J. (1981) 'Management as symbolic action: The creation and maintenance of organizational paradigms', in CUMMINGS, L.L. and STAW, B.M. (Eds) *Research in Organizational Behavior* (Vol 3), Greenwich, CT: JAI Press.

PHI DELTA KAPPAN (1980) *Why Do Some Urban Schools Succeed? The Phi Delta Kappa Study of Exceptional Urban Elmentary Schools*, Bloomington, IN: Phi Delta Kappa.

PINK, W.T. (1989, March) *Effective Staff Development for Urban School Improvement*, Paper presented at the American Educational Research Association Meeting, San Francisco, CA.

POLLACK, S., CHRISPEELS, J.A. and WATSON, D. (1987, April) *A Description of Factors and Implementation Strategies used by Schools in Becoming Effective for all Students*, Paper presented at the annual meeting of the American Educational Research Association, Washington DC.

POLLACK, S., CHRISPEELS, J.A., WATSON, D., BRICE, R. and McCORMACK, S. (1988, April) 'A description of district factors that assist in the development of equity schools', paper presented at the annual meeting of the American Educational Research Association, New Orleans, LA.

PURKEY, S.C. and SMITH, M.S. (1983) 'Effective schools: A review', *Elementary School Journal*, **83**, pp. 427–452.

RAEBECK, B.S. (1990) 'Transformation of a middle school', *Educational Leadership*, **47**(7), pp. 18–21.

RALPH, J.H. and FENNESSEY, J. (1983) 'Science or reform: Some questions about the effective school model', *Phi Delta Kappan*, **64**, pp. 689–94.

RAYWID, M.A. (1989) 'Recentralizing would pose threat to school's success', *Education Week*, **8**(19), pp. 26, 36.

REILLY, W. (1980) 'Effective leaders a major factor in good schools', in BRUNDAGE, D. (Ed.) *The Journalism Research Fellows Report: What Makes an Effective School?* Washington, DC: George Washington University, Institute for Educational Leadership, pp. 40–55.

RENIHAN, F.I. and RENIHAN, P.J. (1991, January) *Pastoral Cosmetic and Participative Considerations in Institutional Image: Implications for School Improvement*, Paper presented at the International Congress for School Effectiveness and Improvement, Cardiff, Wales.

REYNOLDS, D., PHILLIPS, D. and DAVIE, R. (1989, January) *A Highly Effective School Improvement Program*, Paper presented at the second annual meeting of the International Congress for School Effectiveness, Rotterdam, The Netherlands.

ROGERS, V., TALBOT, C. and COSGROVE, E. (1984) 'Excellence: Some lessons from America's best run companies', *Educational Leadership*, **41**(5), pp. 39–41.

ROSENHOLTZ, S.J. (1985, May) 'Effective schools: Interpreting the evidence', *American Journal of Education*, pp. 352–88.

ROSENHOLTZ, S.J. (1989) *Teachers' Workplace*, New York, NY: Longman.

ROSOW, J.M. and ZAGER, R. (1989) *Allies in Educational Reform*, San Francisco, CA: Jossey-Bass.

ROSSMAN, G.B., CORBETT, H.D. and FIRESTON, W.A. (1988) *Change and Effectiveness in Schools: A Cultural Perspective*, New York, NY: State University of New York Press.

ROST, J.C. (1987, November) *The Politics of Instructional Leadership*, Paper presented at the California Principal Conference, Anaheim, CA.

ROST, J.C. (1988 July) *The Nature of Leadership in the Postindustrial Era*, Paper presented at a Meeting of Educational Leadership Researchers at the Center for Creative Leadership, Greensboro, NC.

ROWAN, B. (1988) 'Applying conceptions of teaching to organizational reform', in ELMORE, R.F. (Ed.) *Restructuring Schools: The Next Generation of Educational Reform*, San Francisco, CA: Jossey-Bass, pp. 31–58.

ROWAN, B. and DENK, C. (1984) 'Management succession, school socioeconomic context and basic skills achievement', *American Educational Research Journal*, **21**(3), pp. 517–37.

ROWAN, B., BOSSERT, S.T. and DWYER, D.C. (1983) 'Research on effective schools: A cautionary note', *Educational Researcher*, **12**(4), pp. 24–31.

RUTTER, M., MAUGHAN, B., MORTIMORE, P., OUSTON, J. and SMITH, A. (1979) *Fifteen Thousand Hours: Secondary Schools and Their Effects on Children*, Cambridge, MA: Harvard University Press.

RYAN, W. (1972) *Blaming the Victim,* New York, NY: Random House.

SAMBS, C.E. and SCHENKAT, R. (1990) 'One district learns about restructuring', *Educational Leadership*, **47**(7), pp. 72–5.

SAPHIER, J. and KING, M. (1985) 'Good seeds grow in strong cultures', *Educational Leadership*, **42**(6), pp. 67–74.

SARASON, S.S. (1971) *The Culture of School and the Problem of Change*, Boston, MA: Allyn and Bacon.

SCHEERENS, J. and CREEMERS, B.P.M. (1989) 'Towards a more comprehensive conceptualization of school effectiveness', in CREEMERS, B.P.M., PETERS, T. and REYNOLDS, D. (Eds) *School Effectiveness and School Improvement*, Amsterdam, The Netherlands: Swets and Zeitlinger, pp. 265–278.

SCHEIN, E.H. (1986) *Organizational Culture and Leadership*, San Francisco, CA: Jossey-Bass.

SCHLECHTY, P.C. (1988) 'Leading cultural change: The CMS case', in LIEBERMAN, A. (Ed.) *Building a Professional Culture in Schools*, New York, NY: Teachers College Press, pp. 185–221.

SCHLECHTY, P.C. (1990) *Schools for the 21st century: Leadership Imperatives for educational reform,* San Francisco, CA: Jossey-Bass.

SEELEY, D.S. (1981) *Education Through Partnership*, Washington, DC: American Enterprise Institute for Public Policy Research.

SEELEY, D.S., NIEMEYER, J.H. and GREENSPAN, R. (1990) *Principals Speak-Report #1: Restructuring Schools/School Leadership*, New York, NY: The College of Staten Island/CUNY.

SERGIOVANNI, T.J. (1984) 'Leadership and excellence in schooling', *Educational Leadership*, **41**(5), pp. 4–13.

SERGIOVANNI, T.J. and CORBALLY, J.E. (1984) *Leadership and Organizational Culture: New Perspectives on Administrative Theory and Practice*, Urbana, IL: University of Illinois Press.

SHANKER, A. (1990) 'Staff development and the restructured school', in JOYCE, B. (Ed.) *Changing School Culture Through Staff Development*, Alexandria, VA: Association for Supervision and Curriculum Development, pp. 91–103.

SHOEMAKER, J. and FRASER, H. (1981) 'What principals can do: Some implications from studies on effective schooling', *Phi Delta Kapan*, **63**, pp. 178–82.

SIZEMORE, B.A., BROSSARD, C.A. and HARRIGAN, B. (1983) *An Abashing Anomaly: The High Achieving Predominantly Black Elementary School*, Pittsburgh, PA: University of Pittsburgh Abstract NIE-G-80-0006.

SIZER, T. and HOUSTON, H. (1987) *'Prospectus' of the Coalition of Essential Schools*, Providence, RI: Brown University.

SMIRCICH, L. (1983) 'Concepts of culture and organizational analysis', *Administrative Science Quarterly*, **28**, pp. 339–58.

SMITH, L. and KEITH, P. (1971) *Anatomy of Educational Innovation: An Organizational Analysis of an Elementary School*, New York, NY: Wiley.

SMITH, W.F. and ANDREWS, R.L. (1989) *Instructional Leadership: How Principals Make a Difference*, Alexandria, VA: Association for Supervision and Curriculum Development.

SMYLIE, M.A. and DENNY, J.W. (1990) 'Teacher leadership: Tensions and ambiguities in organizational perspective', *Education Administration* Quarterly, **26**(3), pp. 235–59.

SPARTZ, J.L., VALDES, A.L., McCORMICK, W., MEYERS, T. and GEPPERT, W. (1977) *Delaware Educational Accountability System Case Studies: Elementary Schools Grades 1–4*, Dover, DE: Delaware Department of Public Instruction.

STALLINGS, J.A. (1980), 'Allocated academic learning time revisited, or beyond time on task', *Educational Researcher,* **9**(11), pp. 11–16.

STANLEY, W.B. (1986) 'Critical research', in CORNBLETH, C. (Ed.) *An Invitation to Research in Social Education*, Washington, DC: National Council for the Social Studies.

STANTON, J. and ZERCHYKOV, R. (1979) *Overcoming Barriers to School Council Effectiveness*, Boston, MA: The Institute for Responsive Education.

STEDMAN, L.C. (1987) 'It's time we changed the effective schools formula', *Phi Delta Kappan*, **69**(3), pp. 215–24.

STEVENSON, H.W., LEE, S.Y. and STIGLER, J.W. (1986) 'Mathematics achievement of Chinese, Japanese, and American children', *Science*, **231**, pp. 693–99.

STRINGFIELD, S. and TEDDLIE, C. (1989) 'The first three phases of the Louisiana school effectiveness study', in CREEMERS, B., PETERS, T. and REYNOLDS, D. (Eds) *School Effectiveness and School Improvement*, Amsterdam, The Netherlands: Swets and Zeitlinger, pp. 281–94.

STRINGFIELD, S., TEDDLIE, C. and SUAREZ, S. (1985) 'Classroom interaction in effective and ineffective schools: Preliminary results from Phase III of the Louisiana school effectiveness study', *Journal of Classroom Interaction*, **20**(2), pp. 31–7.

SWEENEY, J. (1982) 'Research synthesis on effective school leadership', *Educational Leadership*, **39**, pp. 346–52.

SYKES, G. (1990) 'Fostering teacher professionalism in schools,' in ELMORE, R.F. and ASSOCIATES, *Restructuring Schools: The Next Generation of Educational Reform*. San Francisco, CA: Jossey-Bass.

TAYLOR, B.O. (1986, April) *Metasensemaking: How the Effective Elementary Principal Accomplishes School Improvement*, Paper presented at the meeting of the American Educational Research Association, San Francisco, CA.

TAYLOR, B.O. (Ed.) (1990) *Case Studies in Effective Schools Research*, Dubuque, IA: Kendall/Hunt.

TAYLOR, B.O. and LEVINE, D.U. (1991) 'Effective schools projects and school-based management', *Phi Delta Kappan*, **72**(5), pp. 394–7.

TEDDLIE, C., FALKOWSKI, C., STRINGFIELD, S., DESSELLE, S. and GARVUE, R. (1984) *Louisiana School Effectiveness Study: Phase Two, 1982–1984*, Baton Rouge, LA: Louisiana State Department of Education.

References

TEDDLIE, C. and STRINGFIELD, S. (1985) 'A differential analysis of effectiveness in middle and low socioeconomic status schools', *The Journal of Classroom Interaction*, **20**(2), pp. 38–45.

TEDDLIE, C., STRINGFIELD, S. and DESSELLE, S. (1985) 'Methods, history, selected findings and recommendations for the Louisiana school effectiveness study, 1980–85', *Journal of Classroom Interaction*, **20**(2), pp. 22–30.

TEDDLIE, C., STRINGFIELD, S. and SUAREZ, S. (1985) 'Classroom interaction in effective and ineffective schools: Preliminary results from Phase III of the Louisiana school effectiveness study', *Journal of Classroom Interaction*, **20**(2), pp. 31–7.

TEDDLIE, C., WIMPELBERG, B. and KIRBY, P. (1987) 'Contextual differences in effective schooling in Louisiana', paper presented at the annual meeting of the American Educational Research Association, Washington, DC.

TEDDLIE, C., KIRBY, P.C. and STRINGFIELD, S. (1989, March) *Effective Versus Ineffective Schools: Observable Differences in the Classroom*, Paper presented at the American Educational Research Association Annual Meeting, San Francisco, CA.

TIMAR, T. (1989) 'The politics of school restructuring', *Phi Delta Kappan*, **71**(4), pp. 165–75.

TOWNSEND, T. (1991, January) *School Effectiveness: A View From the School*, Paper presented at the Fourth International Congress for School Effectiveness and Improvement, Cardiff, Wales.

TRISMAN, D.A., WALLER, M.I. and WILDER, C.A. (1976) *Descriptive and Analytic Study of Compensatory Reading Programs: Final Report*, (Vol 2, PR 75-26), Princeton, NJ: Educational Testing Service.

UNITED STATES GENERAL ACCOUNTING OFFICE (1989, September) 'Effective schools programs: Their extent and characteristics', Washington DC: United States General Accounting Office.

VAN DE GRIFT, W. (1990) 'Educational leadership and academic achievement in elementary education', *School Effectiveness and School Improvement*, **1**(1), pp. 26–40.

VAN METER, E.J. (1982) *Planned Educational Change: A Typology of Overlapping Perspectives*, Paper presented at the meeting of the National Conference of Professors of Educational Administration, San Marcos, TX.

VENEZKY, R.L. and WINFIELD, L.F. (1979) *Schools that Succeed Beyond Expectations in Reading*, (Studies on Education Technical Report No. 1), Newark, DE: University of Delaware. (ERIC Document Reproduction Service No. Ed-177-484)

VILLANOVA, R., GAUTHIER, W., PROCTOR, P. and SHOEMAKER, J. (1981) *The Connecticut School Effectiveness Questionnaire*, Hartford, CT: Bureau of School Improvement, Connecticut State Department of Education.

WALBERG, H.J. (1984) 'Families as Partners in educational productivity' *Phi Delta Kappan*, **84**(6), pp. 397–400.

WALBERG, H.J., PASCHAL, R.A. and WEINSTEIN T. (1985, April) 'Homework's powerful effects on learning', *Educational Leadership*, **42**(7), pp. 76–79.

WARING, M. (1988) *If Women Counted: A New Feminist Economics*, San Francisco, CA: Harper and Row.

WARREN, C. (1978) 'The nonimplementation of EEP: "All that money for Business as Usual"', in MANN, D. *Making Change Happen?* New York, NY: Teachers College Press, pp. 162–84.

WATSON, D.L., POLLACK, S. and CHRISPEELS, J.A. (1987, April) *Developing Reliable and Valid Effective Schools Assessment Instruments*, Paper presented at the annual meeting of the American Educational Research Association, Washington, DC.

WAUGH, R.F. and PUNCH, K.F. (1987) 'Teacher receptivity to systemwide change in the implementation stage', *Review of Educational Research*, **57**(3), pp. 237–54.

WEBER, G. (1971) *Inner City Children can be Taught to Read: Four Successful Schools*, Washington, DC: Council for Basic Education.

WEISS, A.S. (1984) 'The effectiveness of project RISE in raising achievement levels of pupils in milwaukee public school inner-city schools', Unpublished PhD. Dissertation, Marquette University, Milwaukee, WI.

WIMPLEBERG, R.K., TEDDLIE, C. and STRINGFIELD, S. (1989) 'Sensitivity to context: the past and future of effective schools research' *Educational Administration Quarterly*, **25**(1), pp. 82–107.

YIN, R.K. (1984) *Case Study Research: Design and Methods*, Beverly Hills, CA: Sage Publications.

ZALTMAN, G., FLORIO, D.H. and SIKORSKI, L.A. (1977) *Dynamic Educational Change: Models, Strategies, Tactics, and Management*, New York, NY: The Free Press.

ZANDER, A. (1962) 'Resistance to change: Its analysis and prevention', In BENNIS, W.G., BENNE, K.D. and CHIN, R. (Eds) *The Planning of Change*, New York, NY: Holt, Rinehart and Winston.

ZERCHYKOV, R. and DAVIES, D. with CHRISPEELS, J. *Leading the Way: State Mandates for School Advisory Councils in California, Florida and South Carolina*, Boston, MA: The Institute for Responsive Education.

Index

academic focus 21, 131, 165–7
  at Sierra School 70
  at Tahoe School 87–8
  at Whitney School 54–5
  at Yosemite School 112–2
achievement profiles 26, 29–30
Achiles, C.M. 204
administrative leadership 7
Aid to Families with Dependent
    Children (AFDC) 28–9, 40
  at Sierra School 60
  at Tahoe School 77
  at Whitney School 43, 58
  at Yosemite School 98
AIMS (Activities for Integrating Math
    and Science) 55
Aitkin, R. 2, 203
American Federation of Teachers 161,
    162
Andrews, R.L. 11, 14, 59, 139, 197
Aquila, F.D. 208
archival records 19
Argyris, C. 197
Arizona school district 1
Armor, D. 6, 14, 176, 197
Assembly Bill 77, 89
assessment of schools 22, 154–5
Austin, B.R. 171, 197
Austin, G.R. 1, 197
Averch, H.A. 197

Baldridge, J.V. 197
Balkanization 136, 137, 158
Bamburg, J.D. 14, 59, 139, 197
Bancroft, B.A. 206
Barth, R.S. 21, 149, 150, 173, 197
Becker, H.J. 201

Benjamin, R. 14, 198
Bennis, W.G. 14, 140, 152, 198
Berliner D.C. 198
Berman, P. 198
Bickel, W. 198
Bilingual Advisory Committee 107
bilingual tracking 21, 105–6, 137, 144,
    161
Blendinger, J. 198
Blenkey, M.F. 153, 198
Block, J.H. 198
Blumberg, A. 14, 198
Bolman, L.G. 6, 198
Borger, J.B. 198
Bossert, S.T. 14, 198
boundary of open systems 2–3
Brandt, R. 4, 142, 162, 170, 198
Briggs, J. 198
Brookover, W.G. 1, 6, 160, 176,
    198–9
Brophy, J. 199, 202
Brundage, D. 198
Burns, J.M. 14, 199

California Assessment Program (CAP)
    18, 20, 23, 29–30, 99, 129, 134
  and enrollment growth 25–6
  mathematics scores 32, 34, 35–8, 101
  reading scores 31, 33, 35–8 101
California Assessment Program Report
    30, 98, 131
California Business Roundtable 179
California Distinguished School 44
California Mentor Teacher Program 59,
    134
California School Improvement
    Program 17, 24, 77, 171

California School Leadership Academy 69, 73
California Schools 164, 170
California State Department of Education 1, 12, 14, 199
Canady, R.L. 168, 199
Carnegie Forum 135
Carnegie Task Force 4, 149, 162, 199
Carnoy, M. 181, 199
case study design, methodology 16, 19
Casner-Lotto, J. 199
change, in schools 15–16, 140–1
Chapman, J. 199
Chapter 1 76, 77
Chapter VII 77, 97
characteristics of effective schools 7
Chicago schools 124, 163
Chrispeels, J.A. 2, 10, 16, 44, 61, 99, 164, 174, 209
Chubb, J.E. 11, 199
Clark, R. 174, 199
Clark, T.A. 199
Clift, R.T. 200
climate and culture, of school 7–9, 12–14, 21, 42, 123–9, 145, 155–6, 172–80
  at Sierra School 63–8
  at Tehoe School 79–85
  at Whitney School 45–53
  at Yosemite School 102–9
clinical teaching-supervision model 132, 133
Coch, L. 15, 200
Coleman, J.S. 4, 6, 120, 155, 160, 200
Coleman, P. 10, 16, 205
collaboration 13, 21, 72–3, 92–3, 116–7, 136–7, 148–50
collaborative leadership 156–7
Comer, J.P. 173, 200
committee structures to foster collaboration 136–7
communication 22, 151–2, 153
  at Tahoe School 93
  at Whitney School 56–7
  at Yosemite School 117–8
Comprehensive Test of Basic Skills 98, 110
Conley, S.C. 177, 178, 179, 180, 200
Connecticut Questionaire 23, 24
Connecticut School Effectiveness surveys 99, 108, 122
Connecticut schools 170
Connecticut State Department of Education 1, 23

consensus 4, 151
contrived collegiality 136
Cooper, B.S. 76, 201
cooperation 21
cooperative learning 12, 13, 71, 133, 163, 167
Corbally, J.E. 12, 210
Corbett, H.D. 2, 209
core curriculum committee 137
core leadership 92, 97
Corporate Culture (Deal and Kennedy) 125, 200
county effective schools program 44
county effectiveness schools survey 16
Crandall, D.P. 200
Creemers, B.P.M. 8, 127, 139, 210
Crohn, L. 200
cross-case comparison 1, 2, 23, 31–9, 40–2
Cruban, L. 200
Cruickshank, D. 15, 200
culture of achievement 48–50, 129
culture and climate *see* climate and culture
curriculum 7–9, 12, 21
  alignment 12, 54, 69–70, 86, 127, 129–30, 142
  committees 149, 150
  practices 165–72
  teacher delivering 5
Curthoys, A. 178, 200

Dade County schools 145, 163
data sources 17–20
Davis, G.A. 181, 200
Deal, T.E. 6, 12, 13, 125, 177, 198, 200
De Bevoise, W. 14, 200
demographic data 20, 23, 25–9, 42, 144
Denk, C. 11, 138, 210
Denny, J.W. 211
Derr, C.B. 200
Detroit schools 124
disaggregated test data 18, 63, 160–1, 162, 169
discipline plan 47, 80, 153–4
district administration 10
district leadership 44
district variables 10–11
Dorman, G. 201
Doyle, D.P. 76, 161, 177, 179, 201
Doyle, W.J. 5, 163, 201, 205
Dutch schools 139
Dwyer, D.C. 201

Edmonds, R.R. 1, 6, 7, 14, 160, 201, 206
Effective Schools Program 23
efficacy of teachers 12
efficiency in outcome 159–63, 169, 181
Eisner, J. 14, 201
Elmore, R.F. 4, 162, 201
enrollment growth 25, 26
environmental factors 5–6, 7, 10–11
Epstein, J.L. 67, 201
equity in outcome 159–63, 169, 181
Essential Elements of Instruction 61,
    70, 71, 73, 74, 133, 135
Estler, S. 11, 201
ethnic distributions 27, 124
    at Sierra School 61
    at Tahoe School 27, 77
    at Whitney School 27, 43
    at Yosemite School 27, 98–9
Eubanks, E.E. 173, 205
evaluation of students 8–9
Evans, T. 177, 180, 201
Evertson, C.M. 82, 201

federal education influence 10
feminist perspective 152–3
Fenessey, J. 16, 209
Firestone, W.A. 2, 16, 201, 209
Florida schools 164
Foster, W. 139, 201
four track year-round school schedule
    21, 25–6, 39, 118–122, 132, 137,
    144
fragmented individualism 136
frames of reference 6, 7–11
Frederiksen, J.R. 201
French, J. 15, 200
frequent monitoring (FM) 17, 40, 131–3
    at Sierra School 70–1
    at Tahoe School 88–9
    at Whitney School 55
    at Yosemite School 113
Fuhrman, S. 202
Fullan, M. 15, 59, 122, 133, 134, 135,
    136, 140, 141, 142, 143, 172, 202
Fuller, B. 202
Fuller, F.F. 15, 202

GATE teachers 106
Gauthier, J.W. 23, 202
Geary County Schools 164
Gifted and Talented Program 98, 108
gifted track 105–6, 108, 144, 162
Glaser, B.G. 202
Glatthorn, A.A. 202

Glendale school district 1
Glenn, B.C. 159, 171, 173, 202
Good, T.L. 202
Goodlad, J.I. 162, 168, 202
grade level teams 56, 89, 93, 109, 116,
    149, 150
Greenblatt, R.B. 202
Greenfield, W. 14, 198
Gross, N. 15, 203
Guba, E.G. 19, 202

Hall, G.E. 15, 133, 202
Hall, G.R. 1, 14, 160, 205
Hallinan, M.T. 203
Hallinger, P. 10, 11, 19, 121, 138, 139,
    159, 171, 175, 203
Handy, C. 2, 203
Hanna, D.P. 2–3, 4, 203
Hart, A.W. 203
Hawley, W.D. 203
Helgesen, S. 152, 180, 203
Henderson, A. 67, 128, 173, 203
Herriott, R.E. 15, 203
Hersh, R.H. 203
High, R.M. 204
high expectations (HE) 7, 17, 40, 42,
    126–7, 176–7
    at Sierra School 65
    at Tahoe School 81–2
    at Whitney School 49–50
    at Yosemite School 104–5
Hollingsworth, S. 164, 205
Holmes Group 4, 135, 149, 204
home-school relations (HSR) 17, 40,
    42, 127–9, 155–6, 173–4
    at Sierra School 66–7
    at Tahoe School 82–4
    at Whitney School 50–1
    at Yosemite School 106–7
Hopkins, D. 56, 71, 177, 204
Hord, S.M. 14, 15, 133, 142, 202, 204
Hotchkiss, P.R. 168, 199
Houston, H. 4, 168, 211
Huberman, M. 15, 134, 204
Huff, S. 14, 204
Huffman-Carpenter, P. 204
Hutchins, C.L. 204

innovations, implementation of 14, 15
inputs to schools 3–4, 6
instructional leadership (IL) 9, 14, 17,
    40, 42, 138–41, 142
    at Sierra School 73–4
    at Tahoe School 93–5

at Whitney School 57–8
at Yosemite School 118–20
instructional practices 7–9, 12, 21,
    165–72
instructional strategies 114, 121, 127–8,
    133–5, 137, 165–72
interactive process 14, 123
isolation of teachers 1, 11, 13

Japanese education 126
Jencks, C.S. 6, 160, 204
Jenni, R.W. 163, 204
Johnson, F.L. 51, 128, 135, 174, 204
Jones, L.T. 198
Joyce, B. 12, 56, 167, 171, 178, 204

Kanter, R.M. 204
Kearns, D.T. 5, 163, 177, 179, 205
Keith, P. 211
Kennedy, A.A. 13, 125, 200
Kijai, J. 164, 205
Kiltgaard, R.E. 1, 160, 161, 205
King, M. 12, 210
Kouzes, J.M. 205
Kritek, W.J. 207

Lane, J.J. 205
Larkin, M.M. 205
LaRocque, L. 10, 16, 205
Lassen School 24
    results 23–42
leadership 7, 14–15, 145–6, 156–7
learning enriched schools 154–5
Learning Screening Team 87, 97
Leithwood, K.A. 159, 205
LeMahieu, P. 205
Levin, H.M. 181, 199
Levine, D.U. 6, 14, 164, 171–2, 173,
    176, 205
Lezotte, L.W. 1, 6, 42, 199, 160, 165,
    166, 171–2, 173, 176, 205, 206
Lieberman, A. 21, 147, 162, 206
Lightfoot, S. 206
Likert scale 17
Lincoln Y.S. 19, 202
Lipham J.M. 206
Little, J.W. 56, 71, 135, 136, 147, 171,
    206
loft class structure 20, 60–76, 89, 124,
    132
Louisiana schools 166
lower socio-economic status students
    21
    and test scores 37–8

McCarthy, D.P. 199
McClintock, C.C. 206
MacCormack-Larkin, M. 2, 206–7
Macevoy, B. 207
Mackenzie, D.E. 206
McLaughlin, M.W. 152, 207
Mann, D. 206
Mannasse, A.L. 206
Maryland school district 1
Mathematics Monitoring System
    (MMS) 130, 132
Meaney, D. 199
mentor teacher 48–9, 59, 104, 134, 142
Merriam, S.B. 16, 207
methodologies 17–20
Meyer, J.W. 207
Michigan school district 1
Micks, J. 17, 40, 207
Miles, M. 15, 134, 204, 207
Miller, S.K. 11, 207
Milwaukee school district 1
mission statements 51–2, 68, 84, 108–9,
    112, 125–6, 140, 167, 174–5
Moe, T.M. 11, 199
monitoring of schools 154–5
Montgomery school district 1
Montgomery, D.J. 159, 205
Morgan, G. 2, 12, 207
Morrish, I. 207
Mortimore, P. 19, 123, 171, 173, 176,
    207
multi track schools 25, 29
Murphy, J.K. 7, 8–9, 10, 11, 14, 16, 19,
    121, 138, 139, 141, 159, 165, 166,
    171, 172, 175, 176, 207–8
Murphy, M.J. 203

Nanus, B. 14, 140, 152, 198
*A Nation Prepared: Teachers for the
    21st Century* (Carnegie Forum)
    135, 199
National Center for Effective Schools
    Research and Development 208
nationally published textbooks 13
Newberg, N.A. 202
New York schools 124, 163
New York State Department of
    Education 1, 208
non-English speaking students 17, 28–9,
    40, 96, 97, 135
    at Sierra School 60
    at Tahoe School 77, 88
    at Whitney School 43, 58
    at Yosemite School 99

Norman, J. 164, 205
norms of collegiality 134, 152, 176–8
  at Sierra School 68
  at Tahoe School 85, 96
  at Whitney School 52–3
  at Yosemite School 109
norm-referenced tests 13, 169–70

Olson, L. 208
O'Neil, J. 4, 208
open systems model 2–7, 144
opportunity to learn (OLTT) 17, 40,
  90–1, 113–4
Orange County Offices 1
organizational structures and
    procedures 7–9, 11–12, 42, 135–8,
    145, 155, 163–5
  at Sierra School 71–3
  at Tahoe School 92–5
  at Whitney School 56–7
  at Yosemite School 116–8
organizational symbolism 13
outputs 4–5, 6

parent involvement 22, 155–6
parent occupation 27–8
  at Sierra School 27–8, 60–1, 63
  at Tahoe School 27–8, 77
  at Whitney School 45
  at Yosemite School 27–8, 98–9
Parish, R. 208
Passalacqua, J. 206
Patterson, J.L. 208
Pecheone, R. 23, 208
Perrow, C. 2, 208
Persell, C.H. 14, 208
Peters, T.J. 14, 59, 208
Peterson, K.D. 12, 13, 200
Pettigrew, A. 10, 208
Pfeffer, J. 16, 209
Phi Delta Kappa 160, 209
Pink, W.T. 209
Pinyon School
  multi track program 25–6
  results 27–42
Pollack, S. 2, 8, 9, 10, 15, 16, 44,
    61, 164, 165, 171, 173, 174, 176,
    209
Pomfret, A. 133, 202
Pontiac school district 1
population growth 39–40
Posner, B.Z. 205
Prince Georges Counties school district
  1

principals 13, 14, 18, 44, 57–8, 132, 144,
  156–7
problem solving 117
process model 12
Program Quality Review 87, 155
Purkey, S.C. 7, 17, 25, 141, 209
purposeful restructuring 159–82

Raebeck, B.S. 209
Ralph, J.H. 16, 209
Ratner, G. 1, 206
Raywid, M.A. 163, 209
Reading Management System (RMS)
  130, 132
recognition and rewards 124–5, 175–6
  at Sierra School 64–5
  at Tahoe School 80–1
  at Whitney School 47–9
  at Yosemite School 103–4
reflective practitioners 20
Reilly, W. 14, 209
Renihan, F.I. 209
Renihan, P.J. 209
research design and procedure 16–17,
  19
resources for schools 3–4
restructured belief system 20
Reynolds, D. 209
Riverside County Offices 1
Rochester NY schools 145
Rogers, V. 209
"root metaphor" 14
Rosenholtz, S.J. 2, 5, 10, 11, 15, 16,
    19, 52, 59, 120, 135, 136, 140, 147,
    150, 151, 153–4, 156, 157, 159, 163,
    164, 165, 171, 173, 174, 177, 178,
    209
Rosow, J.M. 140, 209
Rossman, G.B. 2, 12, 16, 140, 209
Rost, J.C. 14, 139, 140, 143, 209
Rowan, B. 11, 29, 38, 138, 210
Rutter, M. 1, 123, 210
Ryan, W. 210

Sacramento County Offices 1
safe and orderly environment (SOE)
    17, 40, 124, 173
  at Sierra School 64
  at Tahoe School 80
  at Whitney School 45–7
  at Yosemite School 102–3
Sambs, C.E. 210
San Diego County Effective Schools
    Survey 183–96

San Diego County Offices, schools 1, 145
Saphier, J. 12, 210
Sarason, S.S. 177, 210
Sayre, K.A. 11, 207
Scheerens, J. 8, 127, 139, 210
Schein, E.H. 12, 210
Schlechty, P.C. 5, 21, 149, 173, 177, 210
school effectiveness 18, 123–46
School Improvement Budget 72
school improvement funds 25, 43, 121
School Improvement Plan 65, 72–3, 88, 151, 153–4
school improvement review 23–5, 131
    teacher views 147–58
school mission (CSM) 17, 40, 125, 140
school site council 25, 89, 105, 107, 136, 149, 164, 165
school structures 150–3
school technology 7, 12, 42, 129–35, 145, 153
    at Sierra School 68–71
    at Tahoe School 85–92
    at Whitney School 53–6
    at Yosemite School 109–16
school-wide focus 22
school year schedule 25–6
Seattle school district 1
second chance facilitator 14
Seeley, D.S. 5, 177, 210
segregation of students 117, 118, 137
self-esteem of teacher 12
self-reliance, culture of 1
Sergiovanni, T.J. 12, 210
Sequoia School
    multi track program 25–6
    results 23–42
setting
    Sierra School 60–3
    Tahoe School 77–9
    Whitney School 43–5
    Yosemite School 98–102
Shanker, A. 161
shared decision-making opportunities 22, 72–3, 92–3, 116–7, 137–8, 148–50
shared leadership 74, 141–4
shared learning 143–4
shared mission 21, 125–6, 174–5
    at Sierra School 67–8
    at Tahoe School 84
    at Whitney School 51–2
    at Yosemite School 108–9
shared vision 140

Shasta School 23–42
Shoemaker, J. 23, 208, 210
Showers, B. 135, 171, 204
Sierra School 20, 23–42, 60–76
site-based management 163, 164
Sizemore, B.A. 173, 210
Sizer's Coalition of Essential Schools 4
Sizer, T. 4, 162, 168, 211
Smircich, L. 13, 14, 211
Smith, L. 211
Smith, M.S. 7, 17, 25, 141, 209
Smith, W.F. 211
Smylie, M.A. 211
social context 10, 11
socio economic status 26, 124, 126–7, 138, 156
    and ethnic distribution 27
South Carolina schools 164
South Carolina State Department of Education 1
Spartz, J.L. 1, 211
SPSSX, Inc. 17
staff development 13, 133–5, 142, 144, 154, 171
    at Sierra School 71
    at Tahoe School 89, 91–2
    at Whitney School 55–6
    at Yosemite School 104–5, 114–6
staff interviews 24
staff involvement 149–50
Stallings, J.A. 171, 211
standardized curriculum 12, 13
standardized procedures 5
standardized tests 29, 130
Stanley, W.B. 211
Stanton, J. 164, 211
Stark, J.C. 6, 14, 173, 176, 205
State Compensatory Education funds 77
state influences on schools 10
Stevenson, H.W. 126, 211
statewide curriculum 12, 44, 129
Stedman, L.C. 173, 211
Strass, A.L. 202
Stringfield, S. 11, 19, 176, 212
structure of school 7, 13
student achievement results 20, 155–6
student outcomes, improved 159–63
student progress 7, 154–5, 169–72
Stull Bill Objectives 55, 88
Sweeney, J. 138, 211
Sykes, G. 178, 211
symbols 13, 181

Systematic Training in Effective
  Parenting (STEP) 66
systems theory 181–2

Tahoe Elementary School 21, 24,
  77–97
  results 23–42
Taylor, B.O. 2, 163, 164, 181, 211
teacher as learner 143
teacher empowerment 72–3, 163, 164,
  181
Teacher Expectations and Student
  Achievement (TESA) 25, 65, 71, 82,
  104, 109, 112, 114, 127
teacher interview data 17–18, 22
teacher professionalism 176–8
teacher recognition 48–9, 65, 81, 104,
  125, 176–7
teacher response 41
  at Sierra School 62, 66
  at Tahoe School 79
  at Whitney School 46–7
  at Yosemite School 100
teacher survey data 17, 20
teacher views on improvement 147–58
Teachers Workplace (Rosenholtz) 147
technology of school 13
technology of teaching 7
Teddlie, C. 11, 19, 138, 163, 166, 168,
  175, 176, 212
Tennessee 19
test data analysis 18–19, 142
test scores, use of 130–1, 169
  at Sierra School 68–70
  at Tahoe School 85–6
  at Whitney School 53–4
  at Yosemite school 110–2
theorectical framework 2–11
Thomas, M.A. 181, 200
throughput process 4
Timar, T. 4, 162, 163, 212
time on task (OLTT) 40, 90–1, 113–4,
  168–9
Tomorrow's Teachers (Holmes Group)
  135, 204
Townsend, T. 167, 212

tracking of students 13, 21, 26, 39, 100,
  104–6, 127, 163
transformative process 4
Trisman, D.A. 212

US General Accounting Office 160,
  212

Van de Grift, W. 14, 139, 212
Van Meter, E.J. 212
Venezky, R.L. 159, 176, 212
Villanova, R. 23, 212

Walberg, H.J. 205, 212
Waring, M. 179, 212
Warren, C. 212
Washington school district 1
Waterman, R.H. 14, 59, 208
Watson, D. 2, 17, 209, 213
Waugh, R.F. 213
Weber, G. 1, 14, 160, 176, 213
Weiss, A.S. 2, 213
Wimpleberg, R.K. 159, 160, 213
Winfield, L.F. 159, 176, 212
Winning the Brain Race (Kearns and
  Doyle) 161, 205
Wisconsin school district 1
Whitney Elementary School 20, 24–42,
  43–59
women in teaching 177–80
Workshop Way 128
Writing Project 86, 96, 131, 133

year round schools 25, 39, 98–122
Yee, S.M. 152, 207
Yin, R.K. 16, 19, 213
Yosemite Elementary School 21,
  98–122
  multiple track year-round program
  25–6
  results 23–42

Zager, R. 140, 209
Zaltman, G. 213
Zander, A. 15, 213
Zerchykov, R. 164, 211, 213